WHOLEHEARTED LIVING

AN ENCHANTED JOURNEY FOR YOUR SOUL

365 DAYS OF INSPIRATION

WHOLEHEARTED LIVING

AN ENCHANTED JOURNEY FOR YOUR SOUL

CHRISTIAN SØRENSEN

KATHERINE ECONOMOU

ISBN: 979-8-218-50050-4

To my beloved wife and soulmate, Kalli, who is there with love for me 365 days a year and then some. ~ *Christian*

∞

For Steve and Emilie, who taught me how to live and love with my whole heart.

I am grateful for all of it. ~ *Katherine*

Wholehearted living is about engaging in our lives from places of worthiness. It means cultivating the courage, compassion, and connection to wake up in the morning and think, no matter what gets done and how much is left undone. I am enough.

~ Brene Brown

∞

If we want there to be peace in the world, we have to be brave enough to soften what is rigid in our hearts, to find the soft spot and stay with it. We have to have that kind of courage and take that kind of responsibility. That s the true practice of peace.

~ Pema Chodron

Foreword

Wholehearted Living: An Enchanted Journey for Your Soul was written to encourage us all to live full, joyful, and more fulfilling lives. Looking out into the world, we saw alarming trends of growing hate speech, racism, intolerance, and violence popping up all over. We saw that, in these challenging days, it is becoming more difficult to stay openhearted and live from a place of connection and support for one another. We were inspired to assemble a year-long program to encourage a deeper spiritual walk. The text guides us each back to our hearts and, subsequently, to one another. We believe in the healing power of love and know that cultivating compassion and kindness can begin to bridge the gaps in our society and the world.

The concept of living wholeheartedly was popularized by bestselling author and researcher Brene Brown. She said: "across the board, wholehearted men and women are spiritual people." This doesn't mean they are religious but instead that wholehearted people have "a deeply held belief that we are inextricably connected to each other by something greater than us." When we realize that we are part of the matrix of being and are connected to one another and all of life, it opens our awareness to our true nature and value. We believe by encouraging the realization of our worthiness and purpose, we become the greatest expression of ourselves, thus creating situations of peace and connection rather than chaos and division. In doing this work, we can heal old negative beliefs and wounds that sustain a reactive ego allowing us to create our experience from joy.

Desmond Tutu once wisely said: "there is only one way to eat an elephant: one bite at a time." What he meant by this is that everything in life that seems daunting, overwhelming, and even impossible can be accomplished gradually by taking on just a little at a time. This is the idea behind this daily journal. You will benefit from a bite-sized chunk of inspiration and wisdom to start your day. By engaging with the daily, weekly, and monthly themes, one day at a time, you will have the opportunity to make great changes gradually. Working through this book will reveal the areas of your life that would benefit from some attention and awareness.

This dedicated observation will help you see through your current situation to the possibilities beyond them. There is great value in doing the daily guides when your life is working, and things are happy and right. Consistency and consciously entering into Spirit wholeheartedly when all is well will help you turn to Spirit first when your world is shaken rather than falling into a negative spin. You can start on January 1st or on any day in line with your perfect timing and work through each day of the upcoming year. How exciting it will be to look back after the year and see what amazing learning and growth you have experienced. You could also pick up the book and work on any one month's theme that is calling to you. Or, you could pick it up sporadically and benefit from a random page. This book was created for you, and you are the one to guide your own path.

Wholehearted Living: An Enchanted Journey for Your Soul is an invitation for you to embark on a journey through which you will rediscover your true self and learn to live from an authentic place of expression. It is an enchanted journey that your soul is ready to take. It's up to you to take the first step through the gate and start your journey.

Christian & Katherine

How to Use This Book

Wholehearted Living: An Enchanted Journey for Your Soul was written for you with the intention of helping you connect with your heart and learn to engage and explore new ideas that inspire you to live wholeheartedly.

As an Individual

As you read each entry for the day, journal, doodle, draw, or comment in whatever way that allows you to explore the idea presented. How does it strike you? What do you think about it? How can you engage with it? And most importantly, how can you practice opening yourself to experience the enchanted life that is the Divine Heart, wanting to manifest in, through and as you?

As a Book Club or Small Group

Each month has a theme that is broken into daily topics. Groups can meet weekly or monthly to explore the topics and themes. Meditate on the theme together. Share what you discover in your journal. Discuss deeper practices that will help you and the members of your group. Pray for one another during the meetings and as prayer partners between meetings.

As a Spiritual Community

Using a journal like this allows your entire community to be on the same page for the whole year. Wholehearted Living can be a wonderful annual theme to focus your year around. The theme for the month can also be utilized by the children and youth. Each week's lesson can be based on the topic within each month's theme. When there are five weeks in a month, this allows for an additional deepening into the overall idea being explored. The individual days provide excellent material, quotes, and ideas for weekly lessons or presentations. As mentioned above, weekly or monthly study groups can be formed to support engaging with the material and practicing it more deeply. These can take place at your community location, online, or in members' homes for a more intimate, community-building experience.

Proceeds from the sale of this book go to the Emily Butterworth College Fund.

Contents

JANUARY
Spirituality

January 1-7
Your Infinite Nature

January 8-14
Living in Faith

January 15-21
Practicing the Presence

January 22-28
Raising Your Consciousness

January 29-31
You Are Precious

JANUARY 1

Time to call on Janus

You're off to Great places! Today is your day! Your mountain is waiting, So, get on your way! - Dr. Seuss

Janus was the Roman god of endings, beginnings and transitions. Presiding over passages, doors, birthdays, and transitional periods such as war to peace. He was usually depicted as having two faces looking in opposite directions, one toward the past and the other toward the future.

Love the learning from your journey thus far. Calling in the wisdom of seeing in both directions would be helpful in making choices and transitioning from the old way to a new way.

No longer subject to old thought patterns, step into your new possibilities in the New Year. Open your awareness to the gifts you've learned, insights you've received and understandings of how you've grown from the previous year's experiences. Take some time to review the past year. Take an elevated perspective of the year's journey and integrate your life lessons into what lies before you. Embrace the good from yesterday, but don't allow yourself to be bound by precedent or your past beliefs. Greater good calls you now. Catch the vision, love what you are looking at for this year and get moving!

Spiritual Contemplation: What is my vision, what is my Word that I speak into form for my amazing New Year? Speak it out loud now.

Affirmation: This is my best year ever!

JANUARY 2

In the Beginning

In the beginning was the Word, and the Word was with God, and the Word was God. - John 1:1, NIV

Further along in this passage in Verse 14 you'll find it stating, "that the Word was made flesh." It is exciting to realize that mystical and inner revelations can move into tangible reality. Separation between the divine realm and human expression dissolves. The belief in two disconnected worlds dissipates. "The word became flesh" means it's still the Word and hasn't changed its God nature or essence. It carries the full God vibration. It's just that the Word has become visible as form with all its God qualities.

Form follows consciousness. Your human experience becomes the out picturing of thoughts, beliefs and images that you are speaking into the creative process. January is a powerful time to set your intention for the year. Of course, any time is a good time, but *today* is always the best day to recast and realign your vision for your ever-unfolding life. There is great good in store for you this year, when you speak your Word. It makes a lot of sense to experience it from day one!

Spiritual Contemplation: What is my vision, what is my Word that I speak into form for my amazing New Year? Speak it out loud now.

Affirmation: This is my best year ever!

JANUARY 3

Your Cosmic Umbilical Cord

You have a spiritual umbilical cord that keeps you connected to Source and the vital Life Force Energy you need to sustain your life and existence. - Unknown

We are each connected to the Divine like a cosmic umbilical cord and, through this connection, we receive spiritual nourishment from God in every moment. But most resist this and instead focus on the fast-food quality of nourishment that comes from the material world around us! The 24/7 news cycle, the divisive state of our political system and the ongoing struggles we face daily are all the poison of the world.

When we release the idea that we are separate entities, moving through life alone and trying to make everything happen for ourselves, we disregard the guidance and support that is already here for us. We are being called to remember our direct connection to God and open to that flow of support. We do this by carving out time each day to sit in silence and commune with the presence. Even 10 minutes sitting still and focusing on your breath is enough to begin to allow God to be activated in your experience. Remember that you are always tethered to God and always have Divine support and wisdom available to you.

Spiritual Contemplation: Think about ways that you can accept the support and guidance of God in a greater way in your life. Spend time in silence communing with God as you start and end your day. Notice how you feel afterwards.

Affirmation: I am connected to the Divine at my core and accept all the guidance and support here for me.

JANUARY 4

Remember Whose You Are

The kingdom of God is inside you and outside you. Split a piece of wood and I am there. I am the All: From me all came forth, and to me all are attained. Lift up a stone and you will find me. - Gospel of Thomas

The Divine presence of God is present in all life and in all matter. It is, at the core, the only thing that exists. It was the primordial soup that everything has been created out of, including each and every one of us. Like a flame that sends off sparks, we are one with God. That is unless we remain close to the spirit, we are lost, just as a spark apart from the source dies unless it merges back into the flame. This happens when we forget who and whose we are.

When we get hypnotized by the state of the world, we forget who we are and who sent us. When we live this way, we live according to the ways of the world which are small and limited. But when we remember that God sent us here and we are part of God's life, we benefit from Divine support including guidance, empowerment and infinite blessings. Remember your Divine birthright and you will open to the source and support you deserve, simply because you are you.

Spiritual Contemplation: Take a few moments today to be still. Breathe and remember that you are part of God's life and have been created on purpose, simply to be you. Allow that to resonate within your entire body and being. Journal any thoughts you have afterwards.

Affirmation: I am One with the Divine Life and accept all the guidance and support that is available to me!

JANUARY 5

Potentiality of Possibility

There is no such thing as part of God. In an indivisible unity, all of everything is present everywhere all the time. — Ernest Holmes

The Spirit that is in everything, the unbroken and undivided, cannot express in fragments - only in Wholeness. Within all things is the potentiality of everything. We can never exhaust the potential of possibility. The understanding of Unity compels the acceptance that there is no dividing demarcation. We shall continue to grow and change. Your evolution from where you are to that which you shall become is a natural progression, all taking place within the totality of it all. Dr. Holmes states, "Out of the eternal being comes the everlasting becoming."

The good news is that whatever you might be working on improving in your life, right now its perfect expression is just waiting on your realization of it as your reality. This realization takes place in the Divine Mind. Sri Aurobindo would say, "Transcendence doesn't reconcile; it transmutes." The tide of your divine expression will rise from the depths of the Cosmic Consciousness into your self-expression, naturally bringing about the changes of your wholehearted vision.

Spiritual Contemplation: How do you subjectively embrace dualistic thinking by thinking in parts and segments while attempting to connect to the Infinite?

Affirmation: I am Spirit expressing!

JANUARY 6

From Limitation to Possibility

Believe in your infinite potential. Your only limitations are those you set upon yourself. – Roy T. Bennett

Living a wholehearted life means letting go of the limitations we place upon ourselves and opening the windows of our consciousness to embrace the beauty of infinite possibility for our lives. To do this, we are called to release the judgment(s) we hold on ourselves, our lives and everyone around us. This is because when we judge something, we lock it into a limited perspective, and we use our creative energy to keep ourselves and those we judge tethered to that limitation. But no one is actually limited because there is always possibility and potential around us. We can support the expression of that possibility through our recognition of our life as Divine.

You can move from limitation to possibility through connecting with the Divine presence that lives at the center of your being. Deep below your egoic mind, below your personality and the story of how you got to be who you are, lives your pure essence. This is the place where you and God connect and commune. When you practice connecting with this presence on a regular basis, you will receive wisdom and become more open to impressions and inspiration that will guide you out of limitation and into the possibility that is waiting for you.

Spiritual Contemplation: Take some time in silence today and just breathe. In your mind's eye see yourself journeying down below your ego, personality, and story to that place of connection and peace. Rest in this space for a time and just be. Notice how your day unfolds after this.

Affirmation: I surrender judgment of myself and open to God's guidance and inspiration! I am free!

JANUARY 7

This Too Shall Pass

After a hurricane comes a rainbow. – Katy Perry

Turbulent times are a part of life. No one escapes those moments of tumult and upset. How we navigate these challenges reveals a lot about us and what we believe about ourselves and God. A colleague reminded me that the promise of the bible (and other sacred texts) was not that life would be easy or that we would be able to remove all hardship from our experience, but that God would be with us, and we would never be alone. We may go through a hurricane but the rainbow that shows up after it has passed is glorious and beautiful, just like your life after a challenge.

Challenges, whether in the realm of health, work, or relationships can stir up a lot of emotion and fear. When you realize that these issues have actually come to pass and do not actually stay, it's easier to remember that life will not always be so hard, and you will not always be in pain. Sometimes, they happen to clear your life of those situations that are holding you back from fully experiencing the joy of your life. The question is, can you wait patiently for the rainbow without losing your faith and hope of a brighter day tomorrow? Because it's coming. That's God's promise.

Spiritual Contemplation: Think about the challenges you have experienced in your life and what you gained from them once they passed. What wisdom was revealed to you about yourself and your life?

Affirmation: I stand firm in my faith knowing I am completely supported by God!

JANUARY 8

Sustaining Faith

Faith is to believe what you do not see; the reward of this faith is to see what you believe. – Saint Augustine

Have you ever had a vision sustain you through rough times? Having faith in something greater than the challenges of life doesn't necessarily keep you out of trouble. In the 27th chapter of Acts, God promised the apostle Paul that he would stand before Caesar. When the Romans took Paul by ship to stand trial in Rome, they met a terrible storm at Sea which the apostle Paul had warned them against. This storm was of biblical proportion where the sky disappeared for two weeks. The relentless wind threw the ship around like a cork. It felt that it might never end.

No one would ever cross an ocean if they could have gotten off in the midst of stormy seas. When the crew came to the apostle Paul, asking him what they could do, he told them not to worry; God promised he would stand before Caesar. No matter how large the difficulty, can your vision sustain you through the turbulent times? Can you keep your faith in a vision your soul has revealed and remember to turn your life over to God in the midst of a storm? The crew eventually took down the sails and let control of the ship go to the winds of heaven, allowing those winds to take them to their perfect next step on the way to fulfilling the promise.

Spiritual Contemplation: Are there stormy areas in your life? What vision did you have that had you step into that journey? Do you still have a sustaining faith that will help you weather the storm? If so, proclaim your greater truth and trust where the winds of heaven take you.

Affirmation: I find faith by remembering the vision and promise of my soul!

JANUARY 9

Dating the Divine

God's love is like an ocean. You can see its beginning, but not its end. – Rick Warren

One aspect of living a wholehearted life is embracing God as an integral part of your days. Understanding that you are a spiritual being, with a connection to the infinite Divine Spirit and embracing this truth, opens you to seeing life in a whole new light. It boggles the mind to think that out of infinite possibilities, you were created in the exact unique way, with all your talents and quirks. Out of infinity, God thought "you" and you were created! God is the original lover of your soul and It knew that you were needed by the world. As Ralph Waldo Emerson said: "The fact that I am here certainly shows me that the soul had need of an organ here."

Can you embrace this love of God and welcome it into your daily experience? It is as if you were dating God and building a relationship with the Divine. You do this the same way you would strengthen any relationship you have in your life with time, attention, and connection. Spending time each day in communion with God through meditation and contemplation, spiritual study, and prayer, deepens your relationship and supports your trust and faith in yourself and God, knowing that you are completely supported and loved. Create a date for you and God and see how your life opens to greater love.

Spiritual Contemplation: Make a date for you and God. Spend time listening and communing with the presence and allow the love you have for God to flow through you. Receive God's love and rest in the peace of your connection.

Affirmation: I am one with the Divine Love of God!

JANUARY 10

Unconditional Faith

But seek first the kingdom of God and his righteousness, and all these things shall be added to you. – Matthew 6:33, NKJV

It's easy to have faith when everything is going your way. You are healthy, business is booming, the children are good, and your relationship is passionate and co-creative. When life seems to be going awry, prayers aren't being answered, and the demands of the world are feeling constrictive, it's easy to say, "I'll be happy when everything works out." Your faith becomes conditional. "Once the money starts flowing again, or my children start listening to me, then I'll have faith. God, once you meet my demands on my time frame, I'll have faith once more."

Anything you must have in order to be happy, leaves you out of balance and vulnerable to the material world. It's good to know your direction and goals, but don't allow them to be all-consuming or you will have put something before God in order to be happy. This false idol will now control your ability to be happy and frustration and disappointment will become the ruling energies of your life. Have the faith *of* God, and not *in* God, or in anything else. When the court decision doesn't go your way or the deal doesn't go through - don't lose your happiness. Your life is not based on outcomes. You are able to experience faith, remembering your Source is greater than anything in this world, and somehow this moment in time is taking you on your soul's perfect path.

Spiritual Contemplation: Was there a time in your life that didn't feel good and ended up being a significant part of your path leading to greater good?

Affirmation: My unconditional faith for good prevails in the face of all challenges!

JANUARY 11

Faith

All I have seen teaches me to trust the creator for all I have not seen. — *Ralph Waldo Emerson*

When you live in faith you live with greater possibilities. Consciousness expands, belief increases, enthusiasm comes alive. Faith is more than just a statement. It's demonstrated when there are no longer any doubts lingering in the subjective to challenge what is known to be true in the heart. Awake or asleep, the awareness of the Omnipresent Spirit guides and surrounds every thought. Trusting in the unfolding of Spiritual Truth as your life leaves no room for seemly unbelief. Fears and doubt then have no entry point into your thinking.

When you have a deep abiding faith in the Infinite Intelligence that is God, it is your peace and security. Whatever endeavor you choose to undertake, your trust unfolds with divine guidance and grace. All who come to participate in your vision, do so with the right attitude and are in alignment with what you see. Live in the atmosphere of faith, with a confidence that Infinite Wisdom guides every decision and action, assuring your journey to success. This directing power will always keep you on your right path.

Spiritual Contemplation: Where have you allowed doubts to enter your thinking, moving you away from the joy of your journey? How can you shift your thinking so as to return to the enthusiasm that faith awakens?

Affirmation: I have the faith of God in the intention before me!

JANUARY 12

Keep Your Eye on God

The eye is the lamp of the body. If your eyes are healthy,[a] your whole body will be full of light. But if your eyes are unhealthy,[b] your whole body will be full of darkness. – Matthew 6:22-23, NIV

This scripture reminds me that God must come first in my life. I must keep my eye on the Divine and all that means. To know my connection to a Spiritual Life is to remember that there is nothing from the outside world that can steal my peace of mind. If I give in to the fear that there is not enough and that I need to win at all costs, I lose my ability to see and feel God in my life. My experience can be rocky and difficult, and I feel alone in the world.

The eye, which includes not only our true eyesight, but our knowledge, intuitive knowing, and our heart cannot be split. It must stay singly focused on God and the recognition that we are intimately connected to it. When we realize this, we will be filled with light. Our experience will be filled with that sense of grace, comfort, and ease that we feel when we know that God is operating in our lives. This is the difference between developing Spiritual sight rather than the blurred vision of the human which can lead to a sense of frustration and mental confusion.

Spiritual Contemplation: Today, take the time to pause and remember that God is activated in your life. Affirm Divine presence and welcome the light.

Affirmation: I keep my eye singly on God and my life is filled with light!

JANUARY 13

Growing Faith

A person without a spiritual path is a person walking in darkness. With a path, we are no longer afraid or worried. – Thich Nhat Hanh

A major component of creating and living a wholehearted life is deepening our spiritual walk. This does not mean that we need to be part of any one religion or do any one spiritual practice. It is about the realization that we are connected to something bigger than ourselves; that we are here on purpose and that we can trust the unfoldment of our lives. It serves us well to create a space in each day for a time of communion, meditation or contemplation of those spiritual ideas and presence. When this does not happen, we tend to get stuck in our ego and begin to believe that we are separate and disconnected.

Growing our faith means strengthening our understanding of connection with the Divine Life and acknowledging that there is so much more to this life than what we can see. We get more comfortable in our own skin and with our personal power. We open our hearts more and show kindness and compassion to others and ourselves. Ten to fifteen minutes a day of sitting still and breathing can help expand our faith and open us to living fully and freely!

Spiritual Contemplation: Take a few moments today to sit and breathe and open to your ideas about how the Divine operates in your life. Write your thoughts in your journal.

Affirmation: I embrace the Divine Presence within me and allow it to direct my way! With faith and trust, I step forward as my true self!

JANUARY 14

The Ultimate Prayer

You will never understand who you are until you understand who God is.
— *Billy Graham*

If you want to be healed, it pretty much comes down to emptying out the false sense of self and embrace a willingness to turn within. When you come to feel and realize God within, you have reached the ultimate prayer. By letting go of the false sense of self-healing, forgiveness, and transformation happen. If you are pushing your position on Spirit, you are not available for the higher experience. You can say all you want that 3X3=7, but the principles of mathematics aren't going to take charity on you and finally say, "Ok, this one time I'm going to give it to you."

When you turn to a Higher Power, it must be done wholeheartedly and with a full openness of consciousness in order to receive the shift. It's humbling to acknowledge what you are holding onto is only a belief, not a law or Universal truth. When you understand your belief is no longer serving you, you become available to the experience of Grace and Wholeness. With the realization that nothing of this world has power over you, you free yourself from the dualistic world beliefs of separation.

Spiritual Contemplation: Which beliefs are you holding to be the truth? And what about those beliefs you know are not healthy? Are you willing to be humble enough to let your position go?

Affirmation: I now feel the presence of the Divine within!

JANUARY 15

Martin Luther King, Jr Day

Returning hate for hate multiplies hate, adding deeper darkness to a night already devoid of stars. Darkness cannot drive out darkness; only light can do that. Hate cannot drive out hate; only love can do that. – Dr. King, Sermon: Loving Your Enemies

In 1955, King became the spokesman for the 381 days of continuous peaceful protest of the Montgomery Bus Boycott that resulted in the Supreme Court ruling that segregation in public transport was unconstitutional. Dr. King also led the March on Washington in 1963 to peacefully protest racial discrimination in the labor market. This march was influential in helping the passing of the Civil Rights Act of 1964.

For thirteen years Dr. King was a pivotal advocate for African Americans in the Civil Rights Movement in the United States. His inspiring speeches along with his courageous peaceful protest in the south eventually helped to change many of the laws dealing with the equality of African Americans. In 1964 he was awarded the Nobel Peace Prize. He was assassinated on April 4, 1968 though it was not the first attempt on his life. Since then, 955 streets in the US have been named after him; a man who knew and stood for a nonviolent approach to change.

Spiritual Contemplation: Is there a cause you are so passionate about that you are willing to live full out, stepping through all your fears in order to see your dream come true?

Affirmation: I have a dream that one day (fill in blank) _____!

JANUARY 16

Meaning and Purpose

You do not need to work to become spiritual. You are spiritual; you need only to remember that fact. Spirit is within you. God is within you. — *Julia Cameron*

One of the many gifts that come from committing to live a spiritual life is the sense of meaning and purpose it brings. Many people seem to be wandering aimlessly through their lives jumping from one crisis to another, blaming life or other people for their difficulties, unable to move forward. Spirituality provides a sense of meaning and purpose in life because it connects one to something greater than themselves, whether it be a higher power, nature, or a realization of the interconnectedness of life. This is powerful because it reveals an understanding of their place in the world and in life.

When you awaken to the presence that lives within you and realize that you are connected to something greater, your life starts to shift. You find a deeper sense of peace and well-being when you realize you are meant to be here. Your life has purpose and contributes to the world around you. Spirituality is a personal journey, and it looks different for each of us. If you are looking to understand your life and your place in it, start a spiritual practice and open to the truth that is already sitting right where you are.

Spiritual Contemplation: Do you have a sense of meaning and purpose in your life? In what ways do you connect to a higher power? What images/words best work for you to describe this higher power? (God, The Universe, Nature, Oneness, etc.)

Affirmation: I am One with the Divine and my life is blessed!

JANUARY 17

Log Jam

~~~&~~~

Fear is often our immediate response to uncertainty. There's nothing wrong with experiencing fear. The key is not to get stuck in it. — *Gabrielle Bernstein*

Spirituality is living at the causative level of life. It is not about placing band-aids on issues and hoping problems go away. The Spiritual approach to wholehearted living is delving into a constraining issue presently manifesting in your life and eliminating the cause. Once the constriction is eradicated, the natural flow of nature takes its course. Healing happens, resolution is revealed, and understanding is embraced.

In the old days of logging when the logs would jam up in the river, no longer able to flow downstream, the rookie logger would attempt to eliminate the logjam by working from the edge in to get to the key log of the jam. Knowingly, the veteran logger climbs the tallest tree around, looks up and down the river, spots the logs that are creating the mess. The veteran orders the cause of the jam to be blown-up, allowing the flow of the river to naturally resolve all constriction. You are always at choice as to deal with the cause or their effects.

Spiritual Contemplation: Is there an area of your life you feel constricted? Take an elevated view of your world and identify what is causing this tightening. Decide what to do about the cause and carry out the plan.

Affirmation: My elevated perspective gives me clarity to the causative energies operating in my life

JANUARY 18

Practicing the Presence

*The most holy and important practice in the spiritual life is the presence of God —
that is, every moment to take great pleasure that God is with you.* — Brother
Lawrence

Would you sign up for a marathon and show up on race day without
having done any training? Can you imagine that? Setting out to run 26.2 miles
without having run at all would be a disaster! You wouldn't be able to finish
the race and the pain in your feet and body from the strenuous exercise
would be immense! This is something you would just not do. Similarly, you
can't commit to living a spiritual life without ever doing spiritual practice.
We have been taught that taking time daily for meditation, prayer and
contemplation can change our experience of life and bring us more health,
prosperity, and peace.

As you engage in spiritual practices regularly, you begin to develop a
sense of the presence of God that is with you all the time. The more you
realize this and allow it to resonate within you, when you hit a rocky patch,
you can lean on and depend on Spirit for support. Without that practice, it
is much more difficult when life gets chaotic. Practice the Presence on a daily
basis and soon you will know that you are always connected to God, always
supported by its love, and all is well.

Spiritual Contemplation: Spend some time in silence today communing
with the Presence of God at the center of your heart. Just breathe and allow
that feeling to fill your entire body. Move through your day and notice how
different it feels when you are conscious of your connection.

Affirmation: I breathe into my heart and feel the love of God that has lived
there always.

JANUARY 19

Beyond the Human Hypnotic Trance

Thought can be so seductive and hypnotic that it absorbs your attention totally, so you become your thoughts. — Eckhart Tolle

Part of the human hypnotic trance is attempting to convince God that you have a problem. The Infinite does not get that there is something other than Itself. You don't take heaven by storm. It's not by might or power but by understanding and realizing through communion. You don't have to stir up God on your behalf. All you'll want to do is recognize the nothingness of what's interfering with your life by becoming still and listening to a higher perspective. The spellbinding human perception will dissipate, leaving only Spirit to contemplate.

After some time in this contemplative state, you arrive at a place where thought stops, and you are just basking in a vibration of peace. This Divine frequency has no words or descriptives; it is an experience of well-being. There is only the Presence as you. Communion is gone because there are not two. In this union there is only God and there is nothing troubling going on in this Kingdom. The disconcerting images and stories of the human hypnotic trance dissolve back into the nothingness from which they came. This is how to transform the human condition from disturbance to wholeness.

Spiritual Contemplation: Take some time to bask in the Divine Frequency of peace!

Affirmation: I am the Divine Presence expressing!

JANUARY 20

Eat your Spinach!

When we learn to trust the Universe, we shall be happy, prosperous and well. –
Ernest Holmes, SOM p. 33.3

We all know that dark leafy greens like kale and spinach are good for us. They are packed with nutrients and vitamins that are necessary for our health and vitality. But often, even though we know it's good for us, we don't actually put it into our mouths and eat it, choosing other, less healthy options instead.

Spirituality can be like this. Some people like to talk about spiritual principles and some like to read about and contemplate how they work, but it does no good for the quality of our lives unless we actually put them into action. As we begin this year and this adventure for our souls, let us take one step every day to align our actions with our beliefs and begin to live these principles so that we not only know about God, but we have a deep experience of God. We can begin to trust Life to call to us all the experiences that bring a deeper peace, joy, and well-being. This way, we will experience what Ernest Holmes is talking about in the above quote: we will be happy, prosperous and well.

Spiritual Contemplation: Take a look at your life to see in what areas you are more or less likely to trust the Divine process. How can you practice your knowledge of Spirituality in that area a bit more? (meditation, affirmation, prayer) Commit to doing one thing each day this month to deepen your connection to the Divine.

Affirmation: I trust the Universe. I am happy, prosperous and well!

JANUARY 21

A Remembering Flash

Yea, though I walk through the valley of the shadow of death, I will fear no evil; for Thou art with me; Thy rod and Thy staff, they comfort me. — Psalm 23:4, KJ21

One cold snowy Montana night I walked the quarter mile home through the forest from my closest neighbor's house after dinner. Out of nowhere, a remembering flash caught my awareness of a recent night video footage from my neighbor's camcorder triggered by a mama mountain lion with her adolescent brood of three strolling through their yard. Suddenly, the peaceful starless night stroll home took on a whole other anxious edge that was not as comfortable as the twilight walk over had been.

Crazy how a brief image that pops into the mind can instantly alter the physiological energy that pulses through the body. There will always be lions and bears in the forest or sharks in the ocean. There will be individuals looking to take advantage of others in life. To be aware of those possibilities has its place, but to allow fear to capture your emotions activating the law of attraction in a direction you don't want to go, is not freedom. Replacing the unwanted image that is robbing the moment of its joy, so you can once again be available for the gifts of God that are Omnipresent, is what reclaiming your emotional power is all about.

Spiritual Contemplation: What images are you allowing to fill your awareness? Which ones do not support this year's intention that need to be replaced? What fresh images will you love to empower so they may attract the gifts of God?

Affirmation: I reclaim my power.

JANUARY 22

Living by Vision

Spiritual vision requires that what we see with the eyes of our hearts will be more real to us than what we see with our natural eyes. We must see what is invisible to others. — Rick Joyner

Michael Beckwith is famous for saying we are "pushed by pain until we are pulled by vision." This is a spiritual truth. Life can be rocky until we are connected to a greater vision for ourselves and our lives. There is a Divine perfection to the unfoldment of our lives. But the experience of that unfoldment depends on where we place our conscious attention. Sometimes, that unfoldment can look a little rocky. Situations and experiences shove us forward toward growth and expansion. This can sometimes feel like we are in the middle of the spin cycle of the washing machine. When you live according to Vision, life is different. Vision is a greater idea of what's possible for you. The Vision pulls you – it's an inner urge; a knowing that feels otherworldly. When you hold a high vision for your life, you move toward expansion and greater expression for yourself in a graceful way. Growth happens with ease and joy. This is how God supports you, if you allow it, but it takes a commitment to return to the vision daily; to steep yourself in it and allow it to grow because the vision is alive as part of you. We are called to trust the vision, which means trusting God because God knows you and what you are capable of more than anyone.

Spiritual Contemplation: Today, begin to connect with the Vision for your life and see how everything gets a bit brighter, and your days are steeped in peace, support and ease.

Affirmation: Today and every day I trust God's vision for my life and live in alignment with it!

JANUARY 23

Life's Dynamics

Our minds influence the key activity of the brain, which then influences everything; perception, cognition, thoughts and feelings, personal relationships; they're all a projection of you. – Deepak Chopra

There is a story told of a congregation located across the street from a wild bar. They never liked it and would pray to God for it to go away. One night, lightning struck and burned the bar to the ground. The bar owner sued the church for damages. The church claimed not to be liable. After the judge heard the case, she said that she'd need more time to think about it before a verdict, but it was the first time she had encountered a bar that had more faith than the church members. Our minds influence the key activity of the brain which in turn influences everything--perception, cognition, thoughts, feelings, and personal relationships. They're all a projection of you.

It's always our perception of what has happened that creates our experience. What do you keep telling yourself about what has happened in your life? Is it lifting you up or holding you down? Does it free you or bind you to the past? It takes today's energy to keep the past alive. Are you exhausting yourself with what was or with anxiousness of what could be? Using today's energy to pay the debt of yesterday or tomorrow depletes your energy for now. If a bar owner can change their story about answered prayer, you too can change your perspective to give you the freedom to live wholeheartedly once again.

Spiritual Contemplation: What stories are you telling yourself that deplete your energy? How can you change your interpretation of that experience to lift you up?

Affirmation: I choose a healthier perspective of my life's dynamics!

JANUARY 24

Raise Your Consciousness

There is a gold kernel of truth within each of us. It is the marrow of who you really are. It's right there - your true self, your soul self - shimmering and powerful, free of fear, clean of envy, clear of purpose. — Elizabeth Lesser

In Metaphysics, we learn our belief system outlines what is possible for us in life. If you believe you'll have to fight for everything you want in life, then the universe will reflect those beliefs. If, however, you believe that the Universe is supportive of you, your experience will be markedly different. When you live according to the outside world, you fall under the Law of Averages, meaning 80% of people around you get sick, then you'll probably get sick also. You become a statistic because you believe what you see and what you are being told.

As you shift to a spiritual perspective, you rise above the Law of Averages, and commonly held beliefs no longer apply to you. When you live from a higher place, where the forces of the universe conspire for your good, no matter what, you will be centered in well-being. You will be able to walk through a crowd of sick people and not even catch a cough! You will be prosperous even in an economic downturn! You will be healthy and vibrant no matter how many trips around the sun you take!

Spiritual Contemplation: Today, look for the ways that your understanding of a situation in your world was limited by some external information and journal how you can shift that belief to one of possibility and potential.

Affirmation: I am One with the Divine Mind and affirm infinite possibility as my true being today and every day!

JANUARY 25

Form Follows Consciousness

Spiritual communion is deeper than intellectual perception. The prayer of the intellect may be perfect in form; but this form must be warmed and colored by feeling and conviction. – Ernest Holmes

Communion is not supplication, it's an inward sense of Truth. It is entering into a conscious union with the Infinite Mind. The secret place of the most high is hidden at the center of your being, where in the silence you can connect. In this lowly listening, Divine Images can make their impress known within your awareness. They will reproduce themselves through the principle of Cause and Effect into your physical world, as all form follows consciousness.

The Creative Process reflects the likeness of your thought back to you. Transforming a condition in your body or life then becomes a matter of getting your thoughts aligned with a higher perspective than you are presently holding. You must arrive at a point of certainty in your prayer process in order for the transformation to result in healing the condition you wish to change. You are dealing with a limitless power that is not bound by precedent. Give Infinity a little extra room in your mind and you will soon be manifesting your heart's desire.

Spiritual Contemplation: What conditions in your body and life would you like to see transformed? What thoughts are you holding on to that are keeping the higher perspective at bay? Find a quiet place to commune with the Infinite that is not bound by your condition. What new image of the Truth is impressing upon your awareness?

Affirmation: I am now seeing the transformed state of my body and life from a higher perspective!

JANUARY 26

Matchless Significance

Dream big & have huge ambition, but never forget life is lived in small moments and sustained by simple acts of love. — Cory Booker

The guru asked his disciple to bring him a bucket of water to cool down his tub. After achieving the right temperature, the disciple threw what was left of the water out the window. The teacher pointed out to his student that he could have watered the ashram's plants with the little he had left. In that moment the student realized in his quest for understanding, he was so anxious about finding the big revelations of enlightenment, wisdom and joy that he forgot the ordinary moments. They seemed so small in comparison to his pursuit of the Infinite.

Many devotees become careless in their routine chores. They might forget how much of life's meaning can be found in the slightest of actions, that every thought, word and action hold matchless significance on their spiritual journeys. You are the recipient of matchless significance simply by loving what's before you.

Spiritual Contemplation: Where do you move through life not being fully present? Where are rich soul gifts waiting for you to become more present to them? Go get them by being fully available to receive what they are offering.

Affirmation: I am blessed by the rich gifts of the Infinite Intelligence whether packaged in small or grand moments of my life.

JANUARY 27

House of Mirrors

We live in a house of mirrors and think we are looking out the windows. — *Frederick Salomon Perls*

Sometimes we go along in our lives, hit a rough patch, and can't figure out what is happening or why! Strained relationships that were once calm and harmonious, challenging work situations previously filled with ease, or discomfort in the body where there was once peace are all examples of situations that could wake us up to something being off kilter in our world. One thing we can do is remember that what we see and experience in our lives is a projection of something inside of us — a result of a disturbance in our thoughts and feelings.

All that we see out in the world is a projection of our inner landscape. When our world is rocking, we can be sure that something is calling for attention within. It is a call to align the idea of who we want to be in the world with our choices and actions. As we embrace these truths of ourselves, our world begins to shift and change, and we see things differently. If we have a generous heart, we will see a generous world. If we are kind and compassionate, kindness and compassion will reflect back to us. All our actions and choices, both kind and unkind, move out into our lives and come back to us in ways we can't imagine.

Spiritual Contemplation: If your world is rocking and you're frustrated about how things are going, take some time to contemplate what could be reflecting back onto you. Journal about how you want to show up and see if you can begin to embody this. Then, sit back and see how life reflects back.

Affirmation: I see the world as a reflection of my inner landscape. I embrace and embody love, and the whole universe loves me back!

JANUARY 28

What Voice are You Listening to?

Listen with your heart, listen to your inner voice of wisdom, listen to your dreams. You know what is right for you. – Cheryl Hamada

We each have a few voices in our heads. These voices can be cheerleaders or critics for us. Which voice do you listen to more? The Inner Critic has a lot to say about how you've gotten it wrong along the way. It has some harsh opinions and though it rarely gives suggestions how to get it right, it loves to point out your faults and mistakes. The cheerleader, also known as your Inner Advisor, has some deep wisdom for you and can show you possibilities and guide you to your greatness. The challenge is that the Critic is much louder than the Advisor and it takes attention and focus to ignore the clanging criticism. In lieu of that, listen for the quiet guidance that lives a little deeper within.

It serves us greatly to take the time daily to listen to what is happening within our minds and consciousness. If left unchecked, we can find ourselves feeling ripped apart by life and the world, when the truth is, it comes from our very own minds. When we connect to that still small voice within, we begin to realize that we are more than the critic thinks we are and we are capable of great things. I encourage you to meet and begin a relationship with your Inner Advisor and allow its voice to be the one you listen to most as it will never steer you wrong.

Spiritual Contemplation: Today, as you walk through your day, notice your mind chatter, and observe which voice is guiding the way: your Inner Critic or Inner Advisor. If the Critic has most of your attention, invite your Inner Advisor on a date and spend some time listening and getting to know its voice.

Affirmation: I listen to the wisdom within and allow it to guide me to my greatest expression!

JANUARY 29

You are Precious to Life

Every blade of grass has its angel that bends over it and whispers, 'Grow, grow, grow!' – The Talmud

It's easy to forget that we are Divine beings living spiritual lives when we get caught up in the noise of the world around us. In this fast-paced life, where everyone is in competition with one another to get ahead and succeed, we can forget our true nature. Life is not complete without our participation in it. Each of us is an individual expression and we bring something unique and necessary to life.

Every one of us is important in the grand scheme of life. So much so that the Divine is there to support us with everything we need, including guidance, resources and opportunities. It takes being conscious of this and accepting the Divine support in our daily lives to affirm this truth. When we do this, and realize that we, too, have an angel bending over us whispering blessings, our sense of self increases. Be open to accepting divine abundance as our true nature and our lives flow in harmony, simply because we know we are precious to Life and to God.

Spiritual Contemplation: How would you be living your life differently if you absolutely knew you were 100% supported by God?

Affirmation: I am One with the Divine and a precious part of Life!

JANUARY 30

Season for Nonviolence

We learn to practice nonviolence one step at a time, one choice at a time, one day at a time. Through our daily nonviolent choices and action, the noble and courageous spirit within each of us expresses itself as the skills, wisdom and character of a nonviolent human being. — Barbara Fields

There is a 64-day season for nonviolence that begins with the anniversary of the assassination of Mahatma Gandhi on January 30, ending on the April 4th anniversary of the assassination of Martin Luther King Jr. It is anchored by a mission, statement of principles, and commitments by participants towards living in a nonviolent way.

Peace is found, neither in denial nor by ignoring issues, but by meeting them courageously. Albert Einstein stated, "Peace cannot be kept by force. It can only be achieved by understanding." Peace doesn't mean challenges are eliminated, rather it comes from the capacity to deal with them in a peaceful manner. So slow down, find an inner stillness in which to do what's next. Do not give your power away to the chaos of the world. Do not allow others 'behavior to rob your inner calm. When you are at peace, you bring peace to the world. Do your peaceful part wherever you are and those pieces will engulf the world with the courageous power of peace.

Spiritual Contemplation: Where are you allowing the chaos of the outside world to rob you of your inner calm? How can you slow down, and from a clear awareness, neutralize the inner turmoil, thus returning to a place of peace?

Affirmation: I live my life from the clarity of inner peace!

JANUARY 31

Softening the Heart

It's the hard things that break; soft things don't break…You can waste so many years of your life trying to become something hard in order not to break; but it's the soft things that can't break! The hard things are the ones that shatter into a million pieces! — C. Joybell

In the Book of Exodus, it is recounted that Moses, sent by God, approached Pharaoh to request the liberation of the Israelites who were enslaved in Egypt. However, Pharaoh repeatedly refused to let them go, despite witnessing miraculous signs and plagues brought about by God through Moses. Each time a plague occurred; Pharaoh's heart was described as being "hardened." The story highlights Pharaoh's stubbornness and resistance to change. His heart is portrayed as being metaphorically hardened, which means he was resistant to feeling compassion, empathy, or understanding towards the suffering of the Israelites. His pride, power, and self-interest consumed him, which prevented him from seeing the injustice he was perpetuating.

It is easy to become disillusioned and stuck in pride when Life pulls us in an uncomfortable direction. Our hearts get bruised, and we can become defensive and forget that Life itself is always there for us and we can trust it. Setting an intention to keep a softened heart will support us in moving forward with compassion, which creates opportunities for growth, expansion, and connection.

Spiritual Contemplation: Are there areas of your life where you feel like you have a "hardened heart"? How could you adopt a softer stance and trust that Life is supporting you more than you might think?

Affirmation: My heart is open and receptive to the flow of Life.

FEBRUARY

Love

February 1-7
Love is Who You Are

February 8-14
Live Love

February 15-21
Seeing with the Heart

February 22-28
Loving Yourself

FEBRUARY 1

You are Love

Do not pity the dead, Harry. Pity the living, and, above all those who live without love. — Dumbledore

We have been taught to believe that we only experience love if someone else loves us. We look for relationships to give and receive love rather than realizing that we **are** love. So much time and energy has been wasted trying to make ourselves attractive to others, saying and doing the right things to attract a partner. We put up roadblocks and barriers to how love can come into our experience and consequently, there is a loneliness pandemic happening across the globe.

We all long for greater connection and intimacy, but what we long for already lives within us. The true experience of love comes from the Divine Spirit of God and is then individualized in each and every one of us. God is love and we are made in its image and likeness, which means we are made out of the presence of love. We can never be separated from it. When we begin to embrace this concept, we can get out of our own way, so that God's love flows to us and then through us out into our relationships. When we approach life this way, we come from wholeness and our love blesses those in our lives. We are no longer desperately trying to make someone love us. We welcome and celebrate it and live in an atmosphere of connection and love.

Spiritual Contemplation: What barriers, if any, have you constructed to limit how love comes into your life? Where do you have a difficult time sharing your love? See if you can stretch yourself to open and see love as a way of being in your life. How could your experience of love be different?

Affirmation: I am alive with Love!

FEBRUARY 2

Let God Be God as You

I believe life is constantly testing us for our level of commitment, and life's greatest rewards are reserved for those who demonstrate a never-ending commitment to act until they achieve. This level of resolve can move mountains, but it must be constant and consistent. As simplistic as this may sound, it is still the common denominator separating those who live their dreams from those who live in regret. — Tony Robbins

When the odds appear to be against you, you've got to learn there is greater good in store for you than you have realized. The odds are for you because God is on your side and the odds are about to shift in your favor. The challenge that appears insurmountable is only temporary. Since God has brought you this far in life, you are not going to be abandoned now. You are in the process of learning that, *"this too shall pass"* didn't come to stay - it's transitory! It's moving through like clouds in the sky. Edmund Hillary reminded us, *It is not the mountain we conquer but ourselves."* You are an avenue of the Power which can move mountains, part the sea, and raise the dead. You can go through life stating all the facts why you can't flourish. Or, you can learn to allow God to be God as you. When you love your learning process, you don't get stuck behind the issues. It's your learning opportunity to dig down deep within, pulling forth aspects of your being that would remain dormant. You'll no longer get upset with a challenge and instead find yourself appreciating it for the call to be the Power that can move mountains.

Spiritual Contemplation: What mountains are standing in your way right now? How can God be God as you that will move the mountain that lies before you or give you the feet of faith to climb it?

Affirmation: When I face the opportunities to be more than I have been, I allow God to be God as me!

FEBRUARY 3

Life Loves You

I have found that if you love life, life will love you back. — Arthur Rubinstein

"Life loves us and wants us to have everything we need and desire." I say this to my teenage daughter often and regularly get an eye roll back. On this particular day I continued, "You'll see! Just wait!" I got a "yeh, right" in response and we went along our way. A few weeks later, as I was working on a knitting project, I expressed my desire to connect with my knitting teacher but unfortunately, our local yarn shop closed and I didn't have her contact information. The very next day, leaving an appointment, as we stepped out of the shop, there was my knitting teacher sitting on a bench smiling at us! I looked at my daughter and smiled because I knew the "I told you so" didn't need to be said! She laughed and shook her head at me in that knowing way.

This is a spiritual truth that is important to remember. Life loves us so much that it wants us to have what we need and want. The tricky part of this is that it is according to our beliefs that our experiences align. Can you believe that life is for you and not against you? Can you open your eyes wide to see the ways that life is trying to support you and you may be missing it? I encourage you to play with this idea today and allow the power of Life to bring you that which will bring fulfillment and happiness to your experience.

Spiritual Contemplation: Walk through your day as if this were true and see how the experience shifts to ease and grace. Then, note your observations in your journal so you can begin to collect all the ways that Life is there for you.

Affirmation: Life loves and brings me everything I need and desire!

FEBRUARY 4

Who You Are Is Enough

On a mountain lived a famous tea master. His skill in this art was unsurpassed, and many came from far away to sit at his tea house. One day an impatient samurai burned his tongue on the master's green tea. Enraged, he challenged the master to a duel. As the warrior drew his sword, the master turned to his young apprentice. "I have done nothing but make tea my whole life. This duel is surely my end. The tea house is yours, my student." The student cried out. "No master, take my sword. Face this warrior and raise your weapon in the same way you raise the teapot!" The master walked slowly into the courtyard, and the samurai rushed to attack. Then, the master closed his eyes and raised his weapon steadily towards heaven, with the same grace and strength he would command in the solemnity of tea rituals. At this display of balance, the samurai panicked and thought, "This old man must be a master swordsman!" The samurai fled the tea house, never to return.   — *An Ancient Zen Story*

Your love and dedication to your soul's work will transform your life in ways you couldn't have planned, nor ever dreamed. The single focus of a master in the multitasking world of today has become highly rewarded and appreciated. What counts most is living your joy and doing what you are good at. You'll find your distinct skills will lead you through life's unique moments.

Spiritual Contemplation: How can I give more of myself to what I love to do?

Affirmation: I trust what I love to do is enough to richly bless my life!

FEBRUARY 5

Vulnerability & Love

When someone reveals themselves completely, it's impossible not to love them. —
Stephen Victor

Your ability to be vulnerable and share your authentic self with the world has a big impact on your ability to create deep and intimate connections with others. This can be challenging if you've been hurt in prior relationships and have closed your heart off to others and maybe, even, to yourself. Being vulnerable takes trust and a sense of safety. It is important to be careful choosing those people with whom you can be vulnerable. You do not need to share your presence and all your deepest thoughts and ideas with just anyone. But when you cultivate a safe space to be able to open and share who you are, it is a gift for the other person as well as for yourself.

Authentic sharing leads to trust, emotional bonding, empathy and compassion, and deep connection. True love is the ability to share yourself freely and see the other person for who they are. When you do this, your life will be enriched, and you will create genuine, intimate, and fulfilling connections.

Spiritual Contemplation: Are you able to be authentic and vulnerable in your relationships? Are there people with whom you are more comfortable sharing yourself with? Less comfortable? Explore your ability/willingness to be vulnerable in your life.

Affirmation: I share myself with those I love fully and freely!

FEBRUARY 6

Let Love Lead

Your soul's journey is timeless, limitless and immeasurable. It is unsurprising that you have forgotten who you truly are – a divine being of light. With each lifetime, you are given a fresh start for learning and a unique purpose to your life.
– James Van Praagh

If you were to remember all your past incarnations and things you messed up on or thoroughly enjoyed, you'd be so caught up in attempting to correct mistakes or endeavoring to chase down those good past experiences, you would be unavailable for the gifts and soul lessons of your present life. It's no wonder we've left our memories on the other side; though they are all there for those who learn how to dial into the particulars. You are the accumulation of your soul experiences. Soul lessons are what move with you through time and space.

When you turn from your controlling mind to your expanded self, you'll feel confident in love's guidance. You'll no longer seek to please others. Your concern for what they think of you no longer holds sway over you. You'll be moving in the love vibration rather than fear. You are freed from the constraints of this world, not because "accurate judgment" of others released you, but for the love of yourself that would not allow you to be submerged in the density of the three-dimensional world. Who you are is so much more than the little bit of consciousness that has slipped into your body's present awareness. Let love lead your way on your enchanted journey!

Spiritual Contemplation: Bring your awareness into the stillness that is present right now. Without thought, allow yourself to be immersed in a love vibration.

Affirmation: I am more than what's in this world!

FEBRUARY 7

Spreading Love

Spread love everywhere you go. Let no one ever come to you without leaving happier. — Mother Teresa

The Dalai Lama says one thing that gets in our way of happiness and fulfillment is living with a self-centered attitude. Along the spiritual journey, we do a lot of inner work and focus attention on ourselves and our process, as it should be! Most of our issues begin within our own hearts and minds. Where we get off track is when we forget to balance our self-work with being of service to the world. When we give of ourselves in service, we find a new level of the reality of life for others, and we see ourselves more clearly. Participating in any kind of service opens your heart up and connects you at a deep level to those whom you are serving. It doesn't matter if it is helping at a food pantry, participating in a community clean-up, or delivering a meal to an elder down the street, giving of yourself in service ends up serving you, too. It can be as simple as giving a silent blessing to everyone you meet. You don't need to say anything! As you look at the person, acknowledge their divinity and bless them with love, abundance, and health. Try this for a day and see how much more connected, lighter, and optimistic about life you feel.

Spiritual Contemplation: Think about what kinds of service you would like to do. Research ways to be of service. As you go through your day today, silently bless each person you meet. Journal at the end of the day how it feels to be generous of spirit in this way.

Affirmation: I am a beacon of light and spread love to everyone I meet today and every day!

FEBRUARY 8

Up, Up and Away

Our soulmate is someone who shares our deepest longings, our sense of direction. When we're two balloons, and together our direction is up, chances are we've found the right person. Our soulmate is the one who makes life come to life.
— Richard Bach

When air is heated in a balloon, it expands and the balloon lifts off the ground, rising ever higher into the celestial realm. When you find the one you love, the one who brings you alive, there is a warmth, a lightness, an excitement, a passion and an expansion. You can't help but feel your feet lifting off the ground. When you think of the other person and find yourself floating, this tends to be a good sign if love is what you are seeking. On the other hand, if you are getting a cold shoulder or have a sinking feeling in your gut, obviously things have cooled off between you two. When cool air enters the balloon, it returns to earth. Cold air contracts, becoming heavy, weighing the balloon down.

A relationship can be like a balloon. It's nothing until you put something into it. For best results, you have to heat it up. When the flames are on, there is no hiding it. Everyone on the outside can see what's happening on the inside as you soar high.

Spiritual Contemplation: Where have you let the flame fade that you'd like to see stirred again? How can you bring heat to this situation?

Affirmation: I turn on my heart light and heat up my relationship.

FEBRUARY 9

Be Brave in Love

~~~

A coward is incapable of exhibiting love; it is the prerogative of the brave. —
Mohandas K. Gandhi, presidential address to the First Gujarat Political
Conference, November 3, 1917

One aspect of living wholeheartedly is loving those around you freely and fully. This can be a challenge because we have all been wounded and hurt by love at one time or another. Rejection can be hard, and we are all rejected at some point as we search for those people who are ready for and can accept our love and appreciation. The key is in not allowing the pain of the past to lock up our hearts and pull us away from the power of connecting with others on a deep level.

We are called to be brave in love! We must be bold and daring! If you hold yourself back because of past hurts, you deny yourself the joy, connection, and passion you feel when you share who you are with someone who is ready to see and know you. Sometimes it takes courage to take that first step forward to speak your truth and share your heart. When you do this, you see that it is always worth sharing your love because when you are brave in love and share yourself freely, the gifts and blessings outweigh any pain the past may have held.

Spiritual Contemplation: Think about what experiences from your past may be holding you back from sharing your love fully and freely? How can you step out bravely to open to love in a new way?

Affirmation: I bravely share my love with the world!

FEBRUARY 10

Choose Love

Love never dies a natural death. It dies because we don't know how to replenish its source. It dies of blindness and errors and betrayals. — Anais Nin

Love is the same in the east or the west, no matter whether it be the Northern hemisphere or the south. Love is a nectar that sweetens life. It lies within every human being. This is not something that is brought in or found somewhere else. If anything, the more "cultured and civilized" you become, the more control is imposed on the natural expression of love. Love and its fragrance are the very longing and call that resides in all people. It is your intrinsic nature.

If you could dissolve the cultural conditionings of the appropriate ways on how to love and be in love, then how to love would not need to be taught; only expressed. Humans have created taboos around sexual energy, turning cultural teachings into inner conflicts. The very existence of life depends on the attractiveness of love. A flower in bloom, a bird singing its song and doing its dance, young men and women doing their dances, are all expressions of life's longing for its existence to continue. What is often the starting point of a deeper expression of love is something you are taught to fight against. Love is your true nature, yet "Holy Ones" teach you to battle, often creating a lifelong discomfort around a wholehearted vulnerability to love.

Spiritual Contemplation: Do you remember a time you were taught it was wrong to pursue love or when you were not comfortable with your own vulnerability? How has that programming shut you down in your ability to trust your vulnerability in love?

Affirmation: When I feel love, I choose love!

FEBRUARY 11

A Love that is Unconditional

There is no greater power in heaven or on earth than pure, unconditional love. –
Wayne Dyer

Many religions and spiritual traditions emphasize the power of unconditional love. Unconditional love, or love in its purest form, is a form of love that is given freely with no expectation of anything in return. It is not based on any condition or requirement. It is a selfless love that transcends personal gain, expectation, or criticism.

Unconditional love accepts you for who you are with no judgment. It recognizes the gift that each person is and celebrates their uniqueness without fear of rejection. It creates a safe space for you to be vulnerable and share your authentic self. It fosters compassion and care for one another as it encourages us all to continue to grow and evolve. Though unconditional love can be challenging sometimes, it is a powerful principle to practice. Striving toward living with an attitude of unconditional love in your primary relationships, with your family, kids, and friends welcomes the transformational power of love to be alive in your experience.

Spiritual Contemplation: With whom in your life can you easily practice unconditional love and acceptance? Your partner? Your kids? Your friends? Think about ways you can begin to be more loving, more accepting.

Affirmation: I love those in my life unconditionally. I see the gift they are and celebrate their uniqueness!

FEBRUARY 12

A Transparency for Love

If we give the love of God just a tiny crack through which to enter this world, we shall see how quickly that love will encircle the globe—faster than sound, faster than light. But there must be an entrance made into this world for God, or else God is kept outside. — Joel S. Goldsmith

We all know that this world would benefit from an increased atmosphere of love because we see its positive effects on our young children who thrive when they feel safe and loved, on our animals that share their love freely with us, and even on our plants that blossom and bloom when cared for. The problem is that we are all so entranced by fear that we forget about the healing nature of love and kindness.

The bible teaches that God is love and that God loves each and every one of us. The challenge is that the only way ove can rise into the experience of this world is through us. We are the channel through which love can be expressed, given and experienced. We are called each day to lay down our fears, resentments and anger to open to and embrace love into our experience. Let us become a transparency for love and allow our loving nature to flow forth out into the world. This way, we learn of our own worthiness for love, we share it freely with others and we welcome God into the experience of our lives.

Spiritual Contemplation: Look at your life and see what areas are closed off to God's love. See what old wounds and resentments are keeping you from fully experiencing love in your life. Are you ready to let go of the past in order to fully accept God's love?

Affirmation: I am a Transparency for Love and share God's Love freely in the world!

FEBRUARY 13

Love Enhances

There's no bad consequence to loving fully, with all your heart. You always gain
by giving love. — Reese Witherspoon

Love is the great surrender whereas, instead of leaving you empty, it fills your soul. Mother Teresa said, "Spread love everywhere you go. Let no one ever come to you without leaving happier." The Universal flame of Love consumes fear, melts away the prison bars of apprehension and sets the soul soaring. No reason is required to become loving. It's what your heart yearns for - that which it cannot describe, the ineffable touch of love. Love becomes you when you become love. It graces everything it touches.

One of the crazy things about Love is that it will interpret itself to you only when you love. In the generous giving of love, you go deep into being a receiver. Spirit's Life Force will flow into you, through you and out into your relationships. Recognizing the Divine in those around you lifts the level of your consciousness, making you a love distributor. Every action you take, motivated by the pulse of a fully loving heart, brings the rich blessings of love in amazing ways. Love realizes itself in others and delights in the revelation of the dance of Oneness.

Spiritual Contemplation: Aristotle said, *"Love is composed of a single soul inhabiting two bodies."* Since love's greatest gift is to bless everything, it touches, what can you do to enhance the love in your life?

Affirmation: I love fully with all my heart and all my soul!

FEBRUARY 14

Time Warp of Love

They slipped briskly into an intimacy from which they never recovered. — F. Scott Fitzgerald

Opening your heart and soul for another person to enter is an intimate act of loving trust. The aliveness that comes from the vulnerability of not knowing where you are headed together brings you so vibrantly present that time becomes irrelevant. It stretches into eternity and disappears in the twinkling of an eye simultaneously. When you enter into love, a temporal shift occurs where days feel like moments and moments become eternal. Days turn into weeks, weeks into months, and before you know it, it's next year.

The richness and magic shared in intimacy seem to make a mockery of the concept of time on the clock. The merging of two souls dissolves the boundaries of the mortal realm, opening the gates to celestial delights. It is a connection beyond words and a journey that's out of this world. You experience your beauty being reflected back to you from the mirror of another loving soul. When you awaken from the timeless as if it were morning, you're left wondering if the sacred experience was real.

Spiritual Contemplation: Are you willing to leave all pretense behind and risk being intimately vulnerable with the one you love? What does stepping through the gate look like for you?

Affirmation: I lovingly surrender to the reciprocating intimacy with my beloved as we journey through amazing new realms!

FEBRUARY 15

Accepting What Is

~~~✦~~~

Things are as they are. Looking into the universe at night we make no comparisons between right and wrong stars, nor between well and badly arranged constellations. — *Alan Watts*

One of the most powerful tools we have in our spiritual toolbox is the practice of acceptance. Sometimes we will find ourselves in an uncomfortable moment in life, like a painful, challenging situation that we want to get out of as quickly as possible. This can only happen when we accept the situation as it is and then step forward from that place. If we circumvent that step, we end up living in the energy of avoidance or resistance, which has no creative power and will prevent us from shifting out of the pain. When we accept what is and see our part in creating it, we open to a broader perspective of ourselves and see beyond our own emotional reaction. We no longer fight against the pain creating more pain, but instead, move to embrace the unfolding process and our opportunities to grow. We can see that life is actually for us and the situations that pop up are purposeful in guiding us in the direction of our joy and freedom.

Spiritual Contemplation: Journal about the areas of your life where you have a hard time accepting what is and see if you can uncover the negative beliefs and fears that are holding you back from accepting your life as it is.

Affirmation: I accept my life as it is today and I know that I can create what I truly desire.

FEBRUARY 16

Complain or Clean It Up

An exciting and inspiring future awaits you beyond the noise in your mind, beyond the guilt, doubt, fear, shame, insecurity and heaviness of the past you carry around. — Debbie Ford

There was a worker who opened his lunch box and grumbled, "Not again, another peanut butter jelly sandwich!" The next day as he opened his bag in the breakroom, he let out a big sigh, saying, "These peanut butter sandwiches are going to be the death of me." The following day, the same story, "Why, oh why is it always peanut butter and jelly sandwiches?" Finally, one of his co-workers couldn't take his agony any longer and she asked him, "Why don't you just ask your partner to make you something different?" The man responded with, "I don't have a partner, I live alone." Perplexed, she then asked, "Then who makes your lunch every day?" The worker's response was priceless, "I do."

Do you grumble about the very things you keep placing in your life? I'm talking about those problematic scenarios that you find disturbing that just keep showing up. Is there a pattern there that keeps repeating itself in your life? The same experience with a different face, a different location, but the same outcome. Could you be the master chef whipping up your life choices? If your love doesn't include yourself, it is incomplete. Stop partaking of what makes you sick.

Spiritual Contemplation: Do you have any recurring patterns in your life that you'd rather complain about than clean up?

Affirmation: I easily recognize where I can step it up in my life!

FEBRUARY 17

Spread Loving Kindness

When we practice loving kindness and compassion, we are the first ones to profit.
— Rumi

There are moments in our lives when we will come across someone who may not understand or even like us. We may be met with negativity and unkindness for some reason we don't or may never understand. It could be a co-worker, acquaintance, or someone we meet randomly. This can be challenging, especially when we have set an intention to live whole-heartedly and be a beacon of kindness out in the world.

One way to handle these kinds of experiences is with the Loving Kindness meditation, also known as Metta, which is a popular Buddhist practice that helps us cultivate benevolence. It is a meditation on unconditional love without any expectations of receiving anything in return. This practice directs thoughts of care, concern, and love towards oneself and others and it is easy to do! Just take a few moments to get silent and centered and imagine the person standing before you, and say: May you be filled with lovingkindness. May you be well. May you be peaceful and at ease. And may you be happy. Repeat this a few times and try to feel your best intentions for this person. Then notice how the pain and angst of the situation begins to drain leaving a growing level of peace and contentment.

Spiritual Contemplation: Choose someone who may be causing some discomfort or challenge in your life today and practice the Loving Kindness meditation toward them and then toward yourself. Notice how you feel afterwards.

Affirmation: I am a channel of Loving Kindness and Compassion to all!

FEBRUARY 18

Look Out the Window

It is the mark of an educated mind to be able to entertain a thought without accepting. — Aristotle

Loving to learn will set you up to be the recipient of life's gifts. Learning is not something relegated to the classroom, where you prepare for life. Learning is life itself. It's what creates excitement as your mind expands. Education is not about filling the mind, but about opening it. It's not about being a mirror and reflecting back what has been taught, but being a window where you look out at the horizon of unlimited possibilities.

Learning is the passport to the future. It is meant to free you. The Dalai Lama once said, "When educating the minds of our youth, we must not forget to educate their hearts." The wisdom of the heart allows compassion for other people's thoughts and positions, without having to accept it. Hearing and understanding different views without judgment or need for the battle, "You are either with me or against me," help make the world a better place.

Spiritual Contemplation: Is there an area of your life that expanding your awareness would help you understand something that is not making sense to you right now? Open your heart and mind to learning more on this subject.

Affirmation: I open the window of my heart and mind to learn more of what life has to offer!

FEBRUARY 19

The Eyes of the Heart

~ed&ve~

If what you see by the eye doesn't please you then close your eyes and see from the heart. Because the heart can see beauty and love more than the eyes can ever wonder. — Anonymous

In order to embrace love as a way of life, we need to start to see differently. We need to look with a deeper eye to perceive ourselves, life, and each other from a place of love rather than through the eyes we have been trained to see through. It is a law of the universe that what we put our attention on expands and so it is important that we are conscious of what we are focusing on to support our happiness and well-being.

The question is, with what eyes are you looking at yourself and your life? When you view yourself through the eyes of your egoic self, you see only challenges and limitations, harshly judging your shortcomings, mistakes, and regrets. But if you begin to look through the eyes of your heart, you see from a Divine perspective. From this perspective, you see the whole journey and how far you've come, your potential, and the opportunities that are all around you. You will see the love and appreciation that already exists in your experience. It can be a very different view.

Spiritual Contemplation: When you look around your life right now, what are you seeing? Are you seeing struggle and lack? Conflict and challenge? Or are you seeing abundance, opportunity, connection and peace? Begin today with the idea that you will look at your day through the eyes of your heart and see how differently your day unfolds.

Affirmation: I see clearly through the eyes of my heart!

FEBRUARY 20

Three Seashells for Love

Life shrinks or expands in proportion to one's courage. – Anais Nin

A young brother was watching his little five-year-old sister outside a shop on a family beach vacation. His younger sister was mesmerized by a doll in the window. So, her brother asked the shopkeeper how much it cost. The owner looked at this young pair and asked how much he had. The little guy stuck his hand in his pocket and pulled out all that he had in it: a few pennies, a couple of dimes, and three seashells he had collected from the beach. The gentleman told him that it was more than enough. He said he'd take the seashells, and he could keep the change. The young boy and girl were thrilled. Though the owner's assistant was a bit perplexed and asked why he didn't just give that doll away. The shopkeeper shared that the little boy didn't have a concept of money and that those shells he had collected were precious to him. Someday when he is older, he will remember this moment and hopefully do something kind for someone else.

Life gives you many opportunities to love, be kind, and show you care. It takes courage to step outside the normal behavioral way of how things are done in order to bring love to a moment.

Spiritual Contemplation: Have you ever wished you'd brought love to a moment where it was not expected, but would have made a difference? How would it have felt if you had? Will you deliver the gift of love next time?

Affirmation: I am willing to feel awkward in bringing love to the unexpected moments of my life!

FEBRUARY 21

Loving our Enemies

Love your enemies, do good to those who hate you, bless those who curse you, pray for those who mistreat you. – Luke 6:27-28, NIV

We cannot deny that we are living in extraordinary times. Political and racial divides are causing rifts in families and communities and many people feel as if we will never see eye to eye. The master teacher Jesus taught that we are to love our enemies and bless those who mistreat us. This seems like an impossible task! And it is, from a human perspective. As a human being, it is difficult to love someone who hurts us intentionally. Even those we get along with and love sometimes fail us. This teaching of Jesus is a call to a higher place of relating to one another.

It is only when we look through our divine eyes, that we can see the connections and similarities we hold to those we don't agree with. When we can acknowledge that we are a child of God as they are also, we can begin to build a bridge. We must look through their personality and actions to the seed of divinity that lives at their core. When we do this, we remove ourselves from our connection to the outer world and move into a state of grace, where divine wisdom reveals itself in greater ways. I am not saying you need to be best friends, but by attempting to do this, we open to a path of healing for ourselves and our world. We are each a child of God and deserve to be happy, healthy, and free. Starting from this point, we can begin to heal the divides and learn to live together in harmony.

Spiritual Contemplation: Who do you consider the "other" or "enemy" in your life? Can you see their divinity and acknowledge that they, too, are a child of God? Sit with this and allow your divine self to reveal wisdom and guidance for you.

Affirmation: I love myself, my neighbor, and my enemy. We are all children of God.

FEBRUARY 22

Give Yourself a Little Love

I have an everyday religion that works for me. Love yourself first, and everything else falls into line. – Lucille Ball

In the midst of the busy lives we are living, it's important that we take time to care for ourselves and our physical and mental health and well-being. Caring for ourselves is an expression of love and we cannot truly express our love for others without caring for and appreciating ourselves. Self-care is not only about taking the time to get a massage or pedicure, although those can be nice ways to care for yourself. Self-care begins with how we hold ourselves in our own minds. We need to shift where we live on our own priority lists as most of us put ourselves way down on the bottom after our families, friends, jobs and just about everyone else in the world! When we begin to put ourselves first, to honor the fact that we are a Divine expression of God, the quality of our care increases and we are better able to navigate this life in joy and freedom. This includes the food we eat, how much rest we get, the quality of our relationships and communing with the Divine. When we love ourselves on that deep level, we begin to thrive in all areas and life becomes a joy rather than a chore.

Spiritual Contemplation: What ways are you currently caring for yourself and showing yourself love? Are there one or two more things that you can commit to doing on a daily or weekly basis that increases your care for yourself?

Affirmation: I am a Divine Expression of God and I love myself in all ways!

FEBRUARY 23

A New Conversation

We don't see things as they are, we see them as we are. — Anaïs Nin

Have you ever been knocked off center? You've got your world in balance, all your beliefs lined up happily supporting you when, out of the blue, wham! Something unexpected challenges where you stand. Someone shares a topic from their passion, and you, all of a sudden understand and feel a different perspective. Maybe there is a riot in the streets or in the family, and you hear in a new way - something different. You have taken a position, but now can feel the pain of the other side.

When realizing there is something to "their" viewpoint, life is no longer simply black or white. Coming to see beyond the previous perception, can be shocking to the psyche. Yet, opening the eyes and heart, expands consciousness. It's from an enlarged awareness that a new conversation can honestly ensue, making a new perspective possible. But are you really available for that honest conversation?

Spiritual Contemplation: Where in your life can an expanded perspective help you to understand where someone else might be coming from?

Affirmation: I am available to see and understand beyond what I believe to be true!

FEBRUARY 24

Love Yourself as you would love God

Love holds no expectation on what you will be, it simply values who you are. –
E'yen A. Gardner

How do you care for yourself? If you honestly answer this question, I think some will have to admit that they may be loving toward others but are harsh on themselves. Sound familiar? What does that inner voice sound like when you make a mistake? Can you be compassionate and understanding? Can you self-soothe in a challenging moment or does your inner critic take over and make some Olympic-style judgment that is harsh, angry, and mean-spirited?

One of the best things you can do to honor and love God in your life is to take good care o and love yourself. When you show love for yourself, you are truly loving God because you are God's creation and as such you deserve all love, compassion, and peace. When you show love for yourself, you elevate your spiritual consciousness and connect with God in a whole new way. You also learn how to freely love others with compassion, kindness, generosity, and respect.

Spiritual Contemplation: How can you show love for yourself today? Choose two things that you can do to show yourself love, compassion and care today.

Affirmation: I am the love of God made manifest and I love myself just as I am!

FEBRUARY 25

Here I Am

Life is available only in the present moment. If you abandon the present moment, you cannot live the moments of your daily life deeply. — Thich Nhat Han

One of the gifts that brings your child great pleasure is for you to be content by simply being present with them. They know if your mind is wandering off elsewhere, wanting something more than just them. "Here I am daddy, be with me, not lost in your thoughts where I can't go."

Relax and find peace and joy in your time together. When you are with your child, be one with them. Love the very moment you are in. Don't be anxious to create another moment; drop your agenda and be attainable. Forget the past, don't flirt with the future, allow your heart and mind to be where your body is.

Spiritual Contemplation: Where in your life do you show up with your body, but yet not fully present of mind? How can you be more content and attentive to the present moment?

Affirmation: I am here, fully present in this moment, body, mind and soul!

FEBRUARY 26

You are Loved

What have I done to deserve love like this? — Lauren Daigle

The truth is you are loved. It is the gift of being alive that we are loved by God. To answer the above question posed by singer Lauren Daigle in her song "A Love like This", you haven't done anything to deserve it. You don't need to do anything special to earn the love of God. You are loved just because you are you. You are a Divine emanation of Spirit itself, made in the image and likeness of God, and as it is explained in the bible many times, God is love.

When we see ourselves as part of God, we can begin to accept that we are loved by life. When we soften our hearts and release the harsh judgements we hold about ourselves, we can welcome love into our experience recognizing its healing and transformational nature. We call others of like minds and hearts towards us and observe that Life itself supports us. There is a natural ease to our days and a sweetness to life.

Spiritual Contemplation: Start your day by spending time in meditation and contemplation, allowing yourself to feel the love God has for you. Breathe it in. Fill yourself up with the knowingness that you are completely supported by God and then move through your day noticing how different your experience is from this attitude.

Affirmation: I am loved by God just because I am me!

FEBRUARY 27

What do you Magnify

Weeping may endure for a night, but joy cometh in the morning. – Psalm 30:5, KJ21

Remember the story of Job from the bible? He was cruising through life, a success, vast herds of oxen, camel, he has a big family and good health. Then he lost it all. Thieves stole his herds, killed his children, and painful skin lesions plagued his health. He started focusing on his misfortune and magnifying his problems. Though he never fully gave up faith in God, he complained about his problems, amplifying them. What we reflect on today is Job's losses and faith in God.

What we often overlook is that his time of struggle was just a brief chapter in a long life. Granted it was not a pleasant time, nor do I want to diminish his pain, but for Job, it was not forever and the end. Amen. It is a powerful observation that we still talk about his problems, forgetting when it was all over, God doubled his wealth and resources. Job and his wife had 10 more children, four generations of grandchildren and he lived another 140 years. His brief rough spot in a very long abundant joy-filled life passed and in retrospect, the time of darkness wasn't very long. You, like Job might get caught in a rough patch on your way to your destiny, but it too will pass. Focus on the 140 good years rather than the dark night when the rough patches arise.

Spiritual Contemplation: Is there some struggle you have been magnifying and amplifying with your attention? Knowing spirit hasn't abandoned you, you are the one who can't see the Divine in the dark. Spirit is still there, so start sharing your story of faith to step into your next 140 glorious years.

Affirmation: My struggle is brief compared to the longevity of my glorious life!

FEBRUARY 28

They Will Reach the Stars

Each child is born immaculate on earth
Nor need await some mystic "second birth."
See in that child the offspring of your heart
And like your own let him be counterpart;
For love grows rich the more it is expressed.
— Ernest Holmes, Voice Celestial, page 184

The failure to invest in youth reflects a lack of compassion and a colossal failure
of common sense. — Coretta Scott King

Children arrive with infinite possibilities. It's not our responsibility to limit them but rather to fuel them with empowering love. It's not our place to tell them what is possible and what is not. They will discover on their own what they can and cannot do. Help them stay open to the mysteries of the universe that seek to express through them. Do not limit their perspectives with your boundaries; they are still in touch with the boundless.

Love children enough to encourage them to go beyond what you know. Foster their bravery to explore new frontiers. Do not scold them for their shortfalls. Be there to help dust them off and point them toward their dream once again, rather than returning to the comfort and confines of their previous margins of know-how. Guide without control, help without worry. Look for the child's heart in all things, and you will know how to be what they need to reach the stars.

Spiritual Contemplation: Are there children in your life that you have disempowered with your beliefs of what is possible and what is not? How can you be more encouraging with your language and action in support of their vision?

Affirmation: I remember the passion and excitement of the possibilities of my youth! (Note: For Leap Year, go to End of Book)

MARCH
Relationships

March 1-7
We Are All in This Together

March 8-14
Love's Connection

March 15-21
Setting Boundaries

March 22-28
Choose Your Battles

March 29-31
Seeing Clearly

MARCH 1

What Makes Today Special

Important encounters are planned by the souls long before the bodies see each other. — Paulo Coelho

Many people have moved through your life. Some of those interactions are significant relationships, and others are brief; yet all are important. When building a house, there are many aspects to its blueprints and construction. Some elements are large, others minimal, yet all are important. The various people who have traversed your path are much like those components crucial to building your home - all valuable contributions that have shaped who you are now.

Some will be in your life for a moment or a season, others for the finish line. If someone has graced your world, leaving an imprint upon your heart, be grateful your paths crossed, even if they can't remain.

Spiritual Contemplation: Take some time to open your heart with gratitude to all who have touched your world. Send some love their way.

Affirmation: I honor all who have crossed my path!

MARCH 2

Divine Time in Relationships

People are in your life for a reason, others are there for a season and it's important to realize when those seasons are over. — Tyrese Gibson

Relationships evolve over time, and we are each on a path of continued personal growth and expansion. This means that change is part of our evolution, and we need to get comfortable with this as an important dynamic in our relationships. We each grow and change over time and some relationships reach a point where they no longer support us and our direction.

You want to support the personal development and growth of those you love. Sometimes we can make space for a new way of being in relationship together and sometimes we cannot. Those are the moments when we bless them and let them go. We don't lose the love we have for one another, but sometimes we need to break the old bonds in order to step in the direction we are being called. This can be done elegantly or not, depending on how conscious we are about this process. Holding on to a relationship that no longer serves either participant is a weight that keeps you locked in the past and chained to an old way of being. Blessing the impact the relationship has had in your life and moving on with gratitude makes the process easier.

Spiritual Contemplation: Do you have any relationships that are no longer serving you or your partner? Can you find a new way of being together? Is it time to gracefully step aside and move on? How can you do this with love?

Affirmation: I celebrate my relationships and know they are here by Divine Design and Divine Time!

MARCH 3

Real Family and True Friends

If you live to be 100, I hope I live to be 100 minus 1 day, so I never have to live without you. — Winnie the Pooh

When it all comes down to it, family and friends are about love. Family and friendships open the channels through which love enters the world. You can do all the things expected of a friend or family member but without love the spirit is missing, and the action will convey as empty. When the interactions embody the emotion, souls are touched and connection is felt beyond gesture. Love is Spirit incarnate, splendid and is as lasting in its touch as you are in the lives of those you love.

Family and friends step in when others step out. Sometimes in life the inner flame dwindles, but connecting with a loved one reignites the inner glow. They understand you; they know your past and have faith in your future and love you for who you are now. It's comforting to know, even if time moves family and friendship apart, you still journeyed together, side by side for a long time. A piece of you will always be with them, and they with you.

Spiritual Contemplation: Is there a good friend or family member who you love deeply that you haven't talked to in a while? Give them a call.

Affirmation: I am grateful for the love I feel from my deep relationships!

MARCH 4

You Deserve It All

Friendship is the golden thread that ties the heart of all the world. — John Evelyn

Sometimes you might find yourself in the middle of a challenging relationship with a friend, family member, or partner. Maybe it is a temporary time of challenge or conflict but sometimes you wake up to realize that the relationship has become toxic for you. A toxic relationship is one characterized by patterns of behavior that are emotionally, mentally, or even physically harmful to one or both partners. We choose people to be in relationships with to enhance our lives, not to bring drama and difficulty. It is important to address these kinds of challenges because staying in a toxic relationship or friendship can do great damage to our mental state and well-being.

You are an emanation of the Divine spirit and deserve to be respected, honored, and loved. If open communication, having clear boundaries, or outside support can't help the situation, sometimes the best thing you can do for yourself, and your friend, is to create some space. It is okay to let go of a relationship that is no longer supporting either partner. It is helpful to do our own work and see what part we played in creating the dynamic but that does not mean you need to stay in a painful situation. Sometimes with space, you can begin to see how the relationship served you and you can move forward, calling in the right and perfect next friend or partner.

Spiritual Contemplation: Do you currently have any toxic relationships/friendships in your life? How do you handle them? Are you comfortable setting boundaries in your relationship? Discuss these topics in your journal.

Affirmation: I am an emanation of the Divine and I deserve to be loved, honored, and respected in all my relationships!

MARCH 5

You Are the Abundance of Heaven

It is difficult to make a man miserable while he feels worthy of himself and claims kindred to the great God who made him. — Abraham Lincoln

Do you realize your past mistakes don't devalue you? That's what you did, not who you are. You can create a business or buy an extra vacation home, but that doesn't make you more valuable. It increases your net-worth, not your self-worth. You have been uniquely created, one of a God kind endowed with the traits of the Great Architect. At times, you may feel just ordinary, but because of the divine designer, there is something in you that is extraordinary. Your worth is not based on what others recognize, but what you recognize in yourself. Remember your designer and what is within you can never be taken from you.

Sometimes the knocks in life may feel like they have devalued you. Those heartbreaks and bad breaks, times you've been misled, or denied and turned down, could make you feel less than wonderful. The knocks are just notches for you to step higher. You must remember you are a magnificent expression of God. Don't markdown Spirit as you; you are enormously valuable. Ernest Holmes would remind us, *There is but one ultimate Power. This Power is to each one what he is to it."* To love yourself right now will direct the Power to call forth for you the abundance of heaven on earth. That's how valuable you are, you can call forth the abundance of heaven! So, what are you waiting for?

Spiritual Contemplation: Where do you devalue yourself? Take some time to remember the Divine Designer and all that is within you, and write it down.

Affirmation: I am of Divine Design and of great value!

MARCH 6

Celebrate Individuality

Genuine love recognizes and respects the unique individuality and separate identity of the other person. — Unknown

Maintaining a sense of individuality within a relationship is crucial for personal growth, self-expression, and overall relationship satisfaction. Finding a balance between focusing on yourself and the relationship is integral to not losing your sense of self. It is easy to be swept up in the relationship and lose sight of your own path. When you make yourself a priority, you stay centered and can give your best to the relationship. When you lose yourself, you become overly dependent on your partner for your happiness and sense of self and end up feeling drained with nothing to share.

Maintaining your individuality can be as simple as creating time for your spiritual practice and self-care daily, communicating your needs to your partner, supporting your partner's interests even if they are different from your own, and holding on to your own goals.

By honoring your individuality, while also working on a strong partnership, you create a relationship that is built on mutual respect, support, and love.

Spiritual Contemplation: How are you maintaining your individuality within your relationships currently? How could you create space for your own dreams, goals, and needs? Share your thoughts in your journal.

Affirmation: I create balance in my relationships. I honor my path, goals, and dreams and make space for my partner to do the same!

MARCH 7

You Deserve to Be Someone's Priority

Be with someone who makes you a priority not an option. — Unknown

Maya Angelou once said, "When people show you who they are, believe them the first time." This can be one of life's hardest lessons to learn. You deserve to have friends and a partner who make you a priority in their lives and an important skill in relationship-building is keeping this top of mind. We've all had the experience of knowing someone who wants to make us a priority but due to one circumstance or another, cannot. As we get older, it can be more difficult to foster new connections, and this can make it easier to just accept the quality of your relationships are the best they can be.

Taking an honest look at the quality of your relationships can be revealing as to the level of priority both of you hold each other to. Investing time and attention in connections that enrich your experience and letting go of relationships that don't, will serve you in the long run. You will find yourself surrounded by quality friends who see and appreciate you for who you are and all you bring to their lives and the world.

Spiritual Contemplation: Make a list of your friendships. Rate them with an A, B or C. A: those who invest time and attention in your connection. B: those who try to make you a priority. C: those who say they want to be friends but do not invest in the relationship. Contemplate your list and how you want to proceed with their friendships.

Affirmation: I am a good friend and make my friendships a priority in my life!

MARCH 8

Celebrating Women – International Women's Day

Where there is a woman, there is magic. – Ntozake Shange

Happy International Women's Day! Today is dedicated to recognizing the achievements of women and promoting gender equality worldwide. IWD is a platform to bring awareness about women's rights, challenge gender biases and discrimination, and advocate for a more inclusive and equitable society. Today is a day to highlight the achievements of notable women throughout history and in our society today. It recognizes the progress we've made towards gender parity while reminding us of the work we still have to do in that arena.

International Women's Day is not limited to a single country or region— it is a global observance and has played a crucial role in raising awareness, inspiring activism, and advocating for policies and practices that promote gender equality. It is a platform for women's voices to be heard, their contributions to be acknowledged, and to encourage dialogue and collaboration toward a more inclusive and just world. IWD reminds us that gender equality is not just a women's issue but rather, it's a fundamental human rights issue. It calls on each of us to take action and work together towards a future where women and girls can thrive, free from discrimination and oppression.

Spiritual Contemplation: Who are the women who inspire you and have made a difference in your life? How can you honor their contributions today? What small act can you do to support gender equality?

Affirmation: I honor and celebrate all women today and commit to helping build a world that works for all!

MARCH 9

Thrive or Dive

My dad always said, "Don't fit into the glass slipper like Cinderella did. Shatter the glass ceiling." – Priyanka Chopra

There is no limit to the Infinite Power. Yet, we become so accustomed to calculating power that we begin to wonder if there will be enough to heal and transform a tough situation. Rid yourself of this restrictive view that impacts your results. The Infinite cannot be calculated; there is always enough! Throw off the shackles of limitation and place your sight on the spiritual truth of unlimited omnipresent abundance. You cannot become what you want while holding onto that which you don't want.

Does your thinking take you to where you want to go? If not, why allow those thoughts to remain in residence in your head? It's the thoughts of difficulty that make something difficult. The belief in ease tends to make things easier. Keep your awareness on the high road, and you will find yourself lifted rather than lowered. Where your attention goes, energy flows. A mind that is open to possibilities has breakthroughs, while a mind that is closed has breakdowns. Thrive or dive – the choice is yours!

Spiritual Contemplation: What thoughts will take you where you want to go?

Affirmation: I now choose uplifting thoughts!

MARCH 10

Asking for Help

Don't be afraid to ask for help when you need it. I do that every day. Asking for help isn't a sign of weakness, it's a sign of strength. It shows you have the courage to admit when you don't know something, and to learn something new. — Barack Obama

There are times in our lives when we hit a brick wall. We are humming along, doing well and then suddenly, everything becomes too much, and we hit overwhelm. At this point, even reading all the books of wisdom on the shelf, sitting for hours of meditation, and journaling until the ink runs out won't cut it. We require a greater level of support. This is the time to call on a trusted therapist or counselor to guide us to a greater place of awareness. A good counselor can help us move through the resistance and denial we hold to get in touch with repressed emotions and trauma.

It may be daunting, but realizing we need support and then opening up and sharing our story with a trusted therapist or counselor is the first step in healing. Being truly listened to and validated by a compassionate ear is a tremendous gift that can awaken us to a greater truth that we can't see. We do not need to walk alone in this life. Reaching out for help can be a brave act that shifts our experience and brings greater insight into ourselves and the world.

Spiritual Contemplation: How comfortable are you asking for help? Who in your life would you turn to in a moment of need? Do you have a spiritual counselor or therapist? A trusted friend? Make a list in your journal of those people who are there for you. If you can't come up with any names, maybe it's time to look for a counselor for support.

Affirmation: I am brave and ask for help when I need it.

MARCH 11

Cleaning Up Your Relationships

Friendship is the golden thread that ties the heart of all the world. — *John Evelyn*

Our relationships are some of the most precious gifts in our lives. Whether it is with family or a friend, these connections bring depth, warmth, and love to our experience. They allow us space where we can truly be ourselves and work out our issues and challenges. It is a place of mutual sharing where we give love and support and can receive it.

Relationships, like just about everything in our lives, sometimes need tidying up. Maybe we said some harsh words in a moment of frustration, made false accusations or neglected to honor their point of view. It is important that we examine the state of our relationships and make amends for anything that we did either consciously or unconsciously. When we speak our truth from the heart with an intention for love and healing, making amends can deepen our connections and we benefit from walking the path of life with those whom we love and who love us.

Spiritual Contemplation: Is there anything you need to clean up in any of your relationships currently? Take the time to get clear about the part you played in the situation and write a letter to the person. Decide if you want to send the letter or have a conversation about it.

Affirmation: I take responsibility for the part I play in my relationships and speak my truth with love.

MARCH 12

Love's Connection

Your children will see what you're all about by what you live rather than what you say. — Wayne Dyer

Just past sunset, a gentleman was walking home through the park when he heard a woman fighting and screaming from behind the bushes. As he listened, it was clear she was being attacked. Hesitating for a moment, wondering if he should get involved, if he did, he'd be frightened for his own safety. Thinking it might be best to call the police, but hearing the woman's voice getting weaker, he knew he had to act quickly to help the unknown woman. He found that once he made the decision, there was an instant transformation of physical strength and mental clarity. He jumped into the bushes and pulled the assailant off the young girl. They tussled on the ground briefly before the accoster ran away. The man slowly approached the girl, who was trembling in the bushes. He could not see her face in the darkness, but could feel her fright. So, from a distance, he told her it would be alright, she was safe, and the mugger had run away. After a few moments, he was shocked at her voice, "Dad is that you?" Then he realized the girl was his youngest daughter.

No greater love than dad brought could there have been for his daughter that night. Somehow their connection of love placed him in the right place at the right time. His embrace was the best healing balm God could have delivered in that moment. Love has an amazing way of showing up at the perfect time in the perfect way. It transcends time and space to bring a newfound strength, providing all that is needed.

Spiritual Contemplation: Sit in the remembrance of some of your amazing love stories. Feel the transformative warmth touch you again. Doesn't love truly transcend time and space?

Affirmation: Love now guides me, surrounds me and protects me!

MARCH 13

Building a Strong Spiritual Partnership

Love does not consist in gazing at each other, but in looking outward together in the same direction. — Antoine de Saint-Exupery

Most people desire to have a deep, connected relationship with someone who understands and loves them. Numerous studies have shown that being in a satisfying relationship brings greater levels of happiness and fulfillment. Having someone to share the ups and downs of life with, build memories with and care for, enhance one's overall well-being. Successful relationships take work, and it is important to realize that with time and attention, all your relationships, especially your primary relationship, can develop into something that enhances your life.

Developing relationships spiritually involves nurturing a deep connection and a level of understanding between the couple. Though your spiritual journey is a personal one, there are ways that one can connect with their partner to support their spiritual development. Fostering shared values and a common belief system, respecting each other's differences as well as similarities, and engaging in acts of service together are all ways to walk along your spiritual path together while deepening your connection.

Spiritual Contemplation: Think of three ways that you could work on deepening your primary relationship on a spiritual level. This could be with a spouse, partner, or close friend. What could you do together to develop a spiritual component in your relationship?

Affirmation: I am a spiritual being and connect at the heart level in all of my relationships!

MARCH 14

The Young Apprentice

Sometimes life hits you in the head with a brick. Don't lose faith. — Steve Jobs

The town's blacksmith found a young apprentice willing to do the hard labor of pounding metal for a pittance of a wage. The blacksmith launched into his teachings for the kid. His first directive was, "When I take hot steel out of the fire, I'll lay it on the anvil. When I nod my head, you hit it with the hammer." The apprentice did exactly what he thought he was instructed to do. But the next day, he became the town's new blacksmith.

Mentorships are supposed to end, but this one just may have completed a little too quickly. If you don't feel awkward the first time you attempt something new, then you probably aren't doing it right. The first function of an apprentice is to observe and clarify what you see and hear. Eventually, conflict tends to arise between mentors and mentees, which isn't necessarily a bad thing if the apprentice's desire is to exceed the achievements of the master.

Spiritual Contemplation: Is there anywhere in your life that you didn't start off great at and just quit? Looking back, do you wish you would have stuck with the new endeavor a little longer? Is there anywhere you didn't excel beyond your influencer because of a subjective belief not to exceed their achievements? Where would you be today if you had grown beyond the teacher?

Affirmation: I trust my learning and growth processes are divinely orchestrated!

MARCH 15

What? Can't Read My Mind?

There is no greater agony than bearing an untold story inside you. — Maya Angelou

Have you ever expected your loved ones to know how you are feeling just by osmosis or because you throw a little moody vibe? "Somehow, if they really loved me, they'd know what I was thinking." But they won't know unless you tell them. They may guess something is off, but that could be explained by 1,001 different possibilities. They are not mind and mood readers. Unless you express your feelings, you can assume they are not clear, even if you feel they should be.

Hearts are often broken by words not spoken. What you are feeling might be hanging out in your heart with the pain pleading to be let out. Don't be afraid. It takes great daring to allow it to roll from your lips. Pain locked away never goes away. It must be released in order for you to be free. This doesn't mean to shout out painful affronts in order to retaliate or force a conversation at an inappropriate time. Instead, trust your intimacy and vulnerability with your loved one. Trust that the risk of being honest about what's in your heart will be honored.

Spiritual Contemplation: Are there any areas in your world that have unresolved feelings hanging heavy on your heart? Are you just hoping the other person will guess what's going on? How and when might be an appropriate time to attempt to convey your position?

Affirmation: I allow my heart to be felt by those I love!

MARCH 16

Setting Boundaries

We don't naturally fall into perfect relationship; we create them. — *Nedra Glover Tawwab*

A boundary is a guideline that you establish to care for and protect your own physical, emotional, and mental well-being while in a relationship. Setting boundaries is important not only to protect yourself but to foster mutual respect and maintain a healthy dynamic within the relationship. You want to clearly define and communicate what behaviors are acceptable and unacceptable to you. You want to respect others 'boundaries and expect that they will respect yours.

The goal is to feel safe and supported within the relationship. Setting boundaries is a way to work together with your partner to establish this sense of comfort and safety for both of you. Boundaries take many forms and can include, as examples, the level of emotional sharing you are both comfortable with, time and availability, physical connections, financial agreements, etc. Anything that would allow you to feel safe and more comfortable sharing your true self with your partner can be a boundary. Communication plays a huge part in setting boundaries and the more you can communicate from the heart, the easier the process becomes. This is part of the work of building a sustained relationship that is mutually supportive.

Spiritual Contemplation: What boundaries do you currently have set in your relationships? Are there any that you need to set up now? How can you communicate this to your partner?

Affirmation: I love and respect myself and my partner!

MARCH 17

Bit of a Battle Now for a Better Later

~~ero~~

Chains of causation can be set in motion, individually or collectively which produce their results unless they are changed. They can be changed. — Ernest Holmes, *Seminar Lectures, page 106*

It takes a great deal of bravery to stand up to our enemies but just as much to stand up to our friends. — *J.k Rowling*

Allowing a child to sit at the dinner table engrossed in their phone or laptop is no different from having a TV on during family meals in the past. Communication is sacrificed and interactive exchange is compromised. It may take a bit of a battle at the outset, but the disturbance throughout the meal otherwise makes your endeavor for connectedness worth the effort. Remember, you are the adult here and you set the intention for your togetherness. If screens are allowed at the table, then potential time in conversation lost is not the kids 'fault.

Choosing to tolerate the intolerable creates distance, rather than intimacy. Taking a stand on what's important to you is essential in an honest relationship and expected in parenting. If you don't stand up for what you believe in, you are part of the problem at your table. What's the point of having a voice if you don't speak what's on your heart? The dinner table is the ideal place for heart conversations.

Spiritual Contemplation: Is the media around your dinner table compromising your family's greater connectivity? If yes, are you willing to speak up about your heart's desire to be more present with one another at the table?

Affirmation: I am fully present in the presence of my children!

MARCH 18

Quality Time

～◦∕⋋◦⌒

There's only one thing more precious than time and that's what we spend it on. —
Leo Christopher

An important gift you can give to your partner and your relationship is quality time. Relationships need to be built and this happens with time and attention. When you create a dedicated time, free of distractions for you and your partner, you are setting the foundation for a deep and connected relationship.

This can be challenging in the midst of a busy life where work, kids, and general stress can get in the way. That is why having shared activities, date nights or simply sitting next to one another to watch the sunset are all important activities to add to your daily schedule. You want to create a few moments to disconnect from distractions and focus on nurturing your bond. This will be a time to foster emotional and physical intimacy, show affection, have intimate conversations, and maintain a deep emotional connection with your partner. As you create this space on a regular basis, you will see your relationship begin to improve.

Spiritual Contemplation: Do you have a dedicated time to connect with your partner? How could you create this space to connect and work on your relationship?

Affirmation: I am present in my relationship and create space for connection and intimacy.

MARCH 19

Loss of a Young One

I believe in the incarnation of the Spirit in all, and that we are all incarnations of the One Spirit. I believe in the eternality, the immortality, and the continuity of the individual soul, forever and ever expanding. – Ernest Holmes

The loss of a little one is indescribably painful. Whether at eight weeks, eight years, the age of eighteen, or any age before you, it's important to realize you didn't create life. You were the channel through which life entered into this world. There was some kind of soul agreement before either of you entered into the home of this vibrational plane. Some would call it choosing your parents. The bond of love tends to keep a clan connected before and after the arrival and departure from this earth.

Being you didn't create life; it didn't start at conception or the first breath; life was before either of those moments. At a certain level of soul agreement, this life involves a "sign-up" to be a teacher or facilitator for you, for however long the journey together lasts, including how it unfolds.is. When the "other" has fulfilled their soul's purpose and their soul agreement, the time comes to return to where they came from. In whatever manner they leave the mortal coil behind, their life moves on, alive and aware as ever in their self-expression. Time together here is precious. Be grateful for that time. Memories and insights will be their gift to the veil you see life through.

Spiritual Contemplation: From the pain of loss, what gifts and lessons have you come to discover?

Affirmation: I am blessed by the wake of love that has been left in my world by those I love!

MARCH 20

Communication for the Win

Communication is the lifeline of any relationship. – Elizabeth Bourgeret

Any marriage counselor will tell you that the majority of relationship issues stem from a disconnect in the couple's ability to communicate. Open and authentic communication is crucial for any relationship. Creating a space where both partners feel comfortable expressing their thoughts, feelings and needs is a core skill that is essential. Prioritizing connection and communication in the relationship will help build these skills. I know a couple who has a coffee date before the kids wake up each day at 6:00 am to share how they are doing with one another. Finding a time that works for you on a regular basis will set the space to come together and deepen your connection.

Things to keep in mind when working on your relationship communication skills include sharing authentically from your own perspective (I-statements), actively listening to what your partner is sharing, staying non-defensive, and expressing compassion for your partner. These skills take practice but the benefit to your relationship will be exponential, and these skills will serve you well in all areas of your life.

Spiritual Contemplation: How can you develop communication between you and your partner or close friend? Which communication skills are challenging for you? Which ones come easy?

Affirmation: I am present and communicate clearly in all my relationships.

MARCH 21

Stop Filling in the Cracks!

Before you assume, learn. Before you judge, understand. Before you hurt, feel.
Before you say, think. — Unknown

One thing that gets in the way of our relationships is a habit I call "filling in the cracks". This happens when we hear a piece of a story, with some details missing. Often, we end up filling in the holes of the story with information from our own perspective. This can be a problem because our perspective is limited, and we can never know what someone else is going through. We need to be careful when filling in the cracks because we often ascribe our own bias that may not be valid to a situation. Our misinterpretation of someone else's mood, reaction, or response to us can create more chaos or help to create a deeper connection. When filling in the cracks without checking with the other person first, we are more likely to create more division and the relationship is challenged. If we can become curious and ask questions to clarify those gaps in the story, we learn more about the other person and their situation and they feel heard and seen. Our goal is to become less judgmental and more curious. This will strengthen and deepen our connections to everyone around us.

Spiritual Contemplation: Think about a situation in your life that would have been helped if you hadn't filled in the cracks with your own assumptions. Think of another situation that would have been helped if you were asked to clarify something rather than the other person assuming something about you.

Affirmation: I am present, awake and curious to what is happening around me!

MARCH 22

Family Bonds

Families are like branches on a tree. We grow in different directions, yet our roots remain as one. – Suzy Kassem

Your family is your first tribe. They are your first friends and in its highest form, your family is a launching pad and a safety net for your life. Not all families are supportive, and some can even be detrimental. It is important to wake up to your individual situation and see what ways your family can support you and what ways it cannot.

Working on challenging family relationships is an ongoing and sometimes complex process. When we cultivate empathy and understanding for one another, acknowledging that even though we come from the same family, we may have very different experiences and perspectives and through that recognition we can deepen our connections. Everyone has their own journey and taking the time to understand their individual points of view can help bridge gaps and foster compassion. Active listening, asking questions, and open communication all help to create an atmosphere of respect, acceptance, and love – and that is what family is all about.

Spiritual Contemplation: What is the state of your family relationships? Are there any relationship strategies you could implement to deepen your relationships?

Affirmation: I love my family for who they are!

MARCH 23

As If Soft Music in the Night

~~~

Belief consists in accepting the affirmations of the soul; unbelief, in denying them.
— Ralph Waldo Emerson

Watching over your child's every decision, every effort, and controlling their thoughts to make sure they get it right, will lead to their self-doubt as they learn to look outside themselves for approval. If your child is brought up with threats, manipulations and punishments, they will live in fear. Love and help them to reflect upon their choices without a superior attitude and they will come to discover and believe in their inner guidance. They will learn to listen and hear their inner voice as if it were soft music in the night.

If they stumble, do not impose shame, blame or guilt, but help them to learn responsibility. Show your confidence in their capacities to succeed at their next endeavor, learning from each one in the process. You'll be empowering their self-confidence to blossom as they grow into life, as they learn their choices have impact. You have been entrusted with the possibility to be the first seer of your child's earthly potential. Unconditionally loving your child calls forth their divine nature . . . as well as yours.

Spiritual Contemplation: Where might I have been a bit too controlling in my child's upbringing? Where have I treated myself with that same kind of self-inflicted doubt?

Affirmation: I come to know my inner guidance and trust its direction!

MARCH 24

Choose Your Battles

Be selective in your battles, sometimes peace is better than being right. –
Anonymous

There are times in life when we experience conflict in one of our relationships. Disagreements arise as a natural part of living in a community and will need to be addressed. No matter if it is with a significant other, friend, family member, or co-worker, it is important to be aware of how you handle conflict and to learn ways of fostering harmony and connection. Many are uncomfortable when faced with disagreements and run from conflict at top speed. This is not beneficial in the long run and will leave you with many messes to clean up along your path.

One way to handle these situations differently is through choosing your battles. Not every disagreement needs to be turned into a major conflict. Even if the other person has a high emotional charge on the situation, you can bring an energy of peace if you can stay calm and not get triggered by them. Differentiating between important matters and minor disagreements is a powerful strategy to avoid conflict. Learning to let go of small resentments, and instead focusing on building positive connections, will keep you from getting caught up in unnecessary arguments. Relationships can be blessings in your life and with some attention and forethought, you can keep them harmonious and peaceful.

Spiritual Contemplation: Think about the conflicts you have had in your relationships. Can you see ways that you could have shifted the disagreement and fostered a deeper connection?

Affirmation: I choose my battles in relationships and connect with love and compassion.

MARCH 25

Let Go of the Past with Forgiveness

Forgive others, not because they deserve forgiveness, but because you deserve peace.
— *Jonathan Lockwood Huie*

Forgiveness is a powerful and healing spiritual practice. When we practice forgiveness, it helps us release any righteous indignation we are holding onto and allows the soul to breathe. It supports us in letting go of our judgments and opinions for any given situation. It brings an ability to see the situation clearly, which empowers us to take responsibility for the part we played.

True forgiveness knows that there is a difference between understanding a behavioral choice that someone made and condoning it. We may hold back on forgiving because of the malicious intent of the other person but once we understand how they got to the point where they made that choice, we can start to forgive. We may never get to the place of excusing the choices, and that's okay. But the gift of forgiveness is that we no longer need to carry the pain of the original event. We can move forward freely, no longer held emotional hostage by the past.

Spiritual Contemplation: Who from your past is calling for forgiveness? What old burdens can you lay down as you forgive and let go of what hurt you?

Affirmation: I forgive freely and let go of any attachment to a different past!

MARCH 26

Create a Relationship Ritual

Building relationships is not about transactions – it's about connections. –
Michelle Tillis Lederman

One way to deepen your relationship bonds whether it be with your significant other, family or friends is by creating meaningful rituals that hold spiritual significance for your relationship(s). Recently, at a friend's 50th birthday, we each brought a flower that reminded us of our friend's qualities. We went around the circle and spoke about why we chose each flower and placed them in a vase at the center. It created a beautiful bouquet that represented all the birthday girl's friendships and the support she would be carrying into the next phase of her life.

A ritual can be as simple as lighting a candle together, preparing a special meal, creating a family gratitude jar, or a journal as a couple. These simple rituals bring a sense of sacredness and importance to your relationships. The possibilities are infinite. Taking the time to think about and put together a ritual will bring you closer together and deepen your connections.

Spiritual Contemplation: Do you have any rituals that you already do in your family or in your relationships? How can you incorporate ritual into your relationships in a new way?

Affirmation: I honor my relationships and share in the joy of life with my loved ones through ritual.

MARCH 27

For Parents

We never know the love of a parent till we become parents ourselves. — Henry Ward Beecher

Your child's birthday comes with a flood of reminiscing. Though it's their big day, it's yours as well. To be entrusted to help a new soul get oriented in this world, is an amazing responsibility that comes without instructions. The intuitive heart is awakened, hyper alert is activated and care for the future is on. At some level, soul agreements were made for this relationship, but the memories start stacking up from the first kick in mom's tummy, to baby's first sick day and the sense of helplessness to alleviate the pain. There are profound memories of the first steps, the first bike ride, watching them drive off on their own for the first time, dating, heartbreak, prom, and marriage.

Your child's birthday is an emotionally charged holographic memory book, including more than just the physical senses. You are transported through the past, present and future, quicker than synapses can fire and linger in moments for eternity. Love transcends the logical, enhances remembrances and gives life a passionate meaning that you never knew was possible. Congratulations on your birthing day, your life changed forever as you came to know a new level of love you could never have known before this day.

Spiritual Contemplation: Whatever day this is, create space in your heart to go back to when your child was born and invite the progression of recollections to flood your awareness. There is nothing you need to do with these, other than just be with them.

Affirmation: I am grateful for many parental memories that fill my heart!

MARCH 28

Challenges of Vanity

There is nothing which vanity does not desecrate. – Henry Ward Beecher

There is an Aesop's fable about a crow who finds some cheese in a window and helps herself to it. While enjoying it upon a tree branch, a fox catches the scent and comes to the foot of the tree thinking only of breakfast. The fox asks the crow for a piece of her cheese, but the crow goes on eating. So, the fox tries flattery, "Oh charming creature, what beautiful feathers you have that shine so brilliantly in the sun. You must be intelligent to have found the cheese, and no doubt you have a beautiful voice that would make you Queen of the Birds. If only I could hear your beautiful voice sing, I'd then know for sure that you are the Queen." Listening to these flattering words, the crow forgets her suspicion, as well as her breakfast, for the thought of being called Queen of the Birds is just too alluring. She opens her beak wide to let out a caw and the cheese drops straight into the fox's open mouth.

The flatterer lives at the expense of those who fall prey to them. Not everyone has your best interest at heart, so be aware if flattery comes flying your way. The fox uses the crow's vanity against her. Typically, the crow is considered a smart creature, but this time falls for adulations, leaving her looking foolish. She was so enamored of the flattery that she cared more for the opinion of one she didn't care about. Be careful that vanity doesn't overtake your wisdom and common sense. Your sanity can become severely compromised. Don't allow your vanity to lead your decision-making process, or it will be like quicksand to your reason.

Spiritual Contemplation: When have you allowed flattery to misguide you into incorrect decision-making?

Affirmation: I appreciate the good said about me while remaining centered in who I am.

MARCH 29

The Most Important Task

In raising children, we need to continuously keep in mind how we can best create the most favorable environment for their imitative behavior. — Rudolf Steiner

There is not much more of an important task in the world than raising children. In every culture of every time, children are the treasures, the future and hope. They are the link from the past to the future, carrying the ancestral memories forward into a new era. Their innocence and purity remind you of who you were and the infinite potential of what's possible. You are not here to mold a child into being a great person, rather you are here to remind them of their innate magnificence.

You do not teach by preaching. They may not hear what you have to say, but they will not miss a move you make and will learn through imitation. The more you become yourself, the more they will become who they are. To experience joy in parenting, free yourself of ambitions so you may be free to shift in the ever-changing tides of their dynamics. Guide gently, as there is no need for blame or conquest over a child. They naturally love life, so don't rob that. Their delight is natural, unstructured and free - maybe even inspiring you to remember what that was like.

Spiritual Contemplation: When you are around children, are you aware they are watching and learning from how you are being within every situation? They may not do what you say, but they hear and feel everything said. What kind of lessons for life are they imitating from your behavior in their presence?

Affirmation: I recognize the magnificence and potential of every child I see!

MARCH 30

Clarify

Your assumptions are your windows on the world. Scrub them off every once in a while, or the light won't come in. — Isaac Asimov

People have an uncanny way of listening to one story and understanding another. Recently, a self-improvement training was held, and a presenter made a bold comment which caught his addressees 'attention. He stated, "Some of the best years of my life were spent in the arms of a woman that wasn't my wife!" The crowd was stunned by his disclosure! He followed up by adding, "That woman was my mother!" The crowd burst into laughter and relief. Frequently, things are not what they seem. Moreover, you can get into trouble by jumping to conclusions. Granted, the only way some people get any exercise is by jumping to conclusions.

Assumptions shut down your brain and doors in your life while sincere interest opens doors to greater possibilities. When someone shares something with you, it moves through your filters, making it easy to jump to assumptions. If someone doesn't tell you something, it's also easy to jump to conclusions. What is being called for is clarifying communication and clear listening. In all your relationships, make sure you don't jump to conclusions or engage in the dark dance in your head. When you don't look beyond speculation, you've given up on meeting another in the place of understanding. Do not assume the worst; ask to understand!

Spiritual Contemplation: How has jumping to conclusions gotten you in trouble in the past? Is there somewhere in your life you are not assuming the highest thought for someone or a situation? Attempt to have that clarifying conversation today.

Affirmation: My mind goes to the highest possibility in all situations!

MARCH 31

What Seeds are you planting?

We were planting seeds of change, the fruit of which we might never see. We had to be patient. – Michelle Obama

Two seeds were lying next to one another on the fertile soil. The first seed said, "I want to grow up and put my roots deep down into the soil, spring forth from the ground, feel the warmth of the sun, reach for the heavens, and blossom to fully express myself." This seed grew up to become a beautiful flower, producing many more seeds.

The second seed said, "I'm afraid if I reach my roots into the soil, the ground may be too hard to establish myself. If I'm able to break through the surface, what might I have to face? While my stem is young, it could be damaged by the winds of spring. If I grow flowers, who knows what they might attract? I'd rather wait for a safer time." Thus, while the second seed waited, a chicken came by and added it to its lunch. We will never know what the future holds. When fear holds you back that anxious energy is working to attract its corresponding manifestation.

Spiritual Contemplation: Are you planting seeds of fear somewhere in your life? What thought seeds would you like to change? What are more affirmative phrases you'd like to be holding for yourself?

Affirmation: My thought seeds are now beautifully and courageously blossoming!

APRIL

Caring

April 1-7

Sometimes We All Get Squeezed

April 8-14

Time to Recharge

April 15-21

Flourish and Nourish

April 22-30

Making Change

APRIL 1

Just saying, All Things Are Possible

Everything is funny, as long as it's happening to somebody else. – Will Rogers

People love to laugh and have probably been playing practical jokes on one another since humans arrived on the planet. Slapstick comedies, sitcoms and romantic comedies have kept people chuckling since films started rolling. It's not uncommon on April 1st to see local headline stories talking about silly things like buildings being repurposed, crazy new street names, or a local pub becoming a church.

Imagine if this morning's headline stories read, Flash: It's been decades now since there was a thing called war. Peace has prevailed, borders are irrelevant and everyone loves each other. Caring has become a dominant human trait and money is no longer necessary because all resources are being freely shared. A pandemic of perfect health has broken out all over the planet. Education is now free and all children are lovingly doing what they came to this world to do. The planet has healed herself and Eden has returned. The sky is bright blue, all water sparkles with freshness, and you can drink from the streams or the tap, thinking this is delicious. The oceans are fully restored and vibrant with life, while the recently extinct animals have returned to roam the earth once again. People are living abundantly in balance with the planet. Just saying, all things are possible!

Spiritual Contemplation: If you were to allow yourself to write the perfect headlines to fool people into believing greater good is breaking out all over, what would you say?

Affirmation: I believe the good news that God prevails today!

APRIL 2

Calm the Mind

Daily meditation is the antidote to worries, stress and nonstop thinking, which disturb focus and tranquility and waste mental energy. – Remez Sasson

One key to living a wholehearted life is to create a daily practice for your well-being. Meditation is the perfect way to begin slowing down and awakening the mind to what is happening in your life. Meditation is a state of quiet contemplation, whereby taking a few minutes in the morning or evening to turn your focus inward, you can begin to access a deeper place within. As you become aware of your thoughts you can see what your mind state is. Any change you want to make in your life begins with your thoughts and beliefs. Practicing meditation will show you the areas that need some attention and lead to positive changes. Whether you are in a state of bliss during your practice or sitting in silence watching your thoughts race around, you are benefitting from the practice. You will experience more relaxation and handle adversity better because you are more present. Physiological benefits include an increase in overall well-being with lower stress hormones, a lowered heart rate and blood pressure, and deeper respiration. There is an increase of activity in the brain associated with the ability to concentrate and people who meditate experience less depression and anxiety. Meditation is the doorway to growth. Spend 10 minutes today and see what a difference it can make!

Spiritual Contemplation: Take 10-15 minutes today to meditate. Don't judge your experience, just notice how it feels for you. Try this each day this week and just see how it can support you on your path.

Affirmation: I quiet my mind and open to the wisdom of the Universe!

APRIL 3

The Foundation for Your Day

～ℓ/ℓ√∞～

He comes in beauty and he comes in storm,
But in them both the Presence is revealed
To him who is attuned, and he
Who loves will hear the voice of love.
— Ernest Holmes, Voice Celestial, page 187

Thou wilt keep in perfect peace, whose mind is stayed on Thee — Isaiah 26:3,
KJ21

Prayer is often inspired by a concern. Meditation is not thinking about the self or the concern but the contemplation of Spirit, Divine activities and the nature of God. Because you are part of the wholeness and the Infinite Mind, it is possible for you to tune into the kingdom of God and receive direct revelations. This download of grace naturally fulfills the relevant and real areas of your human concerns.

Throughout your day, perhaps it's go, go, go. The to-do list wants to download the instant your feet hit the floor in the morning. However, you get to decide whether you start your day by taking some time for your Divine Connection or jumping right into the physical world of demands. To be a receiver of God's Guidance, you must hone the ability to quiet the senses during your day. Starting with Spirit in the morning, before anything else establishes the foundation for your day, makes Life sweeter.

Spiritual Contemplation: How can you make your Meditation practice a priority in the morning? Where can you establish a Divine Connection time as a priority on your "To Do" list?

Affirmations: I remember to divinely connect throughout my day!

APRIL 4

Life Breathes Through Me

Those who contemplate the beauty of the earth find reserves of strength that will endure as long as life lasts. There is something infinitely healing in the repeated refrains of nature - the assurance that dawn comes after night, and spring after winter. — Rachel Carson

Meditation is not running away from what's going on in life, it is taking the time to gaze sincerely into yourself and into the circumstances at hand. It's a calming of the thinking and return to the unviolated self. Freed from anger, despair, or concern, you make yourself available to the nurturing aspect of nature. Meditation releases the tension in body and mind and enables availability to review what's going on with as little judgment as possible. From the elevated meditative state, you are more an observer than participant.

Find a sense of peace in your breathing. You'll then bring this peace to the planet by being this peace. The return of balance to the planet begins inside of you. It doesn't come from the outside. It's your awakened awareness recognizing a oneness with the earth and a mindful walking with her, inspiring the restorative practices of balance. In this conscious connection with mother earth, heal yourself, heal the planet. Heal the planet, heal yourself.

Spiritual Contemplation: Find a quiet place to be, whether walking or sitting and bring peace to your breathing. Feel your breath move through your body and into the earth. Pause. Next, breathe and feel the energy from the earth move through your body and out into the world. Repeat.

Affirmation: Life freely breathes through me!

APRIL 5

The Power of Prayer

Prayer is the key that unlocks all the storehouses of God's infinite grace and power. — R.A. Torrey

Prayer as a spiritual practice is found in all religions in one form or another. Creating a sacred time each day for prayer helps us deepen our relationship with God. Sitting in the silence, communing with the Presence and opening our minds to affirm the spiritual truth of a situation, supports us in rising above the challenges of life. Affirmative prayer states the spiritual truth of a situation even though it may be experienced differently. As we know the sun is always shining above the clouds, we can also know the spiritual truth of wholeness, abundance, and harmony, even when we are experiencing illness, financial strain, and strife.

When we make everyday activities a prayer, we realize that every thought we think carries with it the responsibility of an effect on the world. When we realize how powerful our own prayer is and that by simply devoting ourselves to the practice of it, we become the change not only for ourselves but for everyone. Praying is a powerful gift for ourselves and the world.

Spiritual Contemplation: Spend time during your spiritual practice to pray for yourself and others in your life. Affirm the truth of your wholeness, abundance, harmony and love. See yourself and those you pray for as whole, healed and a clear expression of God's presence. Notice how you feel after you pray.

Affirmation: I commune with the Divine and speak spiritual truth into being through my prayer!

APRIL 6

Compassion to Stay

If you want others to be happy, practice compassion. – Dalai Lama

A caregiver took a young Marine to an old man's bedside in the hospital. "Your son is here," she said to an old man who couldn't even open his eyes and was barely able to reach out his hand. All through the night the marine sat holding the old man's hand. The dying man said nothing, only clutching the hand into the night. Toward dawn the old gentleman passed. The Marine informed the nurse who was waiting outside the door. As she extended her condolences, the Marine interrupted her asking, "Who was that man?" The nurse was surprised. "He was your father." "No, he wasn't," the Marine shared, "I'd never seen him before. I was just visiting a friend next door." "Then why didn't you say something?" the nurse asked. "I knew right away there had been a mistake, but I also knew he needed his son. When I realized how much he needed someone, I felt compassion and stayed."

The next time someone reaches out to you to be there for them, do you have the compassion to just stay?

Spiritual Contemplation: Compassion takes time. When someone reaches out to you, will you take the time to allow compassion to work its wonder through you?

Affirmation: I am a compassionate and loving expression of Spirit!

APRIL 7

Sometimes We All Get Squeezed

When you squeeze an orange, you'll always get orange juice. What comes out is what's inside. – Wayne Dyer

One of the most powerful teachings from Wayne Dyer is illustrated in the quote above. He reminds us that when we squeeze an orange, what comes out is orange juice, not grapefruit or apple juice. The question for us is: when life squeezes us or when someone criticizes or puts pressure on us, what comes out? Is it anger, hatred, and bitterness or love and compassion? What comes out is what is alive inside.

When we are reactive and what comes out is not what we want, it is an indication that something is off balance within us. It is a call for some reflection and self-care. When we make self-care a priority and release guilt about taking time to care for our own well-being, we are more centered, calm and loving. We are better able to handle the pressures from the outside, and we can more easily see what is and isn't ours to handle in any given situation. The "juice" that will come out of you when squeezed will reflect those loving and centered qualities rather than the negative ones that come out under stress.

Spiritual Contemplation: What can you do for yourself today to care for your mind and heart? Take some time in nature, nourish your body with some healthy and delicious foods, spend a few minutes with a close friend, etc. Know that as you take time to make yourself a priority, you shift your inner landscape and welcome more peace.

Affirmation: I am a clear channel of Divine peace and love today and every day!

APRIL 8

Being Kind in a Cruel World

Three things in human life are important: the first is to be kind; the second is to be kind; and the third is to be kind. — Henry James

It is very easy to get caught up in the loud chaos of our times. With the 24/7 news cycle and a continual barrage of negativity, a sense of fear and hopelessness is rising, causing many to see the world as a dark, dangerous, and cruel place. Humanity is at a critical juncture and we each have a choice as to how to proceed. Will we allow ourselves to be deluded by the nightmare or will we rise in our creative power to set a new course?

We are being called to wake up and remember that we have the power to create a new way of being with one another. If we wish to see more love, compassion, and kindness in the world, it is up to us to be that in life. Any act of kindness, no matter how large or small, sends ripples out into the world and has far reaching effects we may never see but will definitely feel. People who engage in kind acts become happier, experience less anxiety and depression, have stronger immune systems, and live longer, healthier lives. Let us embrace kindness as a way of being and begin to change the world one small kind act at a time!

Spiritual Contemplation: Engage in some random kind acts today and notice how you feel before, during and after. Think about how your day may be different when you focus on being a channel of kindness in the world.

Affirmation: I share my love freely with all I meet!

APRIL 9

Pause the Pause

It's a transformative experience to simply pause instead of immediately filling up space. — Pema Chodron

It's the space between the words that make them understandable. The lull between the waves allows a surfer to get into position. The story goes "and on the seventh day even God rested". Taking a pause in a "go, go, go" society is important, yet stay alert not to get lost in the break. Some people find it hard to get back into the swing of things after a vacation. During a quarantine, complacency can settle in. Where it was once hard to slow down and step off the track, lethargy now drapes itself over a get up and go, can-do attitude.

Sometimes, you just have to hit the pause button and then get up and get going again. Taking your mind and body out of the game is hard at first, but the recharge can slip into over-relaxed, taking the edge off. This chilled state can become more comfortable than anticipated, requiring a stronger effort to break the hiatus and get you back into the game of life.

Spiritual Contemplation: Taking a break is good, even God does it. But is there or has there been a time where you allowed the pause to become too comfortable, keeping you on the sideline when it was time to get back in?

Affirmation: My pause is appropriate for my recharge to reenter my life with renewed passion!

APRIL 10

Let Yourself Rest

Rest is not idle, not wasteful. Sometimes rest is the most productive thing you can do. – Erica Layne

Many people consider rest a luxury they can't afford and instead throw themselves fully into the fast pace of life. They scream along in their days never feeling completely present, energized, or centered as they constantly deal with stress, anxiety, and the feeling of never being caught up with work! Without appropriate rest, you prevent yourself from fully experiencing the moments of your life.

There is no denying that rest is a key component of health, happiness, and well-being. When we take the time to unplug and rest, we create space in our minds to reset, recharge, and re-evaluate ourselves. Scheduling breaks into our daily schedule promotes well-being, improved mood, reduced stress, increased creativity, and better overall mental health. We are better able to handle our emotions and communicate with more clarity when we are rested. Allowing ourselves time to rest will bring greater satisfaction and happiness to our days.

Spiritual Contemplation: Think about three ways you could add more rest and rejuvenation into your daily schedule. Write them down and commit to doing at least one of them this week.

Affirmation: I allow my mind and body to rest, reset, and recharge!

APRIL 11

Cascading Remembering

A good horse runs when seeing just the shadow of the whip. – Buddha

A deep thinker went to a great master teacher and asked to know "The Truth" without words and without the wordless. The master just stood there for some time in silence. The philosopher bowed to the great one in gratitude saying, "It is with your ancient wisdom, love and compassion that my misperceptions and false beliefs have fallen away and I now know the Truth." Once the visitor had departed, one of the teacher's students asked, what was it the master teacher did in the silence? What did the visitor attain? The wise one's response was simply, "A good horse runs when it sees just the shadow of a whip."

When there is no otherness, there is a connection. In a deep knowing, all is known without having to know anything in particular. It is not theory, thinking or linear unfoldment. It is Truth experienced without image, a peaceful realization of connectivity with the Infinite. It is a sense of well-being not tied to events, irrespective of the external world. Just a gentle hint activates the cascading remembering of Truth of being that fills the present point of awareness.

Spiritual Contemplation: Do you remember feeling a sense of well-being irrespective of external commotion in your world? Feel the shadow of that now.

Affirmation: I gently awaken to remembering who I am in the allness of the All!

APRIL 12

Take Time to Recharge

Rest and self-care are so important. When you take time to replenish your spirit, it allows you to serve others from the overflow. You cannot serve from an empty vessel. — Eleanor Brown

In this fast-paced world, we are faced with a 24/7 news cycle and a divided country grappling with numerous social and political problems. It can feel like we exist in pure chaos, where just getting through a week, or even a day, can feel like treading water and leave us exhausted.

It's important to remember, it is in taking the time and connecting to the heart that our spiritual compass will help us navigate these challenging times with Divine support. We must pause, unplug from the material world's noise and engage in activities that fill us up bringing comfort and rejuvenation. This looks different for each person, and it's up to you to decide what will bring you the feeling of peace and connection. It might be reading, spending time in nature, listening to some inspirational music or even just having a change in scenery that can bring about a feeling of being energized and recharged. Add something to support your own energy each week and see how it can shift your day-to-day experience.

Spiritual Contemplation: Think of one thing you could do this week to help recharge your spiritual batteries. What kind of activity brings you back to your center? Make a list of 5 different activities to add to your schedule on a regular basis.

Affirmation: I honor my needs and take time to connect, rest and recharge my spiritual battery!

APRIL 13

Sharing the Load

Sometimes the only way to carry a heavy burden is to share it with another. —
Jim Butcher

There are moments in our lives when each of us are faced with difficult situations and challenges. Many enter into these moments alone, without the support of friends and family, thinking they do not want to burden them with their troubles. Living a wholehearted life calls on us to open and share our path with those around us. We exist in a community and need to let people in so we can receive their support, but also so we can be a reciprocating support to them when they hit a rough patch.

Sharing our burdens is a healing act that can bring a wider perspective and greater peace. When we allow ourselves to be vulnerable and invite in those closest to us, there is a reduction of stress creating a deeper trust. This leads us each to a place of knowing that, no matter what happens, we aren't ever really alone and together we can get through anything.

Spiritual Contemplation: Today, find one thing that you are currently challenged with and share it with a trusted friend. Notice if it is difficult for you to share your situation and notice how it feels after you share it.

Affirmation: I am open and share my path freely! I welcome the love and support that is already here for me!

APRIL 14

Stop and Look Around

Don't hurry. Don't worry. And be sure to smell the flowers along the way. –
Walter Hagen

Many of us are trained to speed through our days. From the moment
we open our eyes to when we fall into bed at night, we are running at full
speed, trying to keep pace with the world around us. When we speed through
the day, chances are, we are overlooking the blessings in our lives. It takes
time to open our five senses to the world, so we don't miss the shooting star
in the night sky or the words of support from someone we encounter. We
are surrounded by beauty and support, but are you missing it?

We are called to slow down and "practice the pause". Practicing the
pause is exactly what it sounds like: inserting moments of pause into our
days to stop, breathe, and take in the world around us. We slow our breath
and clear the mind so we can be open to inspiration and balance. When we
make this a regular practice, we cultivate a deep inner peace and awareness
and our lives become more balanced and joyful.

Spiritual Contemplation: Take time to practice the pause today and give
yourself 10 minutes to just be. Observe the world around you and be open
to the blessings already present in your life.

Affirmation: As I stop and breathe in this moment, I acknowledge the
blessings all around me right here and right now.

APRIL 15

Why Make It Hard on Yourself?

Don't trouble trouble until trouble troubles you. – Vietnamese Prover

The internet in my home office isn't strong so I tend to spread out on the kitchen table where the connection is better. Recently, my laptop battery wasn't holding its charge, though I kept it plugged into the kitchen outlet. I changed outlets in the kitchen to see if another one closer to the table would work, but it didn't. I took the laptop into the repair shop. They plugged it in and said it worked fine for them. I took it to my work office, plugged it in, and it operated and charged just fine. I packed it up, took it home and plugged it in the next morning. Within a couple of hours, it ran out of juice and wouldn't charge. I meditated on this annoyance and received divine guidance: GFI! I thought I was brilliant, despite my limited electrical knowledge, and I was sure I had figured out the problem—those little switches on some of the outlets! I ran around the whole house, pressing whichever ones I could find. I wasn't sure if I had turned them all on or off. All I knew was that the laptop still didn't work. Just as I was contemplating buying a new laptop, my wife walked in and asked if I'd tried flipping the breaker switch in the closet. Sure enough, it worked!

How complicated do we have to make a situation in our life when the solution is so simple? How much time does one have to waste running around before realizing the remedy is right in front of you? Sometimes the mind naturally goes to the worst-case scenario because it is used to preparing for mishaps. Don't overlook allowing your mind to prepare for the best so it will naturally gravitate to seeing the solutions and gifts that Spirit has already placed before you.

Spiritual Contemplation: Are there places in your life that you are allowing your head to spin a situation into more trouble than it needs to be? How could you allow it to be easier?

Affirmation: I am prepared for the best to come my way!

APRIL 16

Bear of a Situation

~~ⱸ⁄ᕬ⁄ᗞ~~

You're braver than you believe, stronger than you seem and smarter than you think. —Christopher Robin

There is a story of Native American origin about a young man who is to have his own tepee for the first time. As his grandfather escorts him to the edge of the main camp the young one wholeheartedly asks him for some guidance. The young one is worried because it's late spring, and the bears are active around his tepee in the more remote area, which is a 15-minute walk from the main camp. He knows how bears actively scavenge at night, and he remembers how one circled his tepee the previous summer. He asks him what to do if he encounters a bear: "Should I talk to the bear or send it love?" The grandfather pauses, connecting with his grandson's concern, and then answers wisely, "Don't talk to bears, talk to God.

It's always sage advice to connect with the Creator. Fear cannot live where there is no sense of otherness outside of the Divine. The life force that is in and through all things becomes the experience. See what you want rather than seeing what you don't want happening. A funny thing about bears is, bears will be bears. Don't allow the bears in your life, no matter how cute or scary, to disconnect you from what you know to be the truth.

Some bear advice: "I always get to where I'm going by walking away from where I have been." – Winnie the Pooh

---

Spiritual Contemplation: What 'bears' are vying for your attention? Notice, acknowledge, then consciously move your awareness to communing with the Creator.

Affirmation: In every situation, I remember to commune with the ever-available Higher Wisdom!

APRIL 17

Gift of Gaia

Treat the earth well: it was not given to you by your parents, it was loaned to you by your children. We do not inherit the Earth from our Ancestors; we borrow it from our Children. – Native American Proverb

Love the earth, she is neither good nor bad. How is it that when extreme weather like typhoons and tornadoes arise, she is often called bad. Yet, when rain is gentle, clear rivers flow and the soil is nourished, she's called good. Mother Nature doesn't discriminate against who is worthy of her wrath or blessings. The earth does its best to keep herself in balance as she gives the ever-growing population a ride through space. So, spend some time in gratitude for the sustaining stability she provides.

Become conscious of her gifts to you. When you drink water, appreciate the gift from Gaia. When you eat, be gratefully mindful that this too is an offering from the Earth. As you breathe fresh air, become aware this breath of life is a life-sustaining present from the planet. With this expanding mindfulness, a deeper reverence of each moment becomes inherent as your every step becomes a prayer of gratitude for its place to land.

Spiritual Contemplation: Before your next drink of water or bite of food, pause to become mindfully appreciative of its origin, all the hands it took to deliver it to you, and those who are sustained by the earth. Take a deep breath and give thanks!

Affirmation: I realize how blessed I am by the gifts of this planet!

APRIL 18

Flourish and Nourish

When one moves away from nature his heart becomes hard. – a Lakota saying

Real change for the planet will happen when you fall in love with her. Only love reveals how to live in harmony together. When you come to truly realize her qualities and appreciate her gifts your love affair will become impassioned. You would never want to harm her or put her in danger's way. You would never denigrate her. You want to connect and be with her best features, not exploit them. When you love, a longing grows to care for her and yourself so the relationship flourishes and nourishes.

The hardened heart has no room to grow in love or an ability to care. Allow your soul to be filled with the joy and excitement of spending time together. You'll feel nurtured and look forward to giving back. Trust and protection envelop this partnership keeping it safe from any and all betrayal. There is a desire to share all the blessings she brings with your friends. You'll find peace and serenity when you take refuge alongside Mother Earth by breathing in rhythm with her. Surrendering to her loving embrace, healing happens and the heart softens. You are of the earth and the earth is you.

Spiritual Contemplation: Spend some time in Nature. Then, ask your heart how can I care more in my relationship with the earth?

Affirmation: My heart hears the earth's cry and I respond as compassion in action!

APRIL 19

Change Comes from Within

Peace comes within the souls of men, when they realize their oneness with the Universe, when they realize it is really everywhere… it is within each one of us. – Chief Black Elk

When you mindfully take the time to listen deeply, you'll be able to hear the earth's suffering. In the last couple hundred years humanity has taken far more than it has given back to the planet. Exploiting and polluting does not create balance. Listening to what she now needs will give restorative direction. Though humanity must now do more than just listen, compassionate action motivated by the love of Mother Nature can inspire your action. Some people are unwilling to be inconvenienced for the greater good of the planet. They feel defensive, believing their contribution is insignificant compared to corporate greed and the lack of awareness from others. They wonder why they should bother changing their personal habits when no one else is doing the same.

The earth has lost her equilibrium. There is a revolution that must happen and it begins inside each individual. Change doesn't come from the outside, it evolves from within, and will happen when the earth and its people come together as one. When you start treating yourself with greater love and respect, you will no longer exploit and pollute your life and instead, find ways to restore the balance and harmony in your world.

Spiritual Contemplation: Where am I polluting and exploiting myself? How can I be more honoring of who I am in these situations? Do I notice a kinder interaction with the world around me?

Affirmation: My inner and outer worlds are a reflection of a life in harmony!

APRIL 20

Easter

~∿∾

To practice the Presence of God is to awaken within us the Christ Consciousness. Christ is God in the soul of man. The resurrection is the death of the belief that we are separated from God. – Ernest Holmes

The date upon which Easter is held varies from year to year, and corresponds with the first Sunday following the full moon after the March equinox. The word Easter is of Saxon origin, Eastra, meaning the goddess of spring. Often the Easter story of crucifixion and resurrection is considered a symbolic renewal and rebirth telling of the cycle of the seasons, and the return of the sun. It is a story from the beginning of recorded time. Some feel the Sumerian epic myth, the Descent of Inanna, inscribed on clay tablets dated 2100 B.C, influences some springtime celebrations. The legend tells of Inanna's journey through the underworld, in which she is judged, killed and then hung on display. In her absence the earth loses its fertility, crops no longer grow and animals stop reproducing until her return.

It's only one of many returning spring stories. The Babylonians have their story of Ishtar, the Goddess of Love, who descended into the Underworld to find and release her lover, Tammuz. There is the Greek myth of Demeter and Persephone representing the three-phase cycle of descent or loss, search, and with the main theme being the ascent. Other springtime resurrection stories include Egypt's Horus or Persia's Mithras, where the prevailing theme is one of renewal, descent into darkness, and the triumph of light over darkness and good over evil. When a story transcends cultures and time, its personal relevance is worthy of self-reflection.

Spiritual Contemplation: Have you descended into a darker personal time in your life? What have you learned about yourself through your soul searching?

Affirmation: I rise with the spring energies with a renewed passion for life!

APRIL 21

Mother Earth's Wake-Up Call

How sad to think that nature speaks and mankind doesn't listen. – Victor Hugo

It's as if humanity is caught in ecological amnesia, pretending there isn't an environmental crisis looming over our planet. It's time to love Mother Nature enough to wake up and hear her cry. Science points out that if we do nothing different and remain on the current trajectory the planet stands no chance of recovery with us on it. Our children will probably be running and recuperating from climate-driven crisis after crisis. Recovery takes more than casually thinking about it in our spare time. Denial of the severe accumulating physical effects seems easier than taking action. It's no longer enough to simply be upset and say no to those who are exploiting the commons and profiting from disasters. You must love the planet enough not only to take a stand but also to take action in this war between the economic system and the planetary system.

You witnessed how swiftly Mother Earth responded during the spring of 2020, as highly polluted cities enjoyed pristine skies by day and more stars dancing in the night sky than city children had ever seen before. Freeways were void of traffic and animals returned to places they hadn't roamed in years. Mother Nature isn't looking for a conversation, she's looking for our partnership and engagement. She's waiting for us to cut back on the parasitical behavior and focus on restorative actions. It's not too late. The answers to living in harmony with the planet are many and available now. It's time to live them!

Spiritual Contemplation: Feel the cry of the earth. Think about your grandchildren living on this planet and what you have left them. Research some of the many resources available for living in harmony with the planet and start implementing them now.

Affirmation: I love this planet enough to be aware of my impact upon her and to do something to bless this earth!

APRIL 22

Every Day is A Day for the Earth

· Preserve and cherish the pale blue dot, the only home we've ever known. — Karl Rogers

Today we celebrate and honor the only home we've ever known – the earth. Earth Day is dedicated to promoting environmental awareness and encouraging each of us to take action to protect and preserve our planet. It's a global reminder of the importance of environmental conservation and sustainable practices. Earth Day encourages us collectively to make small changes in our daily lives that have a significant impact, such as reducing energy consumption, conserving water, practicing recycling and waste reduction, supporting sustainable businesses, and advocating for policy changes that prioritize environmental protection.

Ultimately, Earth Day serves as a reminder that our planet is a precious and finite resource and that we all have a responsibility to be good stewards of the Earth. It is a time to reflect on the interdependence between humans and the environment and to take action to create a more sustainable and resilient future for all. Every day should be Earth Day.

Spiritual Contemplation: How will you honor the Earth today? What new sustainable practice will you commit to today?

Affirmation: I choose to care for the earth in a new way today and every day! The earth is precious, and I honor it through my actions and choices.

APRIL 23

Wired to Connect

A deep sense of love and belonging is an irreducible need of all people. We are biologically, cognitively, physically, and spiritually wired to love, to be loved, and to belong. — Brené Brown

One of the things we, as a society, learned during the COVID-19 pandemic was that building a strong sense of community for ourselves is tremendously important. We all experienced shock when we were unable to participate in the communities we'd established for ourselves many sank into loneliness, depression and for some, despair. Humanity is wired to thrive in community. In community we can be ourselves, find comfort and solace during challenging times, and serve and live together in harmony.

Many people have one or two communities they think are their own including church, school, friend circles, etc. In truth, we build community wherever we are including in line at the grocery store, on a train and even in the waiting room at a doctor's office. Participating in community gives you a place to give and receive. You can be present for others and at the same time benefit from other's support and kindness. The most important part of building community is embracing the idea that we are all in this together and when we connect at the level of the heart, anything is possible.

Spiritual Contemplation: Think about the communities in which you participate. In what ways can you serve and be served? What are the blessings you receive?

Affirmation: I participate fully and freely in all the communities in my life!

APRIL 24

Persuasion in the Head

We are more or less governed by all our thought patterns, and too many of them have not been created by ourselves but are thought patterns of the ages. — Ernest Holmes, The Power of Belief, page 28.1

Quit terrorizing yourself with scary thoughts, and start inspiring yourself with delightful visions. — Alan Cohen

My son and I first began our hiking adventures on a spring morning at the Manchester Preserve. The waist-high shrubs were spring fresh green rather than summer dry and brown with a dusty trail cut through them. Every few yards the bushes came alive with a constant loud buzzing. At the head of the trail there was a sign with images of critters indigenous to the area. Among them, roadrunner, tarantula, bats, various birds and a big fat long diamondback rattlesnake, who obviously was the star of this gallery since the picture was twice the size of the others, and receiving most of the press. It read: Be careful, dangerous, won't attack you unless... Unless what? The bushes were buzzing with a rattling sound. It was an extremely uncomfortable hike, hearing those sounds coming from such a short distance from our ankles. As soon as we got home, I called a long-time local hiker who laughed as he explained that the sounds we heard were katydids. Unfamiliar, I looked them up to find it's a type of cricket! Wow! I allowed a cricket to ruin the morning as my thoughts created an image far more frightening. Worry is praying for what you don't want, and anxiety is affirming it over and over. I couldn't help but wonder how often I let a scenario rise in my thinking and take over something that isn't so. How about you?

Spiritual Contemplation: What terrorizing pictures and thoughts do I need to release from my awareness?

Affirmation: I now find calm and clarity guiding my thinking!

APRIL 25

Start Your Day with Magic

What nine months of attention does for an embryo, forty early mornings alone will do for your gradually growing wholeness. — Rumi

We have all heard about the importance of self-care. But for most, self-care includes activities like massages, baths, and cozy movie nights on the couch. Though these can be both enjoyable and helpful in letting go of stress, they do not lead to lasting change in terms of increased balance and well-being. One exercise that can deepen your practice of self-care in a real and relevant way is to adopt a Magic Morning Routine. Coined in 2012 by author Hal Elrod in his book *Miracle Morning,* a magic morning is a morning routine that starts your day on the right track so you can begin the day intentionally and creatively.

The Magic Morning includes the following:

M – Movement

A – Alignment

G – Gratitude

I – Intention

C – Connection

How you practice the Magic Morning will be customized to your needs and should include practices that work for you. Examples include yoga or walking for your movement, journaling to set intentions and practice gratitude, and meditation and visioning for your alignment and connection. Setting aside 30 to 60 minutes for yourself on a daily basis sets a strong foundation of self-care and you will feel the difference when you begin your days taking care of yourself.

Spiritual Contemplation: Try to adopt the Magic Morning today and throughout this week. See what a difference it makes in your day.

Affirmation: I start my day with magic!

APRIL 26

What are you Practicing?

The difference between ordinary and extraordinary is practice. — *Vladimir Horowitz*

What you practice, you improve. It's that simple. Just as a blacksmith needs years and countless hours of practice to evolve from making clumsy, imperfect items to crafting beautiful, intricately designed works of art, we also need committed and consistent practice to apply spiritual principles in our lives. Committing to your growth and development isn't always easy, but the hours of self-reflection, meditation, and prayer will pay off in the unfoldment of your life.

So, the question for today is: What are you practicing? Are you practicing how to worry, criticize yourself, or catastrophize about your life? Or, are you practicing trust in the Universe, confidence in your own abilities, and claiming your worthiness? Your mind is always working, and when you think of it as always practicing something, you can better direct your thoughts to those that will nurture and support you in moving in the direction you desire.

Spiritual Contemplation: Today, be conscious and deliberate about what you are thinking and practicing in your life.

Affirmation: What I practice, I get better at! Today I practice knowing my worthiness and know I can build a life of joy.

APRIL 27

Making Change – a 3-step Process

Life will only change when you become more committed to your dreams than you are to your comfort zone. – Billy Cox

A counseling client once asked me if there was a process for making change in one's life. Without hesitating or thinking, I said "Yes! There is a three-step process for changing your life. Step 1: Figure out where you are. Step 2: Figure out where you want to go. Step 3: Figure out how to get there!" We laughed but then started to explore the process and discovered that it works. After a painful divorce, she had just gotten a challenging diagnosis and felt like her life was spinning out of control. Over a short amount of time, we walked through the steps, and she saw how her life started to change. She felt calmer and more centered, even as she went through difficult chemo treatments. She found an inner peace and courage that she had never felt. She even forgave her ex, and they began co-parenting their children together. She shared that this process, though challenging at times, helped her regain personal power to create her life in a way that supported her wants and needs. She was a better parent, as she was more present for her kids and she felt more joy each day than she had in years.

Sometimes doing our spiritual work can feel overwhelming, leaving us feeling lost and unsure of which direction to take. It can be helpful to have small guideposts to direct your way. Over the next three days, we will look at each step of this process and you will receive the tools to begin to make the changes you seek in your life.

Spiritual Contemplation: In preparation for our work over the next three days, think about what is not currently working for you in your life and what area you'd like to work on with this process.

Affirmation: I am open and ready to create a life I love!

APRIL 28

Making Change – Step 1: Figure Out Where You Are

Knowing others is intelligence; knowing yourself is true wisdom. – Lao Tzu.

There are times when we get caught up in the busyness of our lives and can easily lose sight of our dreams and goals. Our days get filled with work, caring for our children and parents, and all the things that encompass a full life. Usually, the first thing that falls off that plate is caring for our mind (emotions and mental state), body (exercise), and spirit (meditation and prayer). We lose sight of our goals and feel lost. The first step for making change is figuring out where we are, and this takes some self-inquiry. Taking some time to be with ourselves and asking questions can open the door to see what isn't working. What am I feeling? Have I felt this way before? When and where did these feelings begin? What part of myself doesn't want to explore this discomfort?

These simple questions with powerful answers will lead you to the place within that is hurting and calling for healing. Everyone carries a wound within. It is part of the human experience that this life brings growth and expansion and it's not easy or comfortable. But this wound is actually a gift because it calls us to a deeper place of understanding ourselves and our life path. We are called to examine the areas where we feel victimized, where we harbor anger and resentment, and where we feel abandoned. By being present with these difficult emotions and treating ourselves with compassion, we gain clarity. This allows us to understand why we are dissatisfied with certain aspects of our lives and what we need to change. When you can observe that ,you are well on your way to shifting it!

Spiritual Contemplation: Take a few moments to breathe and center yourself. Journal your answers to the questions above.

Affirmation: I am Brave! I am True! I am Open to hearing the truth being revealed through me!

APRIL 29

Making Change – Step 2: Figure Out Where You Want to Go

Stop being afraid of what could go wrong, and start getting excited about what could go right. – Tony Robbins

Now that we are becoming aware of what we want to shift in our lives, it's time to figure out what we want to create. When we awaken to what isn't working, and we gain some understanding how we ended up in this situation, we can begin to set course in a new direction. Through self-inquiry and self-compassion, we can begin to create a life of joy and excitement for ourselves. I encourage those I work with to set goals around how they want to feel in their lives rather than what they want to have. This is liberating because it isn't linked to how much money or influence one has.

The goal is to create a life that works for you. How do you want to feel in your life? Do you want to start your day with energy and joy? How do you want to spend your time? Do you prefer being around people who recognize you for your gifts and your presence? How would you feel if you were sharing your true self with the world? Taking the time to vision for the life you desire will open your imagination and creativity and soon you'll find yourself moving in that direction naturally.

Spiritual Contemplation: Take a few moments to breathe and center yourself. Reflect on what came up while journaling yesterday and take some time to journal your answers to the questions above. Again, allow yourself to free-write and don't censor yourself. Let yourself dream big about what life you want to live.

Affirmation: I am living my best life now! I am excited for today and for all that is to come!

APRIL 30

Making Change – Step 3: Figure Out How to Get There

Sometimes the smallest step in the right direction ends up being the biggest step of your life. – Naeem Callaway

Once we figure out what we want to change, and in what direction we'd like to go, we get excited for the possibilities! When we realize we aren't stuck in a bad situation and can actually shift our discomfort, we start to see differently. Maybe we notice a class being offered in a subject that we've always been interested in. Or, maybe we try a new therapy or a new exercise routine. We naturally stop habits that keep us blocked from our joy.

There is no set way of getting to where we want. It's all about our choices and we get to choose about a thousand things each day! From what we eat and who we spend our time with, to how we occupy our days, it is all about choice. We can choose to be around healthy people who support us and see us for who we are. We can choose to create our lives as an expression of our true nature. When we share ourselves from that deep place, the universe responds to us and brings opportunities and experiences that reflect who we truly are. In this way, we move in the direction of our healing and joy just by making choices for our highest expression.

Spiritual Contemplation: Today, as we complete this 3-step process, journal about the choices you have been making for yourself and see if you can shift your choices to be more supportive of growth and development. What are three things you can do to move in the direction of the vision you hold for your life?

Affirmation: I choose my highest and best each and every day!

MAY
Everyday Living

May 1-7
The Flawless Road

May 8-14
Reveal Your Passion

May 15-21
Balancing Your Life

May 22-28
Mindfulness

May 29-31
Waking Up

MAY 1

Stomp Those First Ones

Negative thoughts invade your mind like ants at a picnic. – Dr. Daniel G. Amen

At my ranch in Montana, I had a head gate installed with two towering Ponderosa tree trunks that fork at the top. Another tree trunk lies between the forks, arching across the road at the entrance. The sign, which hangs 14 feet above the ground, is the size of a dining room table with the name of our ranch, Mystic Mountain, carved into it. It's truly a landmark piece I thought would mark the entrance for generations as it's so sturdy a car could run into it and it wouldn't come down. Surprisingly, after a decade it did come down, though not because something big ran into it. Just the contrary. It was due to something so small I didn't even notice them moving in - carpenter ants! Little by little they just kept coming, setting up colonies over time and eating away the inside until the behemoth came down.

Daniel Amen created an acronym for negative thinking that infiltrates the mind. He labeled them A.N.T.s, standing for Automatic Negative Thoughts. At first you may not notice the negative thoughts and over time they just become a repetitive habit until the very foundation of your life crumbles. When the sum total of your thinking can no longer support your magnificence, it becomes imperative you stomp those A.N.T.s, and it's a lot easier if you catch the first few before they compromise your foundation.

Spiritual Contemplation: What negative thoughts have become habitual for you? Get going in stamping them out before ANTs establish an interior colony.

Affirmation: My mind is continually renewed and refreshed with an affirmative approach to living!

MAY 2

Share Your Gifts

In life, it is important to not be afraid to put yourself out there, win or lose. It is all about the spirit of challenging yourself to be open to realizing your highest potential. – Cynthia Bailey

In June of 1944, despite lacking a piano player, a USO troupe entertained soldiers in Normandy from the back of a truck. They called out to the G.I. audience," can anyone here play?" A shy cattle rancher's son from Modesto, California came up and played. He did so well his colonel ordered him out of the line and ordered him to form his own G.I. band. From that, Dave Brubeck's jazz career began.

Can you imagine what would have happened if Dave hadn't stepped forward that day? All of the wonderful music he created might not have made its way into the world. We are each given unique talents and abilities from God and it is our job to develop those abilities and share them with the world. Often, we hold back because we fear being mocked or ridiculed. However, when we have a deep sense of who we are and where we come from—God—we can trust that we are in the right place at the right time and can freely share our true selves with joy. God doesn't make mistakes, and though you may not have discovered them yet, God has given you unique abilities that the world needs. Maybe it's a big talent like the Brubeck story or maybe it's as simple as giving a compliment in the market to a stranger. Remember, God can only show up in life through each of us. So how are you showing up as a channel for God today? As you do so, you will begin to know your worth and experience the joy of full expression!

Spiritual Contemplation: Take some time to contemplate and journal the ways that you may be holding yourself back in the world. How can you begin to share your gifts in a new way?

Affirmation: Today I share who I am fully and freely with the world!

MAY 3

Life's Coming Attraction

I don't like it when a couple argues in public, and I missed the beginning and don't know whose side I'm on! – Anonymous Onlooker

Have you ever walked in on a movie when it was almost over? Everyone seemed happy. The stars get their dream partners, the villains end up where they belong, everything works out, and everyone lives abundantly, laughing and smiling ever after. What you missed was the drama, the struggle and the car chase it took for the couple to arrive in their paradise.

When you see someone, whose life seems charmed, with prosperity flowing and love abounding, what you don't see is what it took for them to reach this destination. It's easy to think, "Some people get all the good breaks; they are so lucky." What you missed seeing is everything they had to go through to arrive at their good fortune - the risks taken, the sacrifices made, the missed family times, the losses incurred, and the hard lessons learned. When you learn to celebrate the good in others 'lives without judgment, you catch a preview of your own life's coming attraction. Good will make an appearance in your life soon.

Spiritual Contemplation: Where do I find myself judging other people's good fortune? How can I shift my perspective to think, 'How wonderful for them'?

Affirmation: I am as happy for others' good fortune as I am for my own!

MAY 4

The Road to Flawless

If you look for perfection, you'll never be content. — *Leo Tolstoy*

One day a young boy was out playing when he saw a grandfatherly man with a sagely looking beard drawing flawless circles in the soil. "Hey, old man, how did you draw such a flawless circle?" asked the youngster. The old man looked at the boy and said, "I'm not sure. I just worked and worked at it. Here, you try." He said as he handed the stick to the child and walked away. The lad began drawing circles in the sand. At first, the circles came out too thin, too oblong, or just too twisted. But as time went by, the circles began to look better and better. He kept working at it, and then, one spring morning, it happened. The flawless circle was drawn into the soil. Shortly thereafter, he heard the voice of a young boy from behind him ask, "Hey old man, how did you draw such a flawless circle?"

If you can look at life as circular, without beginning or end, rather than linearly focused on the final destination, you will find yourself more in love with the present moment of your path. The practice of loving your life now becomes fulfilling rather than daunting on the road to becoming flawless.

Spiritual Contemplation: When has time disappeared for you as you engaged in your creative practice? Is it possible for all of life to unfold in this timeless way?

Affirmation: Time dissolves as I find joy in my practices!

MAY 5

Update the Map

The world we see that seems so insane is the result of a belief system that is not working. To perceive the world differently, we must be willing to change our belief system, let the past slip away, expand our sense of now, and dissolve the fear in our minds. — William James

Recently I was driving my car, which is over 10 years old. It has a screen with a satellite map that shows where I am and where I am going. I glanced at it and noticed, according to the map, I was driving in the middle of a field when I was actually driving on the highway! It made me laugh and then think about the many ways in our lives we use old information to guide us! We are evolving, growing, and unfolding beings but most of us are still following the directions we installed when we were children. It is time to update the map and system, or we will be wandering around our lives blind.

We must look at our core beliefs and see what's not working anymore. Some dated beliefs were helpful and kept us safe as children but are now limiting our ability to express our fullest expression. It's time for a B.S. upgrade. Updating our belief system and letting go of the ideas that have held us back will support each of us in getting to where we want to go!

Spiritual Contemplation: What are some ideas and beliefs operating in your consciousness that no longer serve who you are today? What could they be replaced with that would be supportive of who you are now?

Affirmation: I release the beliefs that no longer serve me, and I accept my Divine Nature!

MAY 6

The Scenery Changed, the Engineer Never Did

Everything I read about hitting a midlife crisis was true. I had such a struggle letting go of youthful things and learning how to exist and have enthusiasm while settling into the comfort of an older age. — David Bowie

As the scenery whizzes by outside your window of a fast-moving train, you rest assured you are on the way to your destination. You enjoy watching the trees passing by. You'd like that beauty to stay in your sight, but you leave it behind as the surroundings change outside your window. A lake comes into view stirring a sense of peacefulness but then you must let it go as well. A city has its own aura, as does the station you pull into. As the backdrops change, the engineer never alters his path, bringing the train home with all the heart and soul of its true nature.

There is an Infinite Intelligence, unchanging in its nature of love. The Divine Engineer gracefully guides you to your destination. There may be experiences of loss along the way, requiring you to let go, but you will never lose the heart that created those connections.

Maybe you once had to let go of a position you held. The consciousness that attracted it into your life is still part of who you are and can attract your greatest next opportunity. Just because the form has changed, doesn't mean the love that guides you is gone. Trust the unfoldment of your life to the love of the Infinite Intelligence that guides the universe.

Spiritual Contemplation: Where have you allowed displeasure and loss to become your guiding personality? Where in your life do you need to let go of something or someone and trust the love of the Divine Engineer hasn't changed?

Affirmation: I let go of what's past and joyously trust what's next!

MAY 7

A Couple of Zen Thoughts

For his 70th birthday, one of his students gave the Zen master a big box with a ribbon around it. When the master opened the box, he found that there was nothing inside. "Aha," he exclaimed, "just what I wanted! — A Zen Story

One Zen student said, "My teacher is the best. He can go days without eating. "The second student shared, "My teacher has so much self-control, he can go days without sleep."The third added, "My teacher is so wise that he eats when he's hungry and sleeps when he's tired."

Teacher number three seems to make the most sense and is less pretentious in the demonstration of control. Why use the Infinite to deny what your body is asking for? It's natural to honor and take care of what you have been entrusted with. You need not be bound through the action of denial to prove your command. You don't need to elevate your awareness through the battle of the lower realm. Your body is the temple of God. In recognizing God knows what It wants, allow your enthusiasm to honor the Divine nudge within you. Simply, say yes to God as your body.

Spiritual Contemplation: How has pretentiousness pulled you down rather than lifting you up?

Affirmation: I say yes to the God knowingness within me!

MAY 8

Reveal Your Passion and You'll Reveal Your Purpose

Don't ask what the world needs. Ask what makes you come alive and go do it. Because what the world needs is people who have come alive. — Howard Thurman

What would you do if you knew you could do anything without failing? This question helps you think big without negative self-talk. I recently asked participants at a retreat this question and the answers I got included ending hunger and homelessness, writing a novel, and starting a business. Attendees were encouraged to dream big and start by musing on their passions. When you realize where your passion lies, you begin to tap into your true self and uncover what you have come to earth to support and create. We all know how hard it is to engage in work that is drudgery. We recognize the toll it takes on our mental and physical well-being. When we begin to connect with our unique passion, we are inspired, energized and excited for each day. As we make this a habit and connect daily with our passions, we move in the direction of our dreams and begin to make them a reality.

Spiritual Contemplation: In your journal, make a list of all the things you are passionate about and love to experience. Try to find a way to engage with one of the items on your list each day.

Affirmation: I connect with my passions and create a life of joy!

MAY 9

Treetop Perspective

If you don't know where you are going, you'll end up someplace else. – Yogi Berra

Cutting a road through a jungle requires a clear vision of where you want to go. You need a treetop perspective to ensure the road is aligned with your intended direction. You can have the biggest and toughest road-cutting crew in the business—strong, fast, and reliable—but without an elevated view of your destination, they might be cutting east when you want to go north, or even circling back through the jungle away from your goal.

Knowing what direction you are heading in life brings clarity to your decision-making. No one has a crystal ball. However, making choices based on your intention for tomorrow with what you know about today is sensible. Whether you are a leader of a business or your family, knowing wholeheartedly where you are going helps to get you there. Without vision, you do not know where you will end up. Proverbs 29:18 says, "Where there is no vision, the people perish."

Spiritual Contemplation: How can your choices today better support your dream for tomorrow?

Affirmation: I am supporting my vision for tomorrow by making wise choices today!

MAY 10

What's Your Why?

The two most important days in life are the day you born and the day you find out why. — Mark Twain

In this life, we are each tasked to figure out why we are here. What is it that makes us unique and special and how are we to share that gift with the world? Those who take the time to figure this out experience greater fulfillment and peace of mind and heart than those who do not. It takes time and courage to do some self-exploration but once we look deeply at what matters and we explore what we are passionate about, we can begin to see how who we are fits into life.

Who do you want to be in the world? How do you want to show up? How do you want to be remembered? Answering these kinds of questions will support you in developing an overarching vision for yourself and what you want to create in your life. Taking the time to inquire within will allow you to see yourself from a different perspective. It will help you understand the 'why 'behind all the things you do. This leads us to a deep realization of who we are and an understanding of what's important to us. When you know your why, you step forward empowered from a state of wholeness and create what you desire.

Spiritual Contemplation: Who do you want to be in the world? How do you want to show up? How do you want to be remembered? What is important to you?

Affirmation: I listen deeply to my heart and open to my why!

MAY 11

It's Already Within

I ask not for a lighter burden, but for broader shoulders. — *Atlas*

According to Greek Mythology, Atlas was a Titan, who was involved in a war between the Titans and their offspring, the Olympians. Fighting against the Titans were a younger generation of Gods; Zeus, Prometheus, and Hades. When the Olympians won the war, they punished their enemies. Zeus condemned Atlas to stand at the western edge of the Earth and hold the sky on his shoulders for eternity. While carrying the weight of the world on his shoulders, Atlas 'plea to Zeus left a lasting and powerful message: "I ask not for a lighter burden, but for broader shoulders."

To this day, some traditions claim that Mount Atlas, located in the western part of northern Africa, is the man Atlas who metamorphosed into the mountain that carries the sky. From time to time, there may be struggles in your life. What is needed already exists within you and is ready to meet every dynamic life throws your way. Allow the Divine metamorphosis to rise with all that is necessary to face whatever is at hand.

Spiritual Contemplation: Where do I feel the weight of my life is too heavy? Rather than being squashed by the burden, how could you be a greater expression than the challenge?

Affirmation: That which is within me is greater than that which is out in the world!

MAY 12

Set Your Goals

It must be borne in mind that the tragedy of life doesn't lie in not reaching your goal. The tragedy lies in having no goals to reach. — Benjamin E. Mays

Goal setting can support you in moving forward in your life. Goals give meaning to life and are meant to continually challenge you to put your talent, skills, and creativity, towards achieving tangible results. When we take the time to write down our goals, it makes it easier to reach our desired destination.

There is power in setting a goal and seeing it to completion, no matter what its outcome. Sometimes you set a goal and never reach its fulfillment, but it is still helpful in revealing greater wisdom about yourself and your life. Witnessing this process will give you an experience of fulfillment increasing your confidence in your own abilities, overriding the idea that you are not good enough. Living wholeheartedly includes setting goals and moving in the direction of your dreams. Start dreaming about what your life could be like and set some concrete goals to let the process of manifestation begin.

Spiritual Contemplation: What are some concrete goals you can set for yourself? Write down three things to work towards in the next few months. Watch how the universe conspires to support you in achieving your goals.

Affirmation: I set goals to express myself fully in my life and watch them come to be with ease!

MAY 13

Hanging On

Some of us think holding on makes us strong but sometimes it is letting go. —
Hermann Hesse

A hiker falls off the side of the mountain and plunges hundreds of feet before grabbing a vine and saving his life. Hanging their hundreds of feet above the ground with no way back up to the top, he prays for the first time in his life. Looking up into the celestial realm, he implores, "Is anybody up there?" A deep voice from the heavens returns, "Do you believe?" To which he responds, "Yes! Yes! Yes!" "Then let go of the vine," comes the reply. The man thinks about it for a moment, then looks up again and eventually asks, "Is anybody else up there?"

Are you unable to reach the next level in your life because you are not ready to let go of where you are? You are ready for a change and know where you are isn't the answer. Yet, despite being unsatisfied and exhausted with your current situation, there's something in you that won't allow you to let go. Sometimes you just need to get comfortable with not knowing and lean into trusting your guidance. It's time to have your action demonstrate you believe in something greater than what you are hanging onto.

Spiritual Contemplation: What in your life are you hanging onto despite knowing it is time to let go? Let Go!

Affirmation: I believe and act based on my inner guidance!

MAY 14

Cultivating Resilience

Man never made any material as resilient as the human spirit. – Bern Williams

Being resilient means having the ability to overcome adversity and bounce back from challenges, mistakes, and losses. It takes a mindful person committed to living a spiritual life to develop resilience. When you live a spiritual life, you understand that you are inexorably connected to everyone and everything around you. You see that life has meaning and purpose, even in the difficult moments. This gives you the perspective to see that you already have the resources within to face any challenge and the strength to handle any setbacks that arise.

Resilient people share a set of common qualities that include: problem solving skills, a willingness to seek help when needed, an ability to take responsibility for their own feelings, and an understanding of the importance of having strong community connections. Working on strengthening these qualities will support you in realizing that you are stronger and more capable than you presume and as you cultivate this resilience, you will persevere in any situation you are faced with.

Spiritual Contemplation: Think about the challenges you have faced and how you bounced back from them. How could you embrace the concept of resilience even more as you move forward in your life?

Affirmation: I am resilient and face every situation of my life with courage, strength and love!

MAY 15

You Are the Divine in Jeans

Don't ask yourself what the world needs; ask yourself what makes you come alive. And then go and do that. Because what the world needs is people who have come alive. – Howard Thurman

When you figure out what you are passionate about, you won't hit the snooze button anymore. Your soul assignment is divinely given, but you must also engage in it here in this dimension. You are the Divine in jeans, answering the call to action, finding something to love and live for. When you have a clear calling, you don't have to force yourself into action. Your passion will drive you. There may be twists, turns and maybe even a U-turn along the most direct route to your destination, but you'll love the journey.

The greatest gift to yourself is in honoring your soul's purpose. It's why you were born, what makes you come alive, and what brings forth your latent strengths and higher qualities. Rumi wrote, *Let the beauty of what you love be what you do."*

Spiritual Contemplation: What are some of your higher, finer, spiritual qualities that come forth when you are living on purpose? How does it feel to be expressing those qualities in your life?

Affirmation: I find what makes me come alive and live that passion!

MAY 16

Unconscious One-upmanship

The one thing you shouldn't do is try to tell a cab driver how to get somewhere. -
Jimmy Fallon

Some people just have to comment on everything. Have you ever been sharing a heartfelt story, and someone one-ups you? You communicate about a project you spent the last year doing and finally proudly completed, and they follow it by telling you about a project they just finished. Maybe you share with a friend some tales of a recent trip to Europe and they immediately start talking about their trip to Paris and dining along the Avenue des Champs-Élysées, "the most beautiful avenue in the world." They redirect the spotlight onto themselves leaving you with a sense they don't really care about your experience at all. That may not be true, but their statement is clear: I'm more interested in sharing than listening. If your light shines, they may feel theirs is diminished. Often those who like to story-top are unaware of what they are doing. They just aren't able to read the social cues and relate to others. This style of interaction feeds their esteem by stealing another's soul food.

Spiritual Contemplation: What did you feel like when you shared something and another person needed to share something better? Do you remember a time you story-topped something important another person was attempting to convey?

Affirmation: My conversational dance with my friends is divine!

MAY 17

Take a Leap!

~~୬ℓℓℓ୬~~

The biggest risk is not taking any risk. In a world that's changing really quickly, the only strategy that is guaranteed to fail is not taking risks. — Mark Zuckerberg

In the 1950s Harland Sanders faced financial ruin and the closure of his restaurant in Kentucky. However, he had a secret recipe for fried chicken that was quite popular. He took a leap of faith and traveled across the country promoting his chicken to other restaurants. He offered the recipe to restaurant owners for a small fee for each chicken sold. This was how Kentucky Fried Chicken, one of the most recognizable fast-food chains in the world, was born. Sanders' commitment and determination allowed him to take the risk that paid off for both him and fried chicken lovers everywhere.

There are times when we are called in a new direction. It may be in your work, relationship, or where you want to live. The issue lies in knowing deep within that we need to change something but we hold ourselves back, fearing failure. It would serve us well to welcome change and learn to leap because we learn a lot about ourselves outside our comfort zone. In trying new things, we gain experience, expand our skill set, and discover new interests and passions. Trust yourself enough to heed the call and leap when it comes!

Spiritual Contemplation: What is calling you to take a risk and leap in a new direction in your life? When have you taken risks before? How did they turn out for you?

Affirmation: I trust myself and I trust life! I leap forward with joy!

MAY 18

Resonance and residence

When you're young, you look at television and think, there's a conspiracy. The networks have conspired to dumb us down. But when you get a little older, you realize that's not true. The networks are in business to give people exactly what they want. — Steve Jobs

There will always be prognosticators of doom. They seem to be turned on as they share their perspectives and the proof that validates their position. Others will walk this world unscathed by the apocalyptic visions pumped into the collective psyche. Their world seems blessed and filled with light. They are happy to share the evidence that validates their position as well. You can live in fear running with conspiracy theories to the right or to the left. The choice is yours. However, those in fear will tell you there is no choice.

You always have the option to move out of the gravitational pull of duality and move into resonance and reside with The Infinite. Evidentially, there cannot be the Infinite and something other than that. In this realization, you free yourself from the terror of fear. As you walk in awareness with the Divine Spirit that is in and through all things, you are released from where you have been mesmerized by form. The "mountaintop view" guides your thoughts to understanding more options than just the battles below.

Spiritual Contemplation: Where in life are you being lured into thinking there are no other options than what are presently being offered? Remove yourself from this place, quiet your mind and look out at your world from a higher, "mountaintop" perspective.

Affirmation: Looking at my life from a higher perspective, I see my options!

MAY 19

Dance with your Resistance in a New Way

~~⁓ℰℰ⁓~~

"Change takes but an instant," goes the old Hebrew proverb. It's the resistance to change that can take a lifetime. – Carolyn Myss

Change is one of the constants in life that we must learn how to approach on an ongoing basis. Just when we get used to a situation in our experience, and particularly those we like, everything shifts. These changes can be difficult to handle, especially when they come in rapid succession. Often, when this happens, our resistance gets triggered and we end up participating in behaviors to avoid the new situation.

When we give in to our resistance, we are living from fear – fear of the unknown, fear that we are not enough to handle the new situation, and fear that the new situation won't be what we want. The goal here is to move from that place of fear to a place of trust and faith. Can you trust Life to bring you the situations that will bring joy and fulfillment? When you begin to build your faith in Life, you begin to live from vision – where you know what's possible and you can already bring forth great joy in life. Let us learn to dance with resistance in a new way. Allow it to show you where you are still holding onto fear and as you let it go, it will serve you in creating a life that you love.

Spiritual Contemplation: Where in your life are you experiencing resistance to change and how can you dance with it differently to create more joy in the process?

Affirmation: I surrender to the unfoldment of my life and trust the Divine process in every way!

MAY 20

It's Either True or It's Not

Once you eliminate the impossible, whatever remains, no matter how improbable, must be the truth. – Arthur Conan Doyle

Truth is simple. There are no great cryptic formulas for Truth. It is either True or Untrue. Degrees of truth don't exist. Truth is, or it is not. There is no mystery there.

If the Truth of Spirit is Infinite, then by definition it includes all things, otherwise it is not infinite. Therefore, your true nature is of Spirit since there is nothing else from which you might have been created from. It doesn't mean you are all of Spirit, but all that you are is Spirit, and your true nature is one of wholeness, abundance and all that God is, you are. Your good unfolds from within, appearing as a person, place, or things in your world. Give up attempting to get and realize you are the perpetual distributor of life. You are the avenue through which the Infinite passes into form.

Spiritual Contemplation: Where are you twisting the truth to make it fit and validate a particular scenario? Truth is simple - it either is, or it is not. Stop complicating it and get back to the simple truth of the matter.

Affirmation: I am a distributor of the abundant truth of Spirit!

MAY 21

Work-Life Balance

There is no such thing as work-life balance – it is all life. The balance has to be within you. – Sadhguru

Work/Life balance speaks to the equilibrium that many strive to create between their personal and professional lives. It requires one to manage their time and energy allowing for professional responsibilities along with ample time for self-care, family, relationships, and leisure activities. Many people struggle in this area giving the most time and energy to their jobs, finding little left for the rest of their lives. Working long hours, high-stress levels, and lack of fulfillment are career issues that can negatively impact one's overall well-being.

Living wholeheartedly includes actively choosing to create a harmonious work-life balance. Prioritizing self-care, setting boundaries, and keeping realistic expectations can support one in finding balance bringing greater peace and enjoyment to both their personal and professional life!

Spiritual Contemplation: How is the state of your work-life balance? What choices could you make to create more space for your self-care and well-being?

Affirmation: I choose to create balance in all aspects of my life!

MAY 22

How Long Are You Going to Wait?

The path to our destination is not always a straight one. We go down the wrong road, we get lost, we turn back. Maybe it doesn't matter which road we embark on. Maybe what matters is that we embark. – Barbara Hall

Several years ago, we bought a beautiful lamp for our living room. After a few years, it stopped working. We tried changing the lightbulb, which didn't fix it, so we left it alone to sit in our living room as a large art piece for over 10 years. I finally got tired of having a broken lamp in our home and decided to fix it. I studied how to rewire a lamp and then bought all the items I'd need. Right before I disassembled the lamp, I considered anything else that might be causing it not to work and discovered a control box within the lamp housing a 1/2-inch fuse that had blown. I ran to the hardware store and bought the $1.65 fuse and returned home to install it. 10 minutes later I had a working lamp again! It just took $1.65 and 10 years!

How many things in our lives could be rectified if we just devoted a little time and attention to them? Assuming our problems are too big to fix or that we aren't capable of doing the work leads us to despair and hopelessness. Truth is, nothing is as bad as our minds convince us it is. We can handle much more than we think and there is no need to put off facing challenges. Sometimes it's as easy as a heartfelt conversation and apology. A little love and attention go a long way. Stop avoiding your problems, face them with love and attention and you'll see how easy it can be to move past them.

Spiritual Contemplation: Is there anything in your life that you are avoiding facing and taking care of? How could you bring love and attention to the situation to move forward in a new way?

Affirmation: I am One with the Divine Flow of Life and face each moment with love and attention!

MAY 23

I Got It, or Do I

✥

Realize deeply that the present moment is all you ever have. Make the Now the primary focus of your life. — Eckhart Tolle

After more than a decade of training, a disciple attained the level of Zen Teacher. Excited to go back and share the news with one of his early Master Teachers, he entered the house where the Master greeted him. The Master asked his student if he had left his sandals and umbrella on the porch. "Of course," the new teacher responded. "Tell me then," the Master continued, "Did you leave your umbrella to the left or the right of your sandals?"

The new teacher realized he did not know the answer, and thus had not yet attained full awareness. He stayed to study with the Zen Master for the next decade. It's not how much you practice something, it's how much of yourself you put into the practice that matters most.

Spiritual Contemplation: Do you learn with your mind and do your work by rote? Or, do you understand with all that you are, then apply all of yourself into your action? How can you become more present in your daily routine?

Affirmation: I am fully present with where I am and what I am doing?

MAY 24

Adjust Your Sails

I can't change the direction of the wind, but I can adjust my sails to always reach my destination. - Jimmy Dean

I have always been fascinated by sailing. It's such a great metaphor for life. Sailboats don't aim directly where they want to go but aim in the general direction because they are working with the forces of nature including the elements of wind and water. They need to work in harmony with the elements to reach their destination!

Life is like this for us all. We have an idea of what we would like to create in our lives and need to learn to move in the direction of that vision while opening to living in harmony with life itself. Bit by bit we begin to see that we are creating moments of what we desire and that encourages us and builds faith in our abilities and in life itself. When we can trust that Life will bring us the experience we desire, we can let go of doubt and struggle and know we are aligned with the highest vision of what's possible. We work with all the elements of our lives and move forward toward what we want, growing and deepening all the while. Then we can adjust our sails and allow the winds of life to take us right where we want to go!

Spiritual Contemplation: What are you dreaming of creating in your life? What are the "elements" of your life that can support you to getting where you want to go?

Affirmation: I open my sails to the winds of Life and allow it to take me to my desired experience!

MAY 25

The Thermostat

You've got to be a thermostat rather than a thermometer. A thermostat shapes the climate of opinion; a thermometer just reflects it. — Cornel West

Have you ever wrestled with remembering how your thermostat works? Do you have a smart heater that needs to be synced with different rooms or does one adjustment work everywhere in the house? Move the switch - is it right or left for auto, on, off, heat, cool or fan? Push the correct buttons for the proper adjustment to set the days of the week with the correct times of day and night and it's handled until daylight savings time. After so many years of doing this, it seems it should be simple to remember from one season to another, and yet for some mysterious reason it's not.

The nature of the thermostat is to work and fulfill its potential. The confusion is within the programmer, not the thermostat. It doesn't withhold its ability to heat or cool the house. It's waiting to cooperate with the direction you give it. You set the temperature and it responds. No matter how smart it is, it can't make the decision on its own. You must first give it direction. So too does the law of cause and effect wait on receiving your direction. Life can get confusing from one year to the next, even if you used the spiritual principles correctly last season. Remember to intentionally and correctly set the climate for your life using the spiritual principle that responds to your intentions. Otherwise, you'll continue to live by old settings.

Spiritual Contemplation: What setting changes could you make to the operation of the law of cause and effect in your life? If you did, what would your new living environment look like?

Affirmation: I now set the perfect climate in which to live my life!

MAY 26

Land of the Free Because of the Brave

Memorial Day is a time for reflecting, respecting, appreciating, honoring, remembering the service and sacrifices of the fallen. – Daniel Paicopulos, US Military Veteran

There was a time when many children couldn't explain the significance of Memorial Day. The responses ranged from when the pools opened to the start of summer. National Moment of Remembrance is committed to increasing the holiday's awareness. It is an annual event that asks Americans, wherever they are and whatever they are doing on the last Monday in May, to pause for a minute to remember those who died in military service to the United States. Some participants include Major League Baseball which halts all their games for that minute, among others including NASCAR, the National Grocers Association, and even Amtrak which silences their train whistles across America.

It's not a holiday where "happy" goes before its name. A veteran, Daniel Paicopulos, states the day "Is for honoring with loyalty and respect to those who lost their own final battle." It is not for honoring current service members or veterans, though they deeply deserve our appreciation. It is for appreciating and remembering those who did not make it home and who believed so deeply in the high ideal of the United States and freedom for all that they were willing to sacrifice their lives for it.

Spiritual Contemplation: Stop whatever you are doing at 3:00 pm this Memorial Day, take a minute to open your heart with appreciation, and remember those who believed in freedom so much that they gave their lives for us!

Affirmation: I honor the fallen by choosing freedom for my life!

MAY 27

Learning How to Slow Down

Nature does not hurry, yet everything is accomplished. — Lao Tzu

In our fast-paced culture, it can be hard to slow down and enjoy life. We are always rushing from one thing to the next and never seem to have enough time in our schedules. We are bombarded with messaging around needing to be more, do more, and have more. But is that what life is really all about? Is a faster pace better?

While being on the go might make us feel productive and important, it can also make us feel incredibly stressed out. This is why we are being called to remember that slowing down and enjoying life is also important. Learning how to say no, not over-scheduling yourself, and practicing Mindfulness, are all strategies for slowing down. When you begin to implement these practices in your day-to-day life, you will see improvements in your health, relationships, and even your productivity will increase! All you need to do is learn how to slow down.

Spiritual Contemplation: Look at your schedule and identify some items that you can let go of. Practice saying no to those things that drain you and bring more stress into your life. What other strategies can you implement to support you in slowing down?

Affirmation: I slow down and breathe and am open to the gift of this moment!

MAY 28

The Power of Mindfulness

We have only now, only this single eternal moment opening and unfolding before us, day and night. – Jack Kornfield

I learned about the practice of mindfulness from a video of a monk drinking coffee. He was sharing how much better the whole experience was when he thought about the beans being grown, the people who harvested them, and all that went into making that simple cup of coffee. It reminded me of how often we run through our days mindlessly hurrying from one encounter to the next without being present to what is right in front of us. We miss so much of life because we live distracted by an unending barrage of thoughts bouncing around in our heads!

When we slow down and become present to what is happening in any one moment, we awaken to the wisdom and guidance that is all around us. We meet ourselves at a deeper level. We hear the concerns and worries of those in our circle. We see through our own issues and can be present to the needs of others in a real way. A Mindfulness practice can lead to more balanced emotions, deeper rest, and greater connection in relationships and peace of mind.

Spiritual Contemplation: Take a look at how you are moving through your days. How can you add a mindfulness practice to slow down and become more present?

Affirmation: I am present in this moment and open to the Divine wisdom here for me!

MAY 29

The Blessing of Community

If you want to go fast, go alone. If you want to go far, go together. — African Proverb

Most have had the experience of the differences between working alone and working together with a group. Each has positives and negatives associated with them and we can see the good and bad in both! Sometimes it's just easier and faster to do a task alone and other times when working in a group makes all the difference. The proverb above speaks volumes to the power of participating in spiritual community.

Spiritual work is geared toward supporting personal development and healing and shouldn't be rushed. Healing takes time, attention, and a willingness to be vulnerable. This is what I equate to "going far". If you want to go far in your life, create a community that sees you for who you truly are. Invite in those who you can be open and authentic with and commit to creating a safe space for them also. This will support you in your healing journey and create a community on which you can depend and in turn support. This is the power of community.

Spiritual Contemplation: Who are the 5-10 people in your life that you feel comfortable sharing your true self with? How can you deepen these relationships and begin to create community together?

Affirmation: I am open, willing, and able to share myself with my community!

MAY 30

Where to Place Your Awareness

Very little is needed to make a happy life; it is all within yourself in your way of thinking. – Marcus Aurelius

Looking at a bookshelf lined with varying options for adventures and explorations of consciousness is an exciting contemplation. Where are you being called to place your awareness for a while? Will it be filled with action, romance, quantum equations, scientific hypotheses, evolutionary thoughts, or historical insights? It's totally your choice.

The shelves of life are lined with adventure awaiting your selection. Will you choose struggle, action adventure, comedy or tragedy? Maybe it will be a textbook waiting to reveal its secrets. How will the protagonist of your novel handle the quest - as a conqueror or one who has been defeated? What's your spin on your evolving story line? No two people read a book the same way. Storylines go through different filters for every individual. No two people have the same understanding from similar experiences. Choose your selection as to where you place your awareness wisely.

Spiritual Contemplation: What kind of adventure do I want to spend some time with?

Affirmation: I choose where I place my awareness wisely!

MAY 31

The Importance of Ritual

Ritual is the passageway of the soul into the Infinite. — Algernon Blackwood

A friend came to see me as her youngest went off to college. She was surprised by the amount of grief she felt as she entered the empty nest experience. After diving into her feelings, we decided to create a ritual to honor her long marriage, a difficult divorce, single parenting, and now the loss of her daily role as a mother. We gathered a small circle of women together and she shared her fears and disappointments of the past and her hopes for the future. We lit candles, burned sage, wrote prayers, and supported her in moving into her new chapter.

Whether it's lighting a candle before you journal or gathering with a group to sing and share, rituals can give your life a sense of meaning and purpose. Rituals can bridge the inner and outer worlds as you step into sacred space. They can bring a sense of renewal and mark major transition points. A ritual can be a simple act or something elaborate but either way it reminds you that you are connected to the larger Life and are not alone.

Spiritual Contemplation: Practice creating a personal ritual around your spiritual exercises this week. Light a candle and read a quote that inspires you before your meditation, reading and journaling and note how you feel in your journal.

Affirmation: I create a personal ritual that serves and inspires me!

JUNE
Wholeness & Health

June 1-7

You Are a Temple of God

June 8-14

Retrain Your Brain

June 15-21

Living on the Spiral

June 22-30

Finding Your Why

JUNE 1

Appreciating Pride Month

Since 1999, the presidents of the United States have proclaimed June to be Pride Month. Pride Month promotes visibility, acceptance, and equality of the world's LGBTQ+. It helps educate people about the challenges and achievements within the movement, while honoring its activists and allies. It's a time to celebrate the freedom of oneself. The Pride events welcome anyone who feels their sexual identity falls outside the mainstream, though all are welcome. It is not about tolerating differences, which would be making yourself recognize differences. Rather, it is about celebrating, appreciating, seeing, and consciously embracing another human being for who they are.

Pride Month is a time to show solidarity and celebrate love and friendship in all its expressions. It is a time to be proud of who you are, no matter who you love. The original organizers chose June to honor the Stonewall uprising in New York City, where a series of raids on a gay club in Greenwich Village escalated into a riot on June 28, 1969. Stonewall soon became a catalyst and symbol for galvanizing a new generation of resistance to social and political discrimination inspiring solidarity within the LGBTQ+ community and its allies.

Spiritual Contemplation: What beautiful aspects of yourself is it time to appreciate and celebrate? How many insults and raids on this beautiful aspect of your being must you endure before you say it is enough? Stand proud of who you are!

Affirmation: I am proud of who I am!

JUNE 2

Caring for Your Body

Keeping your body healthy is an expression of gratitude to the whole cosmos- the trees, the clouds, everything. — Thich Nhat Hanh

With our goal of living a wholehearted life, our health and wellness are the most important things to address as they impact how everything in our lives affects us. Without our health or well-being, nothing is possible. But, when we care for ourselves deeply on the physical level, our bodies become the vehicles through which we can soar in this life.

One aspect of living an awakened life is to become conscious of how we are caring for our physical bodies. What are we feeding ourselves? Are we choosing nutrient rich foods and avoiding the junk? Are we moving and exercising daily? Are we following up with our doctor when something needs attention? Are we appreciating ourselves with words of support and love in our minds? Remembering that this is the only body we've got in this life, it's time to choose to treat it with respect, praising and honoring it as our holy temple.

Spiritual Contemplation: What do you do on a regular basis to care for your physical body? What is one thing you could add on a daily basis to honor your body as a holy temple?

Affirmation: I know my body is a vehicle for the Divine to express as me! I care for it on all levels!

JUNE 3

Purge the Crud

Those who flow as life flows know they need no other force. — Tao Te Ching

Health and well-being are an out-picture of self-expression. When you are true to your heart, soul, mind, and dreams, your body lines up to take care of itself to help fulfill the charge. The life force moves unobstructed through you, continuing to clean out anything unlike itself. In doing that, it refreshes and revitalizes every cell in the body. When you are out of alignment and integrity with your passion, frustration and despair build a blockage that impedes the flow.

Much of our disease, discomfort, and depression comes from a buildup that is blocking the spiritual pipes. When the water pipes coming into your home get clogged, it doesn't matter how big the reservoir behind them is, the water flow won't make it to your home. You must flush the pipes so the water can get through. So too in your life, you have to step into what brings you joy and start doing it to get the spiritual flow going again. This will naturally purge the buildup of crud. Get back to whatever your creative expression is, whether it's art, music, poetry, writing, or volunteering. You could even try physical activity with some yoga, sports or dance to get the somatic energy circulating through your body again.

Spiritual Contemplation: What can you do to flush out your spiritual pipes to restore your energy flow?

Affirmation: Life's energy is now flowing freely through me!

JUNE 4

A Regular Wellness Checkup

Taking care of yourself doesn't mean me first; it means me too. — L.R. Knost

It is important that we periodically take time to check in and see what is happening for us. Often, we get on the hamster wheel of our lives and start running at full speed without realizing that we aren't getting anywhere. This is because we are not taking the time to check in with ourselves to see what is getting in the way of our true wellness.

Setting aside personal time to be quiet and allowing yourself to pause for self-inquiry about how you truly are, can be extremely helpful in creating greater wellness. Pause, breathe and ask yourself some of the following questions: What is going on in your life that is keeping you from being your best? How are your relationships? Are you dealing with any conflict? How is your energy? Are you getting enough sleep? How does your body feel? How's your mind? Spend some time contemplating and journaling your answers and you will gain greater insight into why you may not be feeling your best. The first step to making any change is becoming aware of what is not working, then, you can have a vision for what you want and begin to create it in your life!

Spiritual Contemplation: What gets in the way of you creating what you want in your life? How can you do a regular wellness checkup to support your growth and expansion?

Affirmation: I awaken to my true self and release anything and everything that inhibits my fullest expression!

JUNE 5

Temple of God

Take care of your body. It's the only place you have to live. — Jim Rohn

Some people will treat their bodies like a rent-a-car. They take it out, knock around town in it, not overly considerate or concerned about it. Your body is a temple, it's not a drive-through. You'll want to keep it healthy so it's a fit instrument for your soul to navigate through this world. Treat your body like a temple and not a garage where you store your junk.

Stop hating on your body. How's that 'hate' working for you? Your body hears everything you think and say about it. Your mind is what initiates your body's expression. Healthy mind, healthy body. It's been said your body is the temple of God, which then naturally makes your mind the portal of the Divine expression. The body and mind work together, as taking care of the body supports the mind. Take care of both and your world will be heavenly.

Spiritual Contemplation: What can I start doing today that better supports my body?

Affirmation: I am honoring my body as the temple of God!

JUNE 6

Choose Wellness

Committing to a lifetime of wellness is not a luxury-it's a necessity. You'll never have enough time; you have to make the time. — Oprah Winfrey

It has been said that wellness is the act of practicing healthy habits daily to attain better physical and mental health, so instead of just surviving, you're thriving. Wellness involves every aspect of your being: mind, body, and spirit. Creating true wellness in our lives is a journey of bringing these three dimensions into balance within our experience. A combination of what you eat, how you respond to your body, how you handle your emotions and connect to the larger world drives true wellness.

In New Thought, we know that what we put our attention on, expands. When you bring your attention to how you nourish yourself, how you relate to your body and how you process the experience of life, you begin to awaken to the small changes you can make to enhance your wellness. It's all about choice! As you begin to choose those things that help you align your mind, body and spirit, you begin to create wellness in your life, and you will thrive!

Spiritual contemplation: Choose three things that you can do today to bring attention and support to your body, mind and spirit. Note them in your journal.

Affirmation: My mind, body and spirit are aligned, and I am an expression of wellness! I am thriving in my life!

JUNE 7

Just Move!

~~~

Movement is the essence of life. — *Bernd Heinrich*

Several years ago, my sister opened a Pilates studio in Michigan with the name "MOVE". I was so inspired by that because that one word encapsulates a philosophy of exercise that is so simple and beautiful that it invites everyone in easily. It's not "Crunch" or "Hammer Strength" or any other intimidating name. I love it because everyone can move. No matter your age or ability, there is some way that you can move your body. What my sister knew is that if she can get you to move, you will quickly realize how good it feels and you will see that you are more capable than you think you are, leading to regular practice of exercise that works for you.

This is crucial because we all know that exercise is key for our health and well-being. When you find the movement that works for you and incorporate it in your daily routine, you end up having more energy, more clear thinking and feel better in your mind, body, and spirit. I found yoga, Pilates and dance work best for me. What works for you?

Spiritual Contemplation: As you set your sights on living a wholehearted life, how will you move to support your physical heart and body as well as your metaphorical heart and mind?

Affirmation: Today I move with joy and freedom in my own way!

JUNE 8

Feel Your Feelings

~eﬂﬁ~o~

What you resist persists. – Carl Jung

Living a wholehearted life means being present to our feelings and emotions. This can be a difficult task as many of us struggle with negative emotions like anger or fear. As children, we learned early coping techniques to keep us safe and push away those difficult feelings. Denial and repression helped us to process emotions that were too mature for us to understand as children. The issue arises as we grow into adults and continue to do the same thing. Repressed feelings get stuck in our bodies and can cause depression, anxiety, and even ailments like high blood pressure, digestive issues, and physical pain.

Curious that these repressed feelings never really go away. They lie in wait until we get triggered by some external power and then explode forcing us to face them. The more we try to avoid feeling something, the more life will give us situations to experience it. If we are uncomfortable with anger, we may experience that the entire world is out to make us angry. It will continue until we face and address our anger and deal with it. Being brave enough to sit with our negative emotions – the sadness, anger, fear, and shame – will allow us to see them differently and life will stop bringing situations for us to feel them.

Spiritual Contemplation: What emotions are challenging for you to feel deeply? Journal about this and then take some time to be present with one of the emotions allowing it to move through you. Cry if you need to cry. Scream into a pillow to release your anger. Be present with your fear to see what it is truly about. Then just notice how differently you feel.

Affirmation: I feel all my feelings with love and compassion.

JUNE 9

El Niño

~~⌇⌇~~

Whatever is begun in anger, ends in shame. — Benjamin Franklin

El Niño, "The Boy," is a natural cyclical weather-warming pattern in the Pacific Ocean that makes global weather extreme. As the weather heats up, it creates havoc on the planet. When anger is released in your life, things can heat up, creating chaos. Irritation and offense are natural cyclical occurrences in life. It's how you process them that makes a difference in your world. If the heat accumulates and stress builds, the next irritation could be the one that releases a cataclysmic response that can have a devastating impact on your life.

Focus that energy elsewhere, because El Niño does need to be dissipated. Get mad and get over it. Appropriately direct the energy. One of the transforming remedies for upset is to delay your response. Anger will cloud your mind, blow out your light, and obscure your vision. Do not indulge in your destructive emotions. It is said that you can't get ahead while trying to get even. Life is watching, and responses reflect that. Take your power back from the outside triggers. Did I offer peace today? Did I forgive today? Did I choose to love today?

Spiritual Contemplation: When feeling angry, close your mouth and take a walk.

Affirmation: I am a positive force of nature!

JUNE 10

Ownership of Ailments

Health is not a condition of matter, but of Mind. – Mary Baker Eddy

Listening to the concerns of a client during a counseling session will often lead to the question, "Tell me who you are without these issues?" Too often challenges can get embraced as defining a personality. Ownership of aliments focus the creative attention on the very thing in your life you don't want to be experiencing any longer. Claiming and naming the aches and pains as "mine" is a ticket for them to take a long free ride in your life. Your invitations sound like, my challenges are unique, my prognosis is rare, my struggle is… and the claiming naming list goes on.

When you think of yourself, drop the identification to the human troubles and claim your true divine identity. You are here to express your God qualities. God Consciousness is forever available to express Itself as your life and true identity. Don't allow anything discordant to take a free ride in your awareness or monopolize your conversations. Become aware you are the peace that God is. This harmony that is now at the center of your being permits no doubts to your true identity.

Spiritual Contemplation: Are you claiming any aches and pains as yours? Do you find you are sharing fears as belonging to you? How can you change your language so you don't own your ailments?

Affirmation: I love my healthy body and life!

JUNE 11

Retrain Your Brain

Formulate and stamp indelibly on your mind a mental picture of yourself as succeeding. Hold this picture tenaciously and never permit it to fade. Your mind will seek to develop this picture! – Norman Vincent Peale

Over the past 20 years, neuroscience has taught that our brains retain all the messages we have received throughout our lives. These messages shape the ideas we hold and what's possible for us. If you were told repeatedly throughout your life that you weren't smart, at some point you would probably accept that as truth and see yourself as not being smart. You would get stuck in that rut and call forth situations that prove you aren't smart, when that was just someone's opinion and untrue. This is important because what you believe about yourself affects how you navigate your life and what you think is possible for yourself.

If you want to change anything in your life, you must rewire your brain and create new neurocircuitry (ways of thinking). Spiritual practices like meditation, visualization, affirmations and journaling all aid in retraining your brain and recreating the circuitry. They support you in laying down new ideas about yourself and help dismantle the old, outdated ideas you have been holding onto about who you are. As you embrace new, expansive ideas about yourself and release the old, limiting falsities, you'll experience greater possibilities coming into your experience.

Spiritual Contemplation: What are the ideas you currently hold about yourself? Make a list of your strengths and weaknesses. Read through the list and consider the source of the ideas. Are they true? Rewrite your list of positive attributes and begin to see yourself fully expressed in this way in your life.

Affirmation: I am a Divine Expression of wholeness, peace and love just as I am!

JUNE 12

Don't Rush into It

God screens us evermore from premature ideas. — Ralph Waldo Emerson

A large caravan traveling a great distance came to a forest through which their road led. The elder advised them to be leery of what they ate for this forest had poisonous plants. He suggested they check with him first. Inside the forest was a town and, on its outskirts, grew an enormous fruiting What-is-it tree. Its leaves, flowers and fruit resembled a mango tree. But if the fruit of this tree was eaten, it would assuredly cause death. Remembering the wise one's words, they consulted him and he gently guided them, "This is not a mango tree, it is the deadly What-is-it fruit tree. One bite and you'll die."

What none of them knew was that the racket of some of the villagers was to rob the belongings of those who had died eating the fruit. The villagers would then dump all evidence of the travelers. This time to their great dismay, when the looters came expecting to plunder treasure from the large convoy, they found them all alive and well. The thieves asked why they had not eaten the delicious looking fruit. The Sage's reply was, "When there is a huge tree near a town, easy to climb, filled with ripe fruit, what more evidence does one need? It is easy to determine that the fruit is poisonous."

When out of your element, it is easy to fall prey to the appearances that have been colored by your emotional desire for things to be a certain way. Right seeing can save your life. Remember to slow down when you are in a hurry and check within to see if what you see is true.

Spiritual Contemplation: Where have you jumped to conclusions a bit too quickly and paid the price?

Affirmation: I am comfortable finding time to take a deeper look!

JUNE 13

Choose You at least Once a Day

Whenever you feel compelled to put others first at the expense of yourself, you are denying your own reality, your own identity. – David Stafford

I have seen hundreds of clients for spiritual counseling over the past 25 years and each one has wanted to make some change in their life. Whether it's a change in their relationships, job, or health, almost everyone is unhappy with some aspect of their life and is looking to make a shift. I have come to realize that most of these people were not used to taking care of themselves. They supported their families and friends; had jobs they were responsible for and filled their calendars with so many things that there was very little time left for themselves. This made change difficult. You must create space for yourself. If you jump out of bed first thing and have a day filled with activities to care for everyone around you, but do not create a space and time for your own work, you are never going to be able to make lasting change.

Carving out even a small amount of time for yourself will allow you to realize what you want to create in your life. Setting time daily for meditation, contemplation and journaling will reveal why you want change on a deeper level. Having a weekly coffee date with yourself is a great way to welcome greater creativity and new ideas into your consciousness. Choosing healthy eating and adding movement to your days will support your body in feeling better. Each of these small suggestions can add up to big changes in our lives. As you begin to choose yourself in small and great ways, you will begin to create the life you dream about.

Spiritual Contemplation: What ways do you currently choose yourself daily? What are a few new things that you can add to your day to support yourself more? (Journal, meditate, exercise, eating, etc.)

Affirmation: I choose to care for and support myself each and every day!

JUNE 14

Final Distribution Point

The physician really treats the body as though it were an instrument through which life flows; in doing this he assumes that there is a Life-Principle already existent and perfect, ever striving for an adequate outlet. – Ernest Holmes

As we open our creative channel to the creator, many gentle but powerful changes are to be expected. - Julia Cameron

If you were asked to boil some water, you'd first go to the sink and get some water, then place it on the stove. Where did you get the water? You might say from the faucet. And you'd be right, but there is a bit more to it. The water came from the water tank that was filled from the pipes that came to the house from the reservoir, which gathered the snowmelt, which came from the sky, which evaporated the moisture from the earth, and the final distribution point was the faucet.

When working with a spiritual practitioner, you must realize they don't do the healing. They are a distribution point of an awareness of wholeness. There have been many great healers throughout history, from the first shamans who facilitated the revealing of wholeness to today's practitioners in many modalities. Even modern medicine, which masters many aspects of healing the body, is still a distribution point that waits on nature to do the healing. The key component to all forms of healing is you, as the patient, having faith in the All-Originating Life Force seeking to express through you, above all appearances to the contrary. The other healers are there to help you remember your wholeness.

Spiritual Contemplation: Have you ever given your power away to a healer or medicine thinking it was the source of your return to wholeness? How can your faith play a bigger part next time you turn to the distribution point for assistance?

Affirmation: God is the healing transforming power of my life now and always!

171

JUNE 15

Dad's Gifts

Dads are most ordinary men turned by love into heroes, adventurers, storytellers and singers of song. — Unknown

Dad's unconditional love is essential whether your child is succeeding, stumbling, struggling or soaring. Dads play a vital role in helping their children find strength and courage in themselves. To be there and love is one of the greatest and most lasting gifts dads can give. To know dad's love is there, no matter what, is a gift not only to his child but also to his grandchild. Dad's imprint will last a lifetime. Poet Anne Sexton wrote, "It doesn't matter who my father was; it matters who I remember he was."

Being involved in your child's life only when it's convenient doesn't work. Being there when it's important to them or during challenging times doesn't always come with appreciation, but your love and guidance is remembered. These precious moments allow a glimpse into the future. Dads can see something in their children before anyone else knows it's there. Fathers believe in you even when you don't. Their gift can be more than a thousand teachers. Make sure it's the gift of love.

Spiritual Contemplation: What are some of your dad's gifts that are imprinted on your heart?

Affirmation: I am grateful for the gifts of love from my father woven through my life today!

JUNE 16

Life on the Spiral

The path isn't a straight line; it's a spiral. You continually come back to things
you thought you understood and see deeper truths. — Barry H. Gillespie

Sometimes on the journey to living a wholehearted life, we can come across the same lesson or issue we thought we learned and healed previously. The spiritual seeker can get frustrated thinking that they'd already handled some old issue when they are once again faced with the same thing! Truth is, the path forward isn't a straight line, it's a spiral. We are continually returning to the same issues we've faced and processed repeatedly so that we can put our new awareness into practice and prove to the Universe that we have integrated the new way of being.

Instead of getting frustrated when a familiar issue comes up again, we are called to stand firm in our spiritual knowing and declare the truth that this issue "no longer has any hold over me or my life!" As you affirm your worthiness and divine birthright, you signal to the Universe that you see the situation clearly and create from a higher level of consciousness. This way, it is not the same old issue you started with, it is healed, and you spiral up!

Spiritual Contemplation: Contemplate an issue that has come around in your experience a few times. How have you handled it differently each time you faced it? What have you learned about yourself and your life?

Affirmation: I honor the wisdom of the Universe and know it guides me in all my endeavors!

JUNE 17

Love Your Awareness Open

With mindfulness, you can establish yourself in the present in order to touch the wonders of life that are available in that moment. — *Thich Nhat Hanh*

Mindfulness helps you to see that life is happening through you, not to you. Your outer world reflects the blueprint you hold in your belief system. Reverse engineering leads you back to how it was created. Mind Body Medicine helps you to recognize the interactions between thoughts, emotions, even societal factors and how they directly impact your body. If there is stress in any of those regions, it's important to be aware that chronic stress has a tendency to take form in the body.

Self-awareness, caring for yourself and expressing yourself are keys to physical healing. Let go of the comfort you find in your prior assumptions of how healing must look. Love your awareness out into the open. Welcome your observing self to give you some feedback about stress points in your life. Ask this self-awareness what you could do now to better care for your body and mind. Inquire about what and where you are holding something inside that is asking to be expressed in your life. You are the gatekeeper to your soul; mindfulness is the invitation to see the active blueprint of your life, ready and waiting.

Spiritual Contemplation: What inner stirring is vying for your awareness? What is your body is attempting to tell you? What is seeking to be released?

Affirmation: I hear what my body and mind are telling me!

JUNE 18

Cracking Open

There is a crack in everything, that's how the light gets in. — Leonard Cohen

Along your life's journey, there will be moments when you feel like you are being stretched and tested. Growth is often uncomfortable. I can remember my brother as a teen agonizing over the pain he was experiencing as he grew six inches in nine months. I was amazed at the process of watching him go from a chubby 5-foot-7-inch kid to a lean 6-foot-3-inch man! I have seen the spiritual growth of many counseling clients who have dug deep into their shadow to explore and open to a greater truth about themselves. It can be hard work, but it is always worth it.

Those things we are uncomfortable with about ourselves get stuffed, and we avoid looking at them. We are afraid of what it means about ourselves. But our nature is to grow and evolve, and those things that we stuff down will pop up again because these negative emotions hold the key to our healing. We are afraid that we will shatter into a million pieces, but what happens is that we crack open to a broader view of who we are. We heal when we acknowledge our disowned feelings and allow them to speak into our lives. Then we become deeper and more compassionate points of light in the world. Our healing serves a greater purpose than just for ourselves. When we do the hard work of healing, we make it easier for those around us to do the same. What a gift we can give to ourselves and each other.

Spiritual Contemplation: What are you afraid to look at or address in your life currently? Is there a trusted friend or counselor you could share this with and receive support to do the hard work of looking at your shadow?

Affirmation: I allow myself to crack wide open and let the light of truth into my life!

JUNE 19

Juneteenth

Juneteenth is also known as Freedom Day, and is an annual American holiday celebrated on June 19. It honors June 19, 1865, when Union General Gordon Granger read federal orders in Galveston, Texas, that all previously enslaved people in Texas were free. Lincoln's Emancipation Proclamation formally abolished slavery nearly two and a half years earlier, Texas was the most remote state to be holding human lives in bondage. Part of the day is for remembering and sharing thoughts. It's not enough to just sit back and feel bad for our brothers and sisters who are still being oppressed to this day because of the color of their skin. It's our duty to find the courage to speak out where we see injustice. Part of the honoring of this day is to read to remember injustices and be inspired to speak out. Maya Angelou's poem, *We Saw Beyond Our Seeming*, is a soul stirring call to action and recollection:

We saw beyond our seeming
These days of bloodied screaming
Of children dying bloated
Out where lilies floated
Of men all noosed and dangling
Within the temples strangling
Our guilt gray fungus growing
We knew and died our knowing
Deafened and unwilling
We aided in the killing
And now our souls lie broken
Dry tablets without token

Spiritual Contemplation: Where have you remained silent in the face of injustices? How did that feel? Are you willing to speak out next time?

Affirmation: I find the courage to speak out in the face of injustice!

JUNE 20

Leave it at the Door

It is a common experience that a problem difficult at night is resolved in the morning after the committee of sleep has worked on it. — *John Steinbeck*

A colleague dropped his carpenter friend off at home after work each evening and witnessed him pausing before a pine tree and touching its branches before going into the house. Nightly, he watched him through the window, smiling and hugging his children and kissing his wife. One day when picking his buddy up before work he asked him about his nightly ritual. The carpenter said, "That's my trouble tree. I can't help having issues through the course of my day, but they don't belong at home, so I hang them on the tree before going in at night. Then, in the morning, I'll pick them up. The funny thing is when I do, there doesn't seem to be as many as I remembered hanging the night before."

Spiritual Contemplation: What issues would be good for you to leave at the door and not bring home?

Affirmation: I leave behind the troubles of this day as I step into a glorious new day!

JUNE 21

Litha

~~⋞⋞⋟⋟~~

Are you sure

That we are awake?

It seems to me

That yet we sleep, we dream

— William Shakespeare, A Midsummer Night's Dream

It's fun to open your heart to ancestral stories and practices. One enduring Celtic legend is the battle between the Oak King and the Holly King. These two mighty rulers fight for supremacy as the Wheel of the Year turns each season. At the Winter Solstice, or Yule, the Oak King conquers the Holly King, and then reigns until Midsummer, or Litha. Once the Summer Solstice arrives, the Holly King returns to do battle with the Oak King, and defeats him.

The Sabbath of midsummer is a great time to feel the earth's energies of growth and nourishment that vibrate in nature. Experience the expansion and pulse of life as it flows through the roots and stems into your body. The powers of nature are at their highest point; the pinnacle. The gardens are blooming and summer is in full swing. Take advantage of the extra light of the Midsummer and spend time outdoors connecting with the earth, feeling her renewing power of love.

Spiritual Contemplation: What can I do today to spend some time outside? Plan a barbecue, do some gardening, take a walk in nature, bury your feet in the ground, run through the sprinklers, have a picnic in the park or at the beach, or dance around a bonfire. The list is endless in ways to connect with the earth's energy.

Affirmation: I allow my youthful exuberance to rise and lead me into this day!

JUNE 22

Practicing the Pause

Have patience. Wait until the mud settles and the water is clear. Remain unmoving until right action arises by itself. – Lao Tzu

This quote from Lao Tzu is deep wisdom for us if we choose to put it into practice in our lives. Patience can be difficult to practice when we are caught up in the whirlwind of life's events. When something happens and we get swept up into the chaos and turmoil, we lose our moorings and can't necessarily see straight. Often, we react to situations quickly. We send that email or make that call, which oftentimes is not the highest or best choice for us. If we can take Lao Tzu's advice to pause and wait until the storm calms and the mud settles, we will be able to see what is happening around us and choose to respond from that place of awareness rather than react from fear.

Patience can be a challenging trait to develop. We build our patience muscles by practicing it, which can be frustrating and difficult, but is well worth it. So, the next time you get triggered by someone or some event, practice the pause and allow the natural next steps to rise before you and show you the way.

Spiritual Contemplation: Think of a time when you did not practice the pause and reacted quickly to a stressful situation. Can you imagine how it would have been different if you practiced the pause?

Affirmation: I pause and allow divine right action to rise in every situation of my life!

JUNE 23

Action Behind Belief

Seeing their faith, Jesus said to the paralyzed man, "Be encouraged, my child!
Your sins are forgiven. – Matthew 9:2, NLT

The gospels tell a story of a paralyzed man who wanted to get before Jesus to be healed. This man heard Jesus was doing his teaching and healing nearby and got some of his friends to carry him to the house where the gathering was being held. When they arrived, the crowd was so large they could not get into the room. His buddies were tired and sore from carrying their friend and would have been happy to call it quits. Yet, the paralyzed one insisted they tear off some of the roof tiles and lower him into the room. Which they did. Imagine the spectacle of this man descending from the ceiling and arriving at the feet of Jesus.

It's written that when Jesus, "saw their faith" he said, "Son be of good cheer; your sins are forgiven. Pick up your bed and walk." Why was this man healed that day while others were not? It was because this man boldly showed his faith. He took action and stepped in the direction of his belief. Life could not miss his audacious statement of faith. When you put action behind your belief, you will catch the attention of Life, and it responds with the inevitable outcome of your faith.

Spiritual Contemplation: What issue in your life would you like to see changed? What steps, big or small, could you take in the direction you would like to see this situation move? Put this action into motion.

Affirmation: I now boldly take action to support my beliefs!

JUNE 24

Find Your Why

Don't look for motivation. Find your why, then no excuses will come between you and your goals. – Gym-aholic

There have been times in my life when I have tried to make changes to be healthier with my eating habits and exercise regimen. Like many, I have tried different eating plans and diets or started ambitious exercise plans only to get frustrated and quit after a few days. A regimented program with a high demand on myself never worked for me.

When I realized why I wanted to be healthier and what I wanted to create in my experience, (more flexibility, more stamina and energy) I found that my motivation flowed freely! I was energized and jumped out of bed for my workout. I happily added fresh vegetables and juice to my diet and began to see positive changes quickly. It happened naturally without a ton of stress. It was a joy and not a chore to become healthier!

Spiritual Contemplation: Think of a change you have been trying to make in your life. What is your 'why' for wanting to create it? Journal about your why and create a clear intention statement for what you want and why you want it. Read the intention statement daily and watch as you begin to manifest what you want.

Affirmation: I am awake and aware of what I want to create and why I want it! The Universe supports me in being the best expression of myself today and every day!

JUNE 25

New Cause to Be Cast for Change

In the Infinity of Life where I am, all is perfect, whole and complete. It is safe for me to enlarge my viewpoint of life. — Louise Hay

Say YES to enlarging your world! However, honestly ask yourself: How stubborn am I about changing? Too often, one wants their life to change without having to make the changes. If you want change, you must change. We are talking about changing the inner realm of your thought like your responses and actions for the people, places and things in your world to readjust. An inner shift has to take place before the outer world can reflect it in areas such as finances, career, relationships, home and health. It's all an out picturing of your inner activity.

The good news is that whatever is going on is the feedback for your higher perspective to call a new cause to be cast for change. You are not a victim of your environment; but a participant who can change things anytime you want to be honest with yourself. Give up your self-righteous anger and dive deeper into yourself. Then, think a higher truth about yourself in this situation. But don't just think it! Speak it and take action to support this change.

Spiritual Contemplation: Be wholeheartedly honest with yourself. Where are you being stubborn about not changing something you know needs to be changed? What position do you need to let go of to allow the shift to take place?

Affirmation: I wholeheartedly embrace the changes my life calls for!

JUNE 26

Look at Your Values

Life is good when you live from your roots. Your values are a critical source of energy, enthusiasm, and direction. – Shoshana Zuboff

A spiritual teacher once said that if you want to understand what your values are, look at your checkbook and your calendar. This will show you how you are spending your valuable resources – your money and time. Many of us think that we are living from our values but when we take a good look at our lives, we see that we are actually motivated from need and fear rather than what we know to be true about God and life.

If we think we are generous but hoard our money because we are afraid there isn't enough, we aren't living from the value of generosity. If we think we are loving but there are some people we just can't accept, we aren't living from love. We are being called to align our values and actions in all ways in our lives. When we live in this wholehearted way, we become a channel of these blessings and an inspiration to others to also live from this wholeness. This is how we help heal not only ourselves, but the world.

Spiritual Contemplation: Make a list of the values you think are important in your life. Observe how you are or aren't incorporating them into your life. Make a commitment to live your values in a new way.

Affirmation: I live my life as a channel of Divine Love!

JUNE 27

One Step at a Time

Real change, enduring change, happens one step at a time. — Ruth Bader Ginsberg

When we contemplate our health and well-being, and want to make positive change, many think they need to overhaul their lives! Changing their eating by removing big groups of food that they love is difficult. Starting an exercise regimen with heavy lifting or major cardio can be a lot. Engaging in the latest health fads can be expensive. Is it surprising that so many fall off the path of wellness before they ever get started? It's easy to feel like a failure and give up – and many do.

I have found a different approach works best for me and my clients. Adding one positive thing each day can launch one on the path to greater health and well-being. For me, it was adding one carrot juice in the morning and taking my puppy for a walk down the street. That was it! Then, the next week, I added sauteed spinach (which I love) to my lunch. Then, after a few weeks of adding small things like 15 minutes of meditation, and reading, and drinking more water daily, I began to see that I wasn't reaching for the chocolate quite as much and I wasn't zoning out binging tv shows. I was more energized and craved being outside and active. After a couple of months, I had lost 15 pounds and felt like a new person! Creating wellness in your life doesn't have to be hard. It can be as simple as taking one step each day, choosing something positive for yourself, and soon you will be dancing down the road!

Spiritual Contemplation: What is one goal you have relating to your health and well-being? What is one thing you can do today towards that goal?

Affirmation: I choose one thing for my health and well-being every day!

JUNE 28

Get Up and Dance!

Dance is the hidden language of the soul. — Martha Graham

"Sitting is the New Smoking" is a popular phrase coined by Dr. James Levine, director of Mayo Clinic at Arizona State University, after research released showed how dangerous a sedentary lifestyle is. People who do not move have much higher rates of obesity, cardiovascular disease, cancer and diabetes. Staying still can cause you to get stuck emotionally and intellectually, leading to things being locked up in your body and mind.

Movement is a great way to counteract feeling numbed out, exhausted, stuck or in a rut. Any type of movement or dance will help you begin to increase your ability to move and breathe into those tight places. It's as easy as putting on your favorite music and dancing around your living room! Whether it's intuitive movement, conscious dance, belly dance or ballroom, there are infinite ways to add movement to your days and as you do, you will begin to feel better in your body and calmer in your mind.

Spiritual Contemplation: Take just five minutes out of your day today to move in a new way. Put on some of your favorite music and dance around your living room or put on some meditation music and allow your meditation to flow through your body. Then sit still for a few moments and breathe to see how your body and mind feel.

Affirmation: I move with a freedom of ease and grace!

JUNE 29

Create Space for Peace

The foundations of a person are not in matter but in spirit. — *Ralph Waldo Emerson*

According to the American Psychological Association, stress is currently a leading cause of death, contributing to conditions such as heart disease, cancer, and suicide. We are living in a frenetic culture with a bombardment of demands, news and information thrust upon us and it can be too much to bear sometimes! Thankfully there is something you can do about it. Developing a spiritual practice that works for you is an integral step in relieving stress and finding balance within your mind, body and spirit daily.

I am not the person who gets up at 5:00 am to meditate and journal. If you are – that's great! But I had to let go of years of judging myself because that did not work for me. What works for me is to do my personal practice by getting up at 7:00 am and reading for a half hour. I follow it with some meditation, prayer and journaling. By 8:00 am I am ready to go for the day! I also come back at the end of the day to make some notes in my journal and calm my mind before bed. It's okay to figure out what works best for you. That is the key to developing a regular practice that will help relieve stress and bring you back into balance.

Spiritual Contemplation: Think about what spiritual practice works best for you. Are you an early riser or do you find more peace doing your practice at midday? At night? Find something that you can do daily and see how a simple change can bring great peace.

Affirmation: I open to the best way to connect with myself and Spirit! I am at peace, and all is well!

JUNE 30

Listen to Your Body

And I said to my body softly, 'I want to be your friend.' It took a long breath and replied, 'I've been waiting my whole life for this.' —Nayyirah Waheed

As a teen, I was in an ensemble of dancers that participated in competitions across the Northeast. One year, our group qualified for the finals of the Talent America competition and headed to New York City. We worked hard fundraising in the weeks leading up to the competition so that we could all make the expensive trip. We were thrilled as we boarded the buses in Massachusetts and set off on what was a dream come true for me – I would be dancing in New York! On the bus, I began to feel a little off, and by the time we arrived in NYC, I was not well. But, determined not to miss this event, I ignored the signs my body was giving me. I took all the warm-up classes and prepared to perform with my group. Right in the middle of my performance, I fainted in front of the judges. I had pushed my body too far and ignored the signs that it needed some additional care. I was so embarrassed and felt horrible that I'd jeopardized my group's chances. Lucky enough, we were able to perform again the next day placing first in our division, but I walked away having learned a very important lesson about listening to my body.

Your body is speaking to you all day long. It is telling you what it needs to keep you happy, healthy and well. The challenge is that we have been taught to ignore what our bodies are telling us and, instead, push through our pain and discomfort. Taking the time to pause and be present with sensations in your body will help you reconnect to these signals. That way, you can care for yourself in a way that serves and supports your ongoing health and well-being.

Spiritual Contemplation: When you meditate today, bring focus to your physical body. Ask: What does my body need right now? What can I do to feed, nurture and care for it? Note the answers in your journal.

Affirmation: I listen to my body and care for its needs with love.

JULY

Creative Expression

July 1-7

Healing Through Creativity

July 8-14

Imagine What's Possible

July 15-21

Your Mistakes Are Art

July 22-28

Being Bold

July 29-31

Share Your Gift

JULY 1

Creativity as a Spiritual Practice

Creativity is intelligence having fun. – Albert Einstein

There aren't creative people and non-creative people. There are only creative people who either engage with their creativity or do not. It is our core nature to be creative but sometimes it falls down the ladder of importance in our lives and we don't spend as much time and effort exploring and developing our creativity muscles. When we engage with our creativity regularly, we begin to develop skills that support us in multiple areas of our lives. We gain inspiration, a broader perspective, and new ways of engaging in life with a child-like wonder. These skills will strengthen our self-esteem and relationships, enhance our ability to recognize opportunities, and connect us to our inner voice and intuition.

Add creativity to your daily spiritual practice in any way that feels good to you. Put together a small art kit with some watercolor paints, markers, crayons, pens and even glue sticks and a magazine for collaging. When you sit down to do your practice, make it sacred by lighting a candle and saying a prayer and then allow yourself to be moved to create something for a short time. Try to stay out of your judgmental mind and allow what you are creating to come through without censoring yourself. This practice, a few days each week, will help build your creativity muscles and open you to a new way of connecting to your inspiration and intuition.

Spiritual Contemplation: Take the time to do the above and practice watching your mind as you do. Are you judging and comparing your creations? How can you allow your creativity to flow without judgment?

Affirmation: I am Creative in all areas of my life!

JULY 2

Creativity

No matter what the lips may be saying, the inner thought out-speaks them, and the unspoken word often carries more weight than the spoken. — Ernest Homes

Have you ever walked into someone's home where everything appeared orderly on the surface but you sensed something wasn't right? Perhaps there was some underlying unspoken hostility in the relationship that could be felt. Alternatively, have you ever stepped into a creative brainstorming session where ideas were flying around, getting shot down, only for another crazy thought to captivate the dynamics of the room? It was wild, loud, and chaotic but there was still a sense that everything was alright under the surface. Maybe it was even fun because participants felt supported and encouraged. Despite how it appeared on the surface, it was a safe place to be creative and vulnerable with far-out ideas.

Creativity can be teased out by creating a loving and welcoming atmosphere. That space is something that is felt more often than spoken about. It's not on the surface, but can be more real than what is seen. Creation is the interplay of life upon itself; the manifestation of the invisible. It is not so much a shiny finished product but rather an ever-unfolding, unending emanation looking for its divine available outlet.

Spiritual Contemplation: How can I create a more welcoming mental atmosphere for the divine interplay of life upon itself in my field of awareness?

Affirmation: I am a welcoming space for the divine creativity to be expressed!

JULY 3

Be the Artist of Your Life

We are in the laboratory of the Divine, what then shall we create? — Ernest Holmes (paraphrased)

We are each artists, creating the beautiful expression of our lives. We may not be painters or sculptors but that does not mean we are not creative. As each of us is made in the image and likeness of God, we are each a reflection of God's attributes and that includes us being creators.

Creativity is the way that we interact with the Divine. Your life is your pallet and your dreams and desires are your medium. The experience of life changes when we shift from thinking that life is happening to us to the idea that we are co-creators with the Divine. We are all artists, and our lives are our masterpieces. Instead of approaching life with trepidation and anxiety, let us begin each day with the mindset that we get to create something new every single day! Begin with the question: "What do I want to create today?" and see what arises. When you connect the desires of your heart to the wisdom of your mind, the gift is an abundant and fulfilling life because you are the artist and your life is a masterpiece.

Spiritual Contemplation: Take some time to contemplate what you want to create in your life. Imagine that you are a great artist preparing to create your masterpiece, gathering your supplies, and setting the space to begin. Allow yourself to feel the energy of creativity, excitement and anticipation of the process and write about it in your journal.

Affirmation: I am a Divine Artist Creating my Life in Joy!

JULY 4

4th of July

Proclaim liberty throughout all the land unto all the inhabitants
thereof — Inscription on the Liberty Bell

This verse from the bible, Leviticus 25:10, refers to the "Jubilee" or the instructions to the Israelites to return property and free slaves every 50 years. This inscription provided a unifying cry for abolitionists wishing to end slavery. Beginning in the late 1800s, the Liberty Bell traveled across the country for display at expositions and fairs, stopping in towns small and large along the way. For a nation recovering from wounds of the Civil War, the bell served to remind Americans of a time when they fought together for independence. Movements from Women's Suffrage to Civil Rights embraced the Liberty Bell for both protest and celebration.

On the creative side of the fourth of July celebrations, Erma Bombeck's profound revelation of joyous appreciation over fear reads "You have to love a nation that celebrates its independence every July 4th, not with a parade of guns, tanks, and soldiers who file by the White House in a show of strength and muscle, but with family picnics where kids throw Frisbees, the potato salad gets iffy, and the flies die from happiness. You may think you have overeaten, but it is patriotism."

Spiritual Contemplation: Spend some time contemplating how you use your freedom. Are you using it to limit or express yourself? Feel gratitude for those who have fought for you to have this freedom. Are you honoring them by living the greatest expression of yourself?

Affirmation: My life is a declaration of Joyous Freedom!

JULY 5

Creativity is a Pathway to Freedom

It's not just about creativity, it's about the person you're becoming while you're creating. — Charlie Peacock

Many believe that creativity is only the purview of great and talented artists. Yet, most of us have not been encouraged to develop these talents and skills. It's important to note that art and creativity are not the same thing. Creativity is the desire to express and bring something new into the world while art is the subjective outcome of that urge. We all have creativity because we are creative beings, and creativity is integral to our development.

We are called to say "yes!" to that urge within us to bring something unique forward. The great news is that we can do this in many different ways, not only through artistic expression, including art, writing, sculpture and dance. We can also be creative through our cooking, our relationships, and in our work lives. We can be creative in how we navigate any one day of our lives! There is the potential to engage with creativity all the time and the more we do this, the better off we are because our individual creative expression allows us to become the unique beings we were made to be and herein lies our freedom!

Spiritual Contemplation: Today, find a new way of engaging in creativity. Drive a different route to work, cook something new, try something you've been thinking about. Notice how it feels to stretch a little and embrace something new!

Affirmation: As I live my life creatively, I am free to be me!

JULY 6

Persistence

If your dreams don't scare you, they are too small. — *Richard Branson*

Water cuts through rock to create grand canyons, not because it is stronger than the obstacle but because it is persistent. It's often said that failure is not the opposite of success; it's part of it. When the obstacle in your way seems to have stopped you in your tracks, it's not a failure. It's part of what is calling forth the necessary change so you can move through, around, over or under what's on your path to success. Progress is not possible without some fluidity. The ones who can't embrace the necessary shifts will remain fixated on the obstacle before them. Those who are stuck should get out of the way of those who are in the process of moving through.

There is a power within you that is greater than anything life can throw your way. Those challenges are calling forth a greatness within you that, until now, you have only theorized was there. It is now time to know for sure through dedicated persistence. The Divine Intelligence within not only directs you, but also reveals the confidence and strength necessary for all things to work out for the highest and best.

Spiritual Contemplation: Are there any areas of your work or life where you have come to an impasse and don't know what to do next? Check in with your heart to see if your dream is still on the other side of the obstacle? If yes, then trust the Divine Intelligence within to give you the strength of persistence and the guidance for the way through, over, under or around. What this Guidance is telling you is yours to do now.

Affirmation: I am persistent with the Divine Strength and Wisdom from within!

JULY 7

Getting Un-stuck with Creativity

Happiness consists in activity. It is a running stream, not a stagnant pool.
— John Mason Good

There are moments in life when we each feel stuck and stagnant. Whether it's in our careers, relationships or just how it feels moving through our days, we can hit a rough patch that makes life challenging and leaves us feeling lost and alone. One thing that can help when this happens is to connect to our creativity. When we do this, we begin to feel better, lighter, and happier.

When those dark moments arise, I encourage you to engage in a creative endeavor and watch how it shifts your experience. Something as simple as coloring with crayons, singing (no matter how it sounds!), moving your body and dancing, planting something or writing a poem can shift your energy. You may be surprised how those dark thoughts, worries and feelings begin to lighten and your mood lifts. This is because we are each a channel of Divine creativity and when we engage and make it welcome in our experiences, God's love and joy flow to and through us.

Spiritual Contemplation: Today, try some new form of creativity. Maybe you'll try drawing, writing a poem, or painting with watercolors. It doesn't matter how good you are at something, just participating in the activity will allow Divine Creativity to flow into your life. Notice how it feels to engage with this energy.

Affirmation: I am a channel of Divine Creativity!

JULY 8

The Emerging New

~ero&ree~

Life is a series of natural and spontaneous changes. Don't resist them; that only creates sorrow. Let reality be reality. Let things flow naturally forward in whatever way they like. – Lao Tzu

When you go to the ocean, you expect it to have changed from the last time you visited. The waves might be larger or smaller, and the tide could be in or out. Perhaps the wind is stirring things up, or maybe it's calm like a lake. Is there new debris strewn along the shore? Are you looking at a blue sky or clouds taking on unimaginable shapes? Are the beaches full of diverse people doing their own thing? Yes, it would have changed since the last time you were there. That is to be expected.

Why is it so hard to accept change as a natural occurrence in most facets of life? Life progresses; it is not stagnant. To expect people, places, and projects to be caught in a time warp, is to assume the flow of life has stopped. Creation is the emergence of what is next. You can either be warden to what was, or be beholder of the emerging new. One entails struggle, while the other invites you into the dance with life.

Spiritual Contemplation: Where are you struggling to hold things together?

Affirmation: I say yes to the dance with life!

JULY 9

Imagine What's Possible

Imagination is more important than knowledge. For while knowledge defines all we currently know and understand, imagination points to all we might yet discover and create. – Albert Einstein

Another powerful spiritual practice to make change in your life is visualization. Visualization is more active than meditation as it engages your imagination's faculties to begin pointing you in the direction you want to go. Sometimes it feels like you're stuck in a rut in your life and can't see a way forward out of your current situation. It can be difficult to see beyond the circumstances of your life to even imagine what's possible. This is where visualization comes to the rescue!

When you engage your imagination and spend some time daydreaming about what's possible, you accomplish two things. First, you wake up to what you really want. Often, you need to start by admitting what in your life is not currently working for you. You need to be honest with yourself and see what is calling for a shift. Then, what you really want can reveal itself. Second, you align with your creative abilities to begin moving toward manifesting what you desire. Spending some time each day visualizing your life as you dream about it will help you rise out of your current situation and guide you onto the path of creating what you want.

Spiritual Contemplation: Spend some time today letting your mind wander and imagine what kind of life you want to be living. Let yourself just daydream and see what brings joy to your heart. Jot down some images that come to you. As you allow yourself more time to practice, notice how your relationship to your life will begin to shift.

Affirmation: I open to all possibilities and dream of my perfect life!

JULY 10

What Are You Rehearsing and Rehashing

Enjoy life. This is not a dress rehearsal. – Friedrich Nietzsche

As a performer prepares, they rehearse what they want to deliver in mind and body. They see it, feel it, and then step into it. They practice until it becomes who they are. The experience is so embodied that its out picturing is seen and felt by everyone. Visualizing and practicing is a great approach to manifesting. Make sure you are seeing and exploring what you want rather than what you don't want to happen.

A big challenge for some people is they will rehearse and rehash everything they don't want to experience. They will envision the situation going exactly where they don't want it to go, in every detail repeatedly. They will imagine all the things that could possibly go wrong and replay them through their field of awareness over and over, even sharing the details with others until it demonstrates in their lives. What value does rehearsing what you don't want at 2 am bring? Who is in charge in your mind? Individuals will say in their own defense, "I can't help it, it's just who I am." Have you acquiesced the power over your own thoughts to outside influences? Stop rehearsing and rehashing what you don't want. It is your choice what you choose to view on the screen of your mind. It will end up being the preview of your life's coming attractions.

Spiritual contemplation: What scenes do you keep replaying in your mind that you don't want to happen in your life? Now, stop hitting replay and place a new script into action for your viewing pleasure.

Affirmation: I am divinely guided into seeing as Spirit sees in all scenarios of my life!

JULY 11

Life is a Mirror

Your life is a mirror. Life gives us not what we want. Life gives us who we are. — Robin S. Sharma

How you see yourself is how the world sees you. This can be a hard truth to come to terms with. You are the one who creates your reality and your experience. Your life is a mirror of your inner consciousness. Who you are out in the world begins with how you think of and hold yourself in your mind and heart. This is important to become aware of, especially when you aren't happy with some aspect of your life and want to make a shift. Oftentimes, you'll think it is the outside situation or another person who is the problem or issue, when in reality, a small inner shift within you can make all the difference.

The first step is to become aware of how you think of yourself in your own mind. Then align who you are in your mind with the idea of who you want to be in your life. Visualize how you'd like your life to look and feel and begin seeing yourself as that! Maybe you want to see yourself as happier, more likable, charismatic, or successful. As you begin to see yourself in this new light, your actions and choices shift and begin aligning with that way of being. Slowly, your life begins to shift and you find yourself living the life you dreamed about!

Spiritual Contemplation: As you look at your life today, what parts are reflecting back something you are not comfortable with and want to shift? Journal about what kinds of mental shifts would help you align better to your dreams and desires.

Affirmation: My life reflects back to me the blessing and gift I am to the world!

JULY 12

Remember To Remember

Without leaps of imagination, or dreaming, we lose the excitement of possibilities.
Dreaming, after all, is a form of planning. — Gloria Steinem

When planning an event, it's beneficial to transport yourself to the future and catch a glimpse of what you are about to create. This time travel skill works well for creating parties, classes, seminars, concerts, meetings, dates, and so much more. The list is endless. Where and when will this happening take place? Who do you see in attendance? What kind of vibe do you want to feel and take away for story telling?

This kind of imagining is helpful to remember when those moments of self-doubt start to creep into your planning. Recalling what you saw and felt when you began the journey will pull you out of anxious uncertainty. Don't treat every scenario as if it's a life or death situation or you'll have too many near-death experiences on your road to success. Remember to prepare for spontaneity by leaving space and being flexible for The Divine Creator to drop in on your gig with a few unexpected inspirational party favors. Before long, your body will catch up with where your spirit visited.

Spiritual Contemplation: What are you now in the process of creating? Go back to its genesis and re-energize yourself for your creative process.

Affirmation: I remember what called me into creation!

JULY 13

Living a New Story

Be bold enough to use your voice, brave enough to listen to your heart, and strong enough to live the life you have always imagined. — Unknown

Stepping into a new way of being can be challenging when we are constantly telling the same old lies that we have believed about ourselves since we were children. Sometimes the programming that we receive is still operating and limiting us even though we have evolved beyond the old ideas. It takes courage to see ourselves in a new way and strength to let go of the past and stay focused on what is emerging now.

We do this by awakening to the fact that we are telling stories about ourselves and actually listen to the tone of them. What kind of stories are you telling? Who are you in your stories? Are you the victim? The hero? The damsel in distress? As you cultivate this curiosity, you will start to see what is really happening around you. It opens the door to a greater awareness and broader perspective, allowing you to see the situations before you more clearly. Then you can respond, not from your old limited ego, but from your wholeness and presence. Don't just repeat your past, live your new story.

Spiritual Contemplation: What old, untrue stories are you telling yourself? How can you, more fully, step into your new story and express yourself more clearly?

Affirmation: I release my past and boldly step into my new Life!

JULY 14

Creative Possibilities Still Exist

Don't compromise yourself. You are all you've got. — Janis Joplin

A man told a counselor that he was afraid there was always someone under his bed. He knew it was crazy, but he was still scared. The counselor told him to place himself in his care three times-a-week for the next year. The young man asked how much it would cost. "$150 per session," the therapist responded. The young man said he would sleep on it.

About six months later, the same counselor met the kid on the street and asked him about the fear he had been experiencing. The young man replied, "At $150 a visit, I realized it would cost over $23,000 for a year of therapy. A bartender cured me for $10, and I was thrilled to use the rest to buy a new pickup truck." With a bit of a smug attitude, the counselor said, "Is that so? And how may I ask, did a bartender cure you?" To which the guy shared, "He told me to cut the legs off my bed. I did, and there has been nobody under there since."

Second opinions give you choices. Sometimes, being dialed into thinking a certain way is easier than remembering that you live in a limitless Universe where Infinite creative possibilities exist right now. Stop abdicating your freedom to the experts when there are different creative solutions still to be considered.

Spiritual Contemplation: Is there anybody attempting to convince you their way is the right and only way even though you know wholeheartedly there is another option, even if it hasn't surfaced up until now? Don't compromise yourself.

Affirmation: I stand true to my heart's knowing!

JULY 15

The Stir of the Soul

Imagination is everything. It is the preview of life's coming attractions. — Albert Einstein

Being creative means allowing life to move through you. If you don't listen to your own creativity and give it expression, you betray yourself. Your creativity comes as a seed needing to be nurtured by your love and attention. This seed is surprisingly dropped by a divine muse as an idea, inkling, possibility, image, vision or urge luring you to come play in the creative field. A new playmate catches you unexpectedly, enticing you out of your linear realm into an imagination of unlimited potential.

If you don't believe in your creative expression, it will never see the light of day. It will be challenged with apprehension as your confidence fluctuates. You are an alchemist who brings the hint of the possible into form. The more you illuminate the stirrings of your soul, the more excited you become to bring them to life, regardless of what others think. It has chosen you as its conduit. It will enter this world with your unique characteristics. So be real with what you love into reality. If you don't bring this gift into the world, no one else ever will. It is your contribution to give but without you it would never be expressed.

Spiritual Contemplation: What creative stirring is knocking at your soul, waiting to be expressed? Why haven't you given birth to it yet? What would it take for your new playmate to come to life through you?

Affirmation: I am a confident creative canal for new possibilities to birth.

JULY 16

The Faith Frequency

You cannot swim for new horizons until you have courage to lose sight of the shore. — William Faulkner

Faith is the transportation to your abundant dreams. Faith is a creative and wholehearted vibe that dares to believe in the enchanted journey. It existed long before you arrived. Faith is the part of you that has caught the greater vision and believes in it. Faith will shift your focus away from the past and guide you through the unknown, preventing you from veering off course. You will be challenged not only by your own anxious thoughts and beliefs but also by those who are constrained by their own limiting perspectives. To doubt, would be to use your faith backwards. When you permit your concerns to grow bigger than your faith, you overshadow your dreams.

Raising your faith frequency doesn't make the others go away, because their options will always be a possibility, but it does lift you above the fray frequencies. You'll feel a new option rising with it. You'll catch a new prosperous wave without concern because you'll be sensing your good. Faith is a knowing in your heart, beyond the influence of evidence to the contrary. It is a soul realization of those vibrations above the physical senses. So keep the faith frequency playing, because the most amazing outcomes happen right at the moment you are about to give up. When you have faith, you have everything!

Spiritual Contemplation: Where do you hear the fray frequencies getting louder? If you were to turn the dial of what you are hearing to a new faith frequency, what uplifting relevant message would you be hearing now?

Affirmation: I always keep my heart and soul tuned into Spirit!

JULY 17

Turn a Mistake into Art

Don't worry about mistakes. Making things out of mistakes, that's creativity. —
Peter Max

Growing up, I watched Bob Ross's *The Joy of Painting* on PBS. I never actually painted along but I loved watching him create a beautiful painting during the 30-minute show. He'd start with a blank canvas and without sketching, would paint a beautiful natural scene, often a forest with "happy, little trees" as he famously called them. One of his main lessons about creating art was that mistakes happen. His brush would dab some paint in the wrong place, or he'd scrape some part of the canvas, and his process would be interrupted. But he never lost his cool. He'd shrug and use his creative eye to make something new. Pretty soon, what was a mistake, appeared intentional. It was amazing to watch.

This is also true for our lives. What we label mistakes are actually opportunities to incorporate something new into our lives. What's key is how we react to them. If we get upset we miss the opportunity and end up in a chaotic spiral of emotion. If we could, like Bob Ross, give a little shrug and move into a creative mind-space, we'd see how to relate to the mistake differently. There is always something to learn about ourselves in everything that happens to us. It's up to us to choose if we will use these experiences to create chaos or to make art.

Spiritual Contemplation: Think about a mistake that you made from your past. Look at how you reacted to it and see if there is any other way you could have related to it. What was it trying to teach you?

Affirmation: There are no mistakes in my life! I create art from all my experiences!

JULY 18

You are the Scheduler

The key is not to prioritize what's on your schedule, but to schedule your priorities. — Stephen Covey

If you want to see a change in your life, try creating a new schedule for yourself. Watch how you spend your time each day. How do you feel moving from one activity to another? Are you living under the pressure of demanding performances or are you free to choose how you spend time? Does a phone call or an email regularly grab you, activating your emotions, robbing you of an interval of your morning?

Is it time for you to make some adjustments and be proactive in reprioritizing your schedule? There is nothing wrong with a full or even hectic day if you love that. It can also be beautiful to have open space to be creative in your day or week if that is your joy. Are you being responsible in living the healthiest expression of yourself, or do you just not have the time to do that? It's important to know that you are the scheduler of your day and life. Make sure to place what you wholeheartedly value first in your life, first on your schedule.

Spiritual Contemplation: When was the last time you reevaluated the days in your week? Are there some adjustments you would like to make in order to reprioritize what is most important to you at this point in your life? Then make them!

Affirmation: My actions now place what's first in my heart, first in my life!

JULY 19

Surrender What No Longer Serves

The sculpture is already complete within the marble block before I start my work. It is already there, I just have to chisel away the superfluous material.
— *Michelangelo*

When contemplating creativity in our lives, the above quote from Michelangelo brings much wisdom to mind. I love the idea that what we are creating (our lives, a piece of art, etc.) is already complete in its raw form and our job is to uncover and reveal its beauty to ourselves and the world. One thing that we are called to do is to let go of anything that gets in the way of that process.

Just as Michelangelo let go of the excess marble that wasn't needed for his sculpture, we are called to let go of the excess that gets in our way and isn't needed in the creation of our lives.

This can include our own negative thoughts, judgments we hold about ourselves that we aren't good enough, time commitments we have made that take us away from our goals, and even relationships that do not support us in creating what we desire. When you create the environment for yourself to be focused and connected to your greatest desires and open to the grand vision you hold for what's possible, you reveal the masterpiece that is already there – YOU!

Spiritual Contemplation: Imagine that what you want already exists in your life and instead of trying to make it happen, think about how to reveal it. What is ready to be surrendered to allow this process to happen with ease and grace?

Affirmation: I surrender anything that no longer serves my highest vision and reveal the masterpiece I am here and now!

JULY 20

Drop Your Perfectionist Tendencies

Do not do unto yourself what you would not do unto others. — Tal Ben-Shahar

Perfectionism is a tendency that many carry and are dragged down by. It encourages you to be harsh and mean with yourself as it demands a high standard in all areas of your life. This standard is unattainable all the time, and though some are motivated by perfectionism's tough ways, it is unsustainable over time. Instead, cultivate self-compassion and find a more productive way to encourage yourself forward. Remember that you cannot give true compassion to others without first giving it to yourself.

Self-compassion is cultivated when you can be as kind to yourself as you would be to others who have made a mistake. When you begin to master self-compassion, you'll find yourself showing up as a higher version of who you are, even when you make mistakes. Practicing self-kindness and acceptance during challenging moments, will strengthen your compassion and allow you to be a light for good, not only for those around you but also for yourself.

Spiritual Contemplation: Look around your life and see where you may be operating under perfectionist tendencies. Consider how you could handle that situation differently. Practice acceptance and self-kindness today. Notice how your day flows from this idea.

Affirmation: I love and accept myself just as I am! I embrace myself with compassion!

JULY 21

The Will of a Warrior

When you move, fall like a thunderbolt. – Sun Tzu

A warrior never worries about his fear. – Carlos Castaneda

The warrior goes to battle not because they despise what is in front of them, but because they love what is behind them. They are willing to sacrifice themselves for the good of others. A warrior with a cause is the most dangerous fighter. A warrior lives by action, not by thinking about acting. They are not concerned about what they will be thinking or facing after the battle. When "lighting strikes" the true warrior holds their stance no matter what the circumstance. They have prepared their body, mind, and soul for this moment. The motto of the Navy Seals: "The more you sweat in training, the less you will bleed in battle."

A warrior isn't immune to fear, but they go forth in spite of it. Confucius said, "He who conquers himself is the mightiest warrior." Courage is the first quality of a warrior. Too many people are living their fears rather than their visions. When the battles appear to be going in the wrong direction, the warrior must not allow the emotion of anger into battle. Amanda Gorman said, "There is always light, if only you are brave enough to see it. If only you are brave enough to be it." Warriors must believe in themselves, for that belief is crucial to who they are. They must take care that their spirit is not broken, because nothing can withstand the will of a warrior.

Spiritual Contemplation: Where in your life do you now need the will of the warrior? Call it in! Bob Marley left us with this thought, "You never know how strong you are until being strong is your only choice."

Affirmation: I am ready for whatever life throws at me!

JULY 22

Creativity and Problem Solving

Every problem has a solution; it may just sometimes need another perspective.
— Katherine Russell

Sir James Dyson is the inventor and founder of the Dyson company, known for its revolutionary vacuum cleaners. In the 1970s, Dyson grew frustrated with the inefficiency of traditional vacuum cleaners that relied on bags to collect dust. He noticed that the suction power would decrease as the bag filled up, resulting in a loss of performance. Determined to find a solution, Dyson embarked on a journey of creative problem-solving. Dyson developed a unique bagless vacuum that used centrifugal force to separate dust and dirt from the airflow, eliminating the need for a traditional filter bag. It not only solved the problem of diminishing suction power but also provided more effective and hygienic cleaning. Today, it is one of the most popular vacuums on the market. Dyson's success story stands as a testament to the power of persistence, ingenuity, and out-of-the-box thinking in solving real-world problems.

When you engage in creative activities, you stimulate your cognitive processes and enhance your problem-solving skills. Creativity fosters out-of-the-box thinking and supports generating new ideas and finding innovative solutions. These mental processes can help you develop resilience, adaptability, and a more flexible mindset when facing challenges. Adding just a little bit of creativity will reap great rewards in your life.

Spiritual Contemplation: How can you add creative practices to enhance your ability to problem solve in your life?

Affirmation: I engage in creativity and open to new ways of seeing and being in the world!

JULY 23

The Silver Lining

If you change the way you look at things, the things you look at change. – Dr. Wayne Dyer

From the beginning of time people have explored beyond the boundaries of their present circumstances. New discoveries are what formed the world. It's also true on an individual level. Learn to expand your thinking, particularly when challenges arise. Setbacks are setups for God to show up. When you change the way you look at difficult situations, you throw off your victim glasses. You can't see the silver lining in the darkness. You need some light shed on the situation.

You never know how good a situation might possibly turn out if you are open to allowing some light in. You could get caught in traffic, show up late, miss an appointment, and end up commiserating with a stranger about what you just missed out on, only to marry that person and live happily ever after. Who could have foreseen that unfoldment? You never know what can happen. Do you create space in your field of awareness for divine intervention to lift you to higher ground? We are talking about the Omnipresence, which means infinite possibilities always exist. You are the one who is not available . . . so make yourself available to greater good now!

Spiritual Contemplation: Where are you wearing the victim goggles in your life? Throw them off so you can see the silver lining.

Affirmation: I am available to my greater good now!

JULY 24

Stop Comparing Yourself

Comparison is the thief of joy. – Theodore Roosevelt

As children, we played make believe, drew pictures, built things with legos and expressed our creativity endlessly. At a certain age, we became self-conscious and afraid of being judged. That's when we started to hold ourselves back and our creativity muscles became weak. Some of us have convinced ourselves that we aren't creative at all! But that is not true. Your creativity muscles may be weak, but you haven't lost your ability to be creative.

Letting go of comparison and engaging with our creativity enhances many aspects of our lives. When we are clear channels of creativity, our lives are filled with warmth and color, and we experience inspiration and joy. This leads to stronger relationships because we can show up as our authentic selves. Our work life improves because we can see creative solutions to challenges and feel more centered as we connect with our inner voice regularly.

Spiritual Contemplation: Notice when you fall into the trap of comparison. Just watch the thoughts and the sensations you feel when you are in comparison. Gently bring your focus back to yourself and ask: What is important? What do I want to create? What do I think about the situation?

Affirmation: I am the pure expression of me always and in all ways!

JULY 25

Flexibility

Freedom and happiness are found in the flexibility and ease with which we move through change. – Gautama Buddha

Flexibility is one of the more important qualities to a happy family life. Inflexibility can be a reflection of insecurity, often leading to mood swings and shouting matches. Being mentally rigid is not a good thing and doesn't tend to sow a happy free-flowing family dynamic with those you care most about. It's been said, blessed are the flexible, for they will not allow themselves to be bent out of shape

Flexibility is being mindfully aware of the present moment and open to new possibilities, while being accepting of new experiences. Seek to maintain a broader perspective while faced with challenges. Flexibility allows you to maintain your contact with deeper values despite setbacks. If a parent maintains their value of compassion and kindness, and their child is screaming and the moment is not invoking a loving response, flexibility invites them to see how to mindfully respond in a way that matches their value instead of flying off on a tirade. Bear in mind that sometimes this choice is easier said than done. But then, this life is a school room for learning no matter what age you might be.

Spiritual Contemplation: Where are you being too rigid in your life? How can you be true to your values and still be flexible in your approach with another?

Affirmation: I am mindful of my greatest values with others and am flexible in their delivery!

JULY 26

Well-being through Art

Art doesn't reproduce what we see. It makes us see. — *Paul Klee*

Over the past number of years, Art Therapy as a psychological endeavor has become more prevalent and available. Art Therapy is a therapeutic process that supports the individual in exploring both mental and emotional challenges through the viewpoint of creative expression. An Art Therapist can help one find ways to explore and express their emotions, learn new ways of communicating, cope with stress, and work through traumatic experiences. The benefits include improving one's personal relationships and achieving greater self-fulfillment.

While working with a professional can be helpful and important if you're facing significant mental challenges, you don't necessarily need to go to a therapist to experience the positive effects of creativity in your world. Finding an art class in person or online, or cultivating a regular practice of self-expression will give you the benefits of creativity. You can discover your true self, express your emotions, regain a sense of control, and more. The power of creativity is in its ability to tap into the innate human capacity for growth and transformation, which sits right at the center of your being.

Spiritual Contemplation: In what way can you find an artistic expression to work through your current challenges? Try something new this week to expand your creative toolbox.

Affirmation: I welcome the joy and freedom that comes from expressing myself through creativity!

JULY 27

Bold Enough to Be Found

Art and life are subjective. Not everybody's gonna dig what I dig, but I reserve the right to dig it. — Whoopi Goldberg

A powerful part of creativity is the courage to be real and true to your own self-expression. To be free to offer the gifts of your soul, you must move beyond concern of what others might think or say. You must learn to allow the spark of the imagination to catch fire. This happens not through attempting to please others but by losing yourself to the lure of the depth of the unknown. There is someone who needs your inspirational offering. Are you living your life boldly enough so they may find it?

You are the one who is making the invisible visible by giving it form, dimension, sound, and pigment. You are standing up and exposing your spirit. Only in sharing your gift will you ever know the satisfaction that comes from being a divine deliverer. It may not result in instant gratification, but there is a relief that emerges from getting your spirit out of the self and into the world. It's a time where the unknown exceeds assurance.

Spiritual Contemplation: Where in your life are you not being bold enough with your creative self-expression because you are concerned about what others may think and say? How would you like to be more true to yourself in these situations?

Affirmation: I find great joy in expressing my creative self for all the world to see!

JULY 28

Your Body Talks

~⚬⚭⚬~

When the eyes say one thing, and the tongue another, a practiced man relies on the language of the first. – Ralph Waldo Emerson

I speak two languages, Body and English. – Mae West

People communicated through body language before there was speech. How you eat says a lot about you. Do you appreciate and enjoy your food? Or do you quickly get the food down? Does this correlate with how you savor each moment of life or mindlessly rush through it? Your walking style is a giveaway as to your mood. It is easy to spot a head held high with confidence and self-assurance. Short, quick steps can indicate impatience, if not impulsiveness. Steady, consistent steps can be an air of calm. Slouched shoulders do not bode well for finding someone with confidence and energy.

Punctuality can reveal a potentially organized person who respects your time, whereas one who is consistently late shows signs of unreliability and a lack of value for your time. Anyone who chooses to be conscious reads your body's messages from the moment they see you. Your body language tells a lot about your personality and your feelings. While Interpretations may vary, there is still an energetic projection that can be read like a book. You are your body, mind, and soul. Be conscious of how they line up. Otherwise, your body goes on autopilot to replicate where your mind and emotions are hanging out. Make sure this is what you want to be projecting to the world.

Spiritual Contemplation: Be conscious of what your body is conveying to the world. Is this the message you want to project?

Affirmation: My body, mind, and soul are now in perfect alignment!

JULY 29

Learn Something New

Anyone who stops learning is old, whether at twenty or eighty. Anyone who keeps learning stays young. – Henry Ford

Every year I try to learn something new. One year it was learning to speak Spanish, another year it was learning how to build things with power tools, and yet another year I learned how to cook Indian food at home. I would sit down at the beginning of the year and think about what I had an interest in and pursued it by setting aside some time each week to engage in my new endeavor. This practice has fed my passion for learning new things and having new experiences.

When we commit to being a life-long learner, we become a student of life with thirst and enthusiasm. We learn more about ourselves, uncover more of our potential, and connect on a deep level to the wisdom of life all around us. Read a book on a new topic, take a class, study a language, learn an instrument, or visit another country and culture. It doesn't matter what you do, but by exposing yourself to something new, you open fresh channels in your brain, expanding your perspective and perhaps even enabling a connection with others of like mind.

Spiritual Contemplation: Contemplate what you would like to expand your knowledge about. Set some time aside each week to learn something new. Buy a book or look for a class on a topic you are interested in.

Affirmation: I am open to learning about myself and the world around me!

JULY 30

Healing Through Art

Art is a wound turned into light. — Georges Braque.

When Maya was a child, she experienced great trauma leaving deep emotional scars that affected her into adulthood. One day, Maya stumbled into her local community center's art classes. Intrigued, she stayed even though she had no experience in painting or any artistic medium. What she found was a channel for her emotions to flow, and she felt the deep pain she had carried through her whole life begin to ease. She continued with classes, and over the months, she discovered a newfound sense of empowerment and self-expression. She began to heal and transform her life of difficulty and pain to one of joy and freedom. She started teaching art as a healing modality and began to share the growth she'd experienced.

Creativity provides a way of working through and expressing complex emotions. Through art, in all of its forms, you can explore your feelings, face your fears, and release stuck emotions in a safe and constructive way. For those who have experienced trauma, artistic expression can be a way to reinterpret experiences and reclaim personal power. This is a path to empowerment and healing.

Spiritual Contemplation: Think of a challenging situation that you have been faced with. Think of a way to explore this situation and your feelings about it through creative expression. Maybe make a painting, work with clay, write a poem, or make a collage. Use your creativity to explore your emotions and share it in your journal.

Affirmation: I allow my emotions to flow freely through my artistic expression!

JULY 31

Don't Let Someone's Opinion Steal Your Creativity

You can't use up creativity. The more you use, the more you have. – Maya Angelou

When I was in second grade, my art teacher refused to hang up a painting I made with the rest of the class's art because she said it was "messy and not good enough." This broke my heart and caused a lot of shame and self-doubt to rise in me. I handled it as any other 7-year-old might; I began to get sick each week on art class day. It took just under two months of staying home from school each Tuesday for my parents to catch on that something needed to be addressed. After meeting with the principal, I shared my story, and the healing process began, though it took years for me to regain my love for creating art without harshly judging myself.

Each of us is a unique channel for creative expression. Whether it is through artistic means or through creating our life, we are constantly bringing new ideas, experiences, and forms into being. Be it through painting or writing, cooking, or how we dress, we are the artists of our own lives. Learning to trust yourself, your ideas, and ways of expressing yourself strengthens your ability to stand strong in the face of someone else's judgment of you. Their ideas about who you are stem from their own insecurities and judgments and have no bearing on who you are and what gifts you have to share in this life.

Spiritual Contemplation: Think about a time when someone else's ideas about you had an impact on how you navigated your life. Were you able to stand strong in the face of someone else's criticism? How could you have handled that situation differently? How would you handle it now?

Affirmation: I am the artist of my life, sharing my creativity freely with the world.

AUGUST
Playfulness

August 1-7
Being Curious

August 8-14
Time to Play

August 15-21
Let's Laugh

August 22-28
Walking & Talking with God

August 29-31
The Joy of Being

AUGUST 1

In for an Adventure

Jobs fill your pockets; Adventures fill your soul! – Jaime Lyn Beatty

One question I often ask anyone who comes to me for spiritual support is, 'What kind of adventures have you had lately?' Most people look at me quizzically and respond, 'Well, I'm here to talk about my relationship", or they mention a work situation, self-esteem issues, etc. But the subject doesn't really matter. Your soul incarnates into this life to have an adventure and if you haven't created space for any adventure, that may be the reason your relationship, or work, or self-esteem are suffering.

Adventure requires us to step out of our comfort zone and take a leap of faith into the unknown. These kinds of experiences show us what we are capable of and help us develop some latent talents that haven't been expressed yet. It reminds us that we are supported in ways that we don't yet realize. There is no real safety net in the outside world, but we are 100% supported from within by the Divine presence. Embrace the kind of adventure that shouts to the world ' I am alive! I choose to live fully!"

Spiritual Contemplation: Think back to adventures you experienced that forced you to step out of your comfort zone? What was that like? And what did you learn about yourself? What kinds of adventures are calling in now? Plan an adventure for your soul.

Affirmation: I am alive! I choose to live fully!

AUGUST 2

Is It Work or Is It Play

Your purpose in life is to find your purpose and give your whole heart and soul to it. — Buddha

One of the great secrets of life is to thoroughly enjoy what you are doing while you are doing it. You wouldn't call it work, you'd call it play. Doing what you love is the foundation for an abundant life. Sometimes work becomes so hectic that it becomes easy to sell out your life in order to make a living. Don't forget the saying, "No one on their deathbed says they wish they would have spent more time at the office."

Spending time doing what you love is called passion, and working at what you don't like is called stress. Find what you love and do it. Life will find ways to compensate you for your gifts. It takes an inner drive to start a new endeavor and work to keep it going. The reward is that work becomes joyful and the compensation is more than you can imagine. Amazing things will occur for you.

Spiritual Contemplation: If money were no object, what would you be doing?

Affirmation: I love my work and what I do!

AUGUST 3

Make Space for Fun

The most important thing is to enjoy your life – to be happy – it's all that matters. – Audrey Hepburn

One can get pretty serious about their personal development and forget that the main point of all of this is to be happy and enjoy the life they have been given. This is why I always remind my clients to make space for joy and fun in their lives every day. Making space to engage in fun activities brings an energy of light-heartedness to life. It loosens us up, shakes out the stress that we carry and reminds us that life is supposed to be joyful! When you laugh and get silly with friends, you will actually feel the stress lifting off your shoulders. We were not meant to be so serious all the time!

How can you make space for more fun in your life? It doesn't matter what the activity is. Going for a bike ride, hosting a game night, playing pickleball or engaging in your favorite hobby are all great ways to increase your level of fun. Scheduling fun time gives you something to look forward to and bonds you deeper to your family and friends awhile making lasting memories of the joy that is here for you. When you do this, you will feel the simple gift of being happy and have a greater appreciation for your life.

Spiritual Contemplation: What are the activities that bring you great joy? Make a list and begin to add one thing each day that is fun for you. You deserve to be happy.

Affirmation: My life is filled with joy! I am happy! I am free!

AUGUST 4

Harmonious Flow

In a state of grace, the soul is like a well of limped water, from which flow only streams of clearest crystal. – Saint Teresa of Avila

A young woman learning martial arts was having difficulty surrendering to the flow of the moves. She was allowing herself to be distracted by the other students in the dojo. The instructor asked what the issue was. She said, "As much as I work on the moves, I can't seem to get them down." The teacher took her out of the classroom and explained that she first had to understand the harmony of flow. He asked her, "Do you see those rocks in the way of the stream?" He continued, " when the water comes up to them, it simply and harmoniously flows around or over them, moving on to what is next before it. Be like the water and simply flow through your moves irrespective of who is watching or standing before you."

Take the wisdom of harmonious flow to heart. Soon, you'll hardly notice what's in your way.

Spiritual Contemplation: Where do you allow the concern of who is watching you or what is in your way to knock you off center? Remember how much you love being in the flow of your self-expression? Return to the simplicity of that and its flow will carry you around or over the apprehensions.

Affirmation: I relax into the harmonious flow of the life force that now moves through me!

AUGUST 5

Be Curious!

Be curious, not judgmental. Ted Lasso

Though the above quote was incorrectly attributed to Walt Whitman in the popular television show Ted Lasso, it is still a great piece of advice. When we adopt an attitude of curiosity rather than judgment, we open ourselves to a whole new world of possibility and potential. Curiosity is a fundamental aspect of our nature as humans inspiring exploration and learning. If we are stuck in our judgment of people and situations in our lives, we will never be able to find creative solutions or ways to connect with one another in a supportive and empowering way.

Adopting a playful, open demeanor can serve us well along this journey. Getting curious encourages us to see things from different angles, explore alternate ideas, and embrace a more inclusive mindset. When we approach life with curiosity, we are more receptive to unfamiliar ideas, perspectives, and challenges. This openness allows us to learn and adapt, expanding our understanding and promoting personal growth.

Spiritual Contemplation: How can you get curious about your life in a new way? Take some time today to try to see from a new perspective. Ask questions. Open yourself to seeing and experiencing life in a new way.

Affirmation: I am curious about life and release any judgment that I hold!

AUGUST 6

The Gifts of the Present

We've become such a multitasking society that just paying attention to the road doesn't seem to be that important anymore. I have to remind my kids all the time that that's what you're supposed to be doing in the car. – Andie MacDowell

A pupil of martial arts asked her teacher about the value of training in another form of the martial arts to improve her skills. "Besides studying under you, I think I should practice with another instructor as well, so as to learn a different style. Do you think that's a good idea?" The master teacher's reply was clear, "A hunter who tries to chase two rabbits will catch neither."

It's been said that if you want to dig a well and discover water, digging several shallow wells in multiple places doesn't work. In this era of multitasking, too many are missing the depth and gifts of being fully present and giving all to what's at hand. The Love of life allows you to discover the richness from finding depth where you are.

Spiritual Contemplation: Where are you getting impatient and losing focus because your mind won't stay fully present in the moment? Do you feel that being fully present matters?

Affirmation: I discover untold riches from the depths of the present moment!

AUGUST 7

Ordinary Curiosity

When love is accompanied with deep intimacy, it raises us to the highest level of human experience. — *Leo Buscaglia*

Have you ever seen a couple at a restaurant who are interacting very little? They are polite enough, but their energy is neutral. They likely have blank expressions, focus their gaze to some distant horizon and engage in almost no dialogue. They're wearing wedding rings, and are cordial, but their liveliest moment occurs when one of their cellphone's rings. They've lost their natural curiosity for one another.

Now think about when you first fell in love. You wanted to know everything about the other person, up to and including the most intimate details, yes? You wanted to share special aspects about yourself with them, too. You discovered more about yourself in the new vulnerability. You'd get together in the afternoon and soon enough the sun had set and risen again. You couldn't wait to communicate the next day, eagerly anticipating their response. You'd want to know about every facet of their day. Yes, passion cycles, but don't fall into thinking you know this person as the frozen image you have in your mind after many years together. Be curious and interested in your beloved as an ever-evolving story. Even after all these years, you still care to know more about your treasure.

Spiritual Contemplation: The person you have dinner with tonight will be different than when you were last together. Get curious and allow your desire for greater intimacy to show up as caring to know their thoughts and feelings.

Affirmation: I care and find time to inquire how my loved ones truly are!

AUGUST 8

Verify and Clarify

My therapist told me the way to achieve true inner peace is to finish what I start. So far today I have finished two bags of chips and a chocolate cake. I feel better already. – Dave Berry

All things are up for interpretation. There are as many ways to understand a moment as there are people. This is why clarification is essential. The subjective understanding of your reality makes you a unique expression. The world is full of influences from biased media outlets, amplified to manipulate your emotions and make you believe their perspective is your own.

Independent thinkers who broaden their perspective with various viewpoints are scary to those who want to direct the narrative. Whether it is a bully who wants to get to you through fear or a clever and artful storyteller who emotionally moves you, remember to verify and clarify. Not all you read, hear, and see is true. It's your responsibility to get clear on what's important to you.

Spiritual Contemplation: When have you not gone back to get clarification and it got you into trouble? Where would it be helpful to get clearer on something? Go back and clarify before you make a wrong assumption.

Affirmation: I understand deeper than words!

AUGUST 9

Don't Take Yourself So Seriously!

Don't take yourself so seriously. No one else does.   Regina Brett

There are moments when we need to take responsibility and face challenges. This can be difficult as it calls us to face our mistakes, failures, and ways we may have fallen short of what we intended at the outset. This process can take its toll, and many experience self-doubt, anxiety, and even depression.

Embracing a playful attitude can help us navigate these moments gracefully and bounce back more easily. Incorporating playfulness in our lives helps cultivate resilience by teaching us not to take everything too seriously, including ourselves. Playfulness helps us find humor in challenging moments, reducing stress, and encouraging emotional well-being. If you find yourself in a down moment, try to find a way not to take it all so seriously and see how laughter and play can open the door to a new path of joyful living.

Spiritual Contemplation: Think about a situation in your life that you consider to be serious. How can you find some lightness within the situation?

Affirmation: I am open to seeing life with more joy and lightness!

AUGUST 10

The Magic of the BBQ

When I figured out how to work my grill, it was quite a moment. I discovered that summer is a completely different experience when you know how to grill. —
Taylor Swift

Summer is time to clean off the barbecue and call some friends over. Those hot afternoons and warm summer nights bring with them the defining scent of the grill. It's time for conversations, storytelling and laughter all around the rising smoke of the barbecue. Make plans with the clan, and enjoy the warm season together.

Nature is inviting you to plan for fun, starting now! You are entering a time of a cosmic pause where anything is possible and so much happens. Every kaleidoscopic twilight sunset is different, reminding you of the many variations your summer can take. The ritual of the barbecue is the perfect place to plot your late psummer foray. Barefoot summer afternoons liberate the soul, setting your spirit to flight.

Spiritual Contemplation: Call some friends, plan a barbecue, plot your summer adventure but leave some room for spontaneity.

Affirmation: My body, mind and soul feel so relaxed this summer!

AUGUST 11

Go Out and Play!

We don't stop playing because we grow old; we grow old because we stop playing. — *George Bernard Shaw*

Including moments of play on a regular basis is critical in our stress-filled days. Play reminds us of the importance of laughter and fun in our lives. Playing board games, sports or engaging in anything recreationally that brings you joy counts as play! It brings an experience of the sacredness of joy, renewal and relaxation and allows us to connect deeply with our friends and family.

Play has been shown to release endorphins, improve brain functionality, and stimulate creativity. It helps to keep us young and feel energetic. Studies show that play improves memory and stimulates the growth of the cerebral cortex. Play isn't just a luxury. It's a necessary function of life and our health and well-being are increased when we engage in it on a regular basis. So, get outside today and go play!

Spiritual Contemplation: What are the playful activities you engage in or would like to engage in on a regular basis? Plan a game night with some friends and allow yourself to enjoy the experience of connection and play!

Affirmation: I am open to the joy of life through play!

AUGUST 12

Recharging Your Soul

Summer's lease hath all too short a date. – William Shakespeare

Lying on the grass watching the stars go by on warm summer nights releases the imagination to infinite realms of the inconceivable, where anything is possible. Summer brings an ease and respectability to the art of relaxation. It's also a time when the mental model is patterned into your memory so you might recall, in the midst of winter or dark times, that you can relax and imagine your way through.

There is great value in recharging your soul and cells with the spirit of delight. Don't give yourself a hard time for going out with playmates and revitalizing your spirit. Take in the summer scents, dance to the music of the outdoor concerts, and enjoy the tastes and sounds of summer while laughing with friends. That fun and joy will be planted in the depths of your being today to be called upon when the burden of the cold pushes in during long winter nights. Plant the joy of living deep within you today, as the sun calls you to play. Expose yourself to the pleasure of the light and feel the kiss of the sun upon your skin.

Spiritual Contemplation: Make a list of what will recharge your soul during this season of sun.

Affirmation: I feel good about permitting myself to let go and allow my spirit to roam free this summer!

AUGUST 13

Take a Break

We must always change, renew, rejuvenate ourselves; otherwise, we harden.
– Johann Wolfgang von Goethe

It can be easy to jump on the fast track of life and keep going without taking a break. There will always be more work to do, projects to work on, and situations to handle. There will always be something calling for your time and attention, and this can wear you down and zap your energy, creativity, and sense of joy.

Taking regular breaks for play can provide a much-needed break for the brain. Playfulness allows the mind to relax, recharge and rejuvenate. It triggers the release of endorphins, which are hormones that boost one's mood and promote relaxation. Returning to life after a playful break enhances focus, creativity, and productivity. The best thing you can do to increase a sense of fulfillment and satisfaction in life is to take a break and play for a while!

Spiritual Contemplation: How often do you allow yourself to take a break and play? What kinds of activities do you enjoy? (puzzles, brain teasers, board games, creative arts, etc.) Find something you enjoy and give yourself a break.

Affirmation: I give myself a break to play and enjoy life!

AUGUST 14

Have a Good Laugh

If you can laugh at it, you can heal it. – Alice Bandy

A friend once shared her spiritual practice of Laughter Yoga with a class I was teaching. She stood in front of the room and, after leading us through deep breathing and gentle stretching exercises, she started to laugh with a series of booming "HA! HA! HA!" laughs. We all followed, and what began as a contrived sense of laughter turned into genuine giggles, chuckles, and about 10 minutes of real contagious laughter! We couldn't stop! It was playful and fun, and we all felt the release you get from a good, deep laugh.

Laughing has numerous benefits for stress reduction, as it releases tension, improves mood, and boosts the immune system. Humor provides a fresh perspective, helps us find lightness in challenging situations, and encourages a more positive outlook. Intentionally including time for humor and laughter in your days by reading or watching something funny or practicing laughter yoga can be as important for your well-being as meditation and exercise. Find something funny today and laugh!

Spiritual Contemplation: What do you find funny that makes you laugh? How can you incorporate a time each day for lightness and laughter?

Affirmation: I embrace the joy of this moment and allow myself to laugh fully and freely!

AUGUST 15

Peace, Love & Rockin 'Roll

We are stardust, we are golden and we've got to get ourselves back to the garden.
— Joni Mitchell, song-Woodstock

On August 15th, 1969, Woodstock Music Festival opened. It was the year we put a man on the moon. Butch Cassidy and The Sundance Kid was released in the movie theaters. The Beatles were breaking up. The Stonewall Riots were happening in New York, and Vietnam protests were going strong. That summer, there were many improbable reasons for the celebration of Peace, Love, and Music on Max Yasgur's dairy farm not to happen. The original venue was canceled just prior to the event and the festival was moved. Woodstock organizers ran out of time to put up fencing around the new venue. Nonetheless, word got out, and the crowd of festival attendees went from 50 thousand people paying $6 per day to over 400 thousand storming the concert for free.

The Guru of Woodstock, Swami Satchidananda, prayed with attendees on Friday afternoon. Many were already there as they finished building the stage around him. Still, there were throngs of people stuck in the legendary traffic jams on the country roads including the opening acts. It necessitated improvisation with the order of performers. The music continued 24-hours a day, ending with Jimmy Hendrix's performance at 11:10 on Monday morning the 18th, confirming the event's success. There were apocalyptic rainstorms, the feeding of the multitudes and bankrupted organizers. Yet, somehow, this event became a defining chapter in the story of the emergence of a new generation that believed in love, peace, freedom, and music.

Spiritual Contemplation: Where do you feel that the odds are stacked against you? Despite that, do you believe in a vision greater than all the "no's" on your path?

Affirmation: I hear the celestial music of my soul!

AUGUST 16

The Power of Play

Play is the royal road to childhood happiness and adult brilliance. – Joseph Chilton Pearce

Research now shows that engaging in play on a regular basis is not a luxury but a necessity for us to reach our greatest human potential. Having time for play puts us in an altered state where we can just be ourselves without purpose, lose track of time, and be fully present in the activity. Anything you do recreationally that brings you joy can be considered play whether it's throwing around a ball, playing board games, writing poetry, or playing sports.

The benefits of play include reduced stress and increased overall well-being. Research shows that playful adults tend to do more enjoyable activities and have a more active way of life than less playful adults. Cultivating a play mindset will bring more fun and creativity to all the areas of our lives.

Spiritual Contemplation: Create a regular time for unstructured play in your schedule. Get outside. Dance. Play games. Throw a ball. Free your inner child! Engage with the activities you loved as a child. Notice how different you feel in your mind, body and heart.

Affirmation: I play with joy and abandon!

AUGUST 17

Laugh More

~~~⚬⚭⚬~~~

Laughter is an instant vacation. — Milton Berle

Laughter is the closest distance between two people. — Victor Borge

Laughter unlocks the cage of the mind and helps you transcend beyond your concerns. At least for the moment, laughter makes one forget. Humorous stories connect strangers, create bonds among friends, and help heal emotional and physical wounds. Smiles, laughter, and love benefit not only those who receive but also those who give. Laughter is God's quick fix.

Help keep that carefree child alive in you. Watch a silly romantic comedy, subscribe to the joke of the day, or do something unexpectedly silly. Your world won't fall apart if you are not so solemn every moment of the day. It's impossible to be belly laughing and feel angry at the same time. Picture yourself attempting to laugh and being angry at the same moment … It's kind of funny!

Spiritual Contemplation: To get laughter rolling, just ask someone to share a humorous or silly tale from their past. You will be amazed at how everyone has a story to tell. Laughter and love will fill the room.

Affirmation: I love laughing a lot!

AUGUST 18

Take Time to Daydream

A daily dose of daydreaming heals the heart, soothes the soul and strengthens the imagination. — Richelle E. Goodrich

Albert Einstein was a genius, but his childhood teachers didn't think he would amount to much because he daydreamed so much. Yet, within this seeming absentmindedness was when Einstein did his most creative problem-solving. It was the time he took each day to slow down that allowed him to become the most creative and productive physicist of our time.

It is easy to assume that daydreaming is a waste of time and energy, but it's a mistaken assumption. Not only has daydreaming been shown to reduce stress and anxiety, but it also helps with problem-solving and enhancing creativity. It creates space in our overcrowded minds and allows our thoughts to flow freely. Many have experienced spontaneous solutions to their challenges in the midst of daydreaming. Even a few minutes of allowing the mind to wander can bring forth its benefits.

Spiritual Contemplation: Take 5-10 minutes today to allow your mind to wander. Just let the thoughts flow without judging them. Notice how you feel during and after this exercise.

Affirmation: I release my thoughts and allow my mind to wander. I am open to fresh ideas and new perspectives!

AUGUST 19

Play to Reduce Stress

It is a happy talent to know how to play. — *Ralph Waldo Emerson*

According to the World Health Organization (WHO), stress has been classified as the health epidemic of the 21st century. The general level of worry and unhappiness in the modern world is becoming part of the "new normal" causing a decrease in productivity and an increase in health problems including high blood pressure, diabetes, arthritis, and inflammatory disease all of which are made worse by chronic stress.

Play has a significant impact on stress reduction and can serve as a powerful antidote to the pressures of everyday life. Engaging in playful activities helps reduce stress by providing a mental and emotional break from daily pressures. Playfulness activates the release of endorphins, which boost one's mood and promotes a sense of relaxation and happiness. Incorporating playfulness into your life creates a positive feedback loop where stress levels decrease, allowing more joy, creativity, and overall well-being into your experience.

Spiritual Contemplation: How do you currently handle your stress? Can you think of alternate ways to include play in your stress reduction strategies? Think of three things you can do this week to play with this concept.

Affirmation: I welcome joy in my life and release stress through play every day!

AUGUST 20

Wholehearted Living with A Four-Legged Friend

The best therapist has fur and four legs. – Anonymous

When it comes to wholehearted living, our four-legged friends are great teachers. They lead us on an enchanted journey of the heart. They teach us to play, love unconditionally, live in the moment, communicate without words, show loyalty, dedication, and even to forgive. They have a way of making you feel special and can get you to laugh and shift your mood with ease. They bring joy, calm your nerves, and soothe your soul.

As a member of the family, your pet, who thinks he/she is your child, brings you unconditional love, offering it at your feet as if it's the morning paper. This caring is a special bond that words cannot describe, yet your furry friend understands you with all its heart and soul. This kind of unwavering love is sometimes hard to find in a human relationship. Coming home to a wagging tail or purring cat can help dissolve the issues of a day, sometimes better than a deep conversation. This reciprocal loyalty is a Divine exchange between a human and a divine companion. It is Spirit made manifest.

Spiritual Contemplation: Take a moment to allow your heart to fill with a special memory of a beloved pet you have journeyed with. Allow that enchantment to warm your soul now.

Affirmation: I still feel the love I shared with my pets.

AUGUST 21

Playing Together

Being playful is a key component in making us happier, healthier, more present and connected in all of our relationships. — Meredith Sinclair.

After twenty-years of marriage, John and Sarah's relationship had hit a rough patch. They had been consumed with their careers, raising children, and taking care of all the things adults need to do and, as a result, they lost their connection. As a last attempt to turn the tide of their relationship and reconnect, Sarah planned a weekend away to their favorite beach town. They agreed to leave their issues at home and just spend time together like they did at the beginning of their relationship. They built sandcastles at the beach, rode bikes, explored the town, and even played carnival games at a local summer festival. By focusing on play for the weekend, they rediscovered the joy, laughter, and lightheartedness that brought them together. Playfulness became the glue that reconnected them and supported them in re-establishing their strong bond.

Playfulness supports you in building stronger connections and deeper relationships. Playful interactions with friends, family, and romantic partners create positive memories and strengthen bonds. Having a playful attitude encourages laughter, lightheartedness, and connection, which creates a sense of closeness and trust. Want to strengthen your relationships? Start to play!

Spiritual Contemplation: How comfortable are you with play and being playful? In what ways can you make space for more play in your relationships?

Affirmation: I am joyful with an attitude of playfulness in all of my relationships!

AUGUST 22

Patience in Nature

Climb the mountains and get their good tidings. Nature's peace will flow into you as sunshine flows into trees. The winds will blow their own freshness into you, and the storms their energy, while cares will drop away from you like the leaves of Autumn. —John Muir

Be present by living fully in each season as it is. Participate in the excitement blossoming in the spring and allow the fruits of the summer to drip sweetly upon your tongue. Consent to fall's magical shift moving through you and the rejuvenating wonder of winter's stillness to stir your soul. Be patient and observant with each season. Mother Nature has her cycles, each different from the previous, with a timing all her own.

She invites you to calmly enter her rhythm. There is no influencing her cadence to hurry in finishing off a season before it's time. You are as much a part of nature as the trees, the animals or any other living expression of life on this planet. Patiently surrender to her pull, feeling the pulse of the wild in your soul. Find the pleasure in the pathless way through and she will reveal more to you than any book can convey. Mother Nature will soothe, heal, and put your senses right.

Spiritual Contemplation: How can I spend more time in nature? Make it your intention to do so.

Affirmation: I practice patience in my time with nature!

AUGUST 23

Walk and Talk with God

Go forth under the open sky, and list to Nature's teachings. — William Cullen Bryant

Taking a walk is medicine for the soul. It's hard to stay stuck in negativity when you're outside, moving through fresh air. You feel lighter, unsure if the air is lifting you or if you've left the weight behind. It's instant upliftment, and it costs nothing to step away from your burdens. Kids instinctively know this; they're always ready for recess—running, playing, and getting their blood pumping. They don't dwell on what they left inside. They return red-faced and smiling.

Do you still remember to take a recess to reset—stepping outside, stretching, and getting your blood flowing? Have you become so serious with work that you've forgotten to go outside, even for a few minutes? A good laugh is medicine for your soul, and being outside helps you lighten up and reconnect with the infinite nature of your being. In this stress-free state, good things can come your way. It's essential to consistently reconnect with your source. "I and the Spirit are one." Throughout the day, we can easily forget our oneness with Spirit. Step outside, and you'll remember instantly. That bit of fresh air and movement will do more for your productivity than any prescription for lackluster living.

Spiritual Contemplation: Make taking a walk a priority in your busy day. Schedule it in your calendar. Is reconnecting with your Life Force more important than depleting it?

Affirmation: I enjoy making walking and talking with God a priority in my day!

AUGUST 24

Enhance your Creativity with Play

Almost all creativity involves purposeful play. — *Abraham Maslow*

Creativity and play are closely related and have a reciprocal relationship. Playfulness enhances one's creativity and creativity inspires play, which creates a cycle of exploration and expression. When we engage in play, we learn to embrace spontaneity and tap into our imagination in new ways. We learn to let go of rigid structures and rules and explore new ideas, possibilities, and perspectives. This sense of freedom encourages creative and out-of-the-box thinking, which translates to different areas of life.

If you are feeling stuck and long for change in your world, start to embrace a playful attitude and incorporate play in some way in your life on a regular basis. Not only will you have more fun, but you will also be open to new possibilities for yourself. By embracing playfulness, you will foster fertile ground for creativity to flourish right where you are.

Spiritual Contemplation: Are you currently faced with a challenge that could be solved with a fresh perspective? In what ways could you include more play and playfulness in your life to support your creativity and creative thinking?

Affirmation: I embrace play each and every day and open to new ways of thinking and being in the world!

AUGUST 25

The Wishing Tree

You become what you think about all day long. — Ralph Waldo Emerson

A traveler thought she found paradise when she sat under a tree and discovered it was the famed wishing tree. It was said that under this tree, one came to realize all their thoughts were instantly fulfilled. The traveler was hungry from her travels and thought it would be nice to eat. To her amazement, she found a banquet table with dishes of her most favorite foods laid out before her. She thought, "This is amazing! This can't be happening!" Then, in the next moment, the table, with all its delights, was gone. She thought she had better rethink this and mused on how nice it would be to have it back. Before she knew it, the banquet table was back. While enjoying the food, she felt some fine beverages would enhance the meal. There she was, drinking and eating in paradise. On her stomach, lying fully in the shadow of the tree, she began to wonder how things could be so good. It was probably some evil spirit playing tricks on her, she thought. Suddenly a ghostly figure appeared looking more terrible than she had imagined. Now afraid she was going to lose her life from this creature, she did.

We live in the world of our creation. It just may be a little slower to manifest than this journeyer's discovery. But don't be fooled, form follows consciousness, and you live in the out-picturing of your thoughts.

Spiritual Contemplation: Where are you being less than conscious with your thoughts? How can you reframe them so they bring a positive experience?

Affirmation: I am aware that my life-affirming thoughts are now bringing good into my life!

AUGUST 26

It's All in the Interpretation

Everything you can imagine is real. — *Pablo Picasso*

A man traveling a long distance by horseback became tired, so he tied up his horse and took a nap. When he woke up, he discovered that his horse was missing and there were strange footprints where his horse had been. Realizing someone had stolen his horse, he grabbed a thick stick and headed into the nearby village. In the center of town, he began swinging the club-like stick and saying, "If my horse is not returned I will have to do what I did the last time someone stole my horse." Hearing this, the thief became scared for himself and the town. He anonymously released the horse who then appeared wandering down the street. The traveler jumped on his horse, tipped his hat and began to ride out of town when the thief curiously asked him what he did the last time his horse was stolen. The traveler said, "Nothing, I bought another horse to ride out of town. "

Your mind is creative. You can be freed or trapped by your imagination. As John Lennon said, "Reality leaves a lot to the imagination." How do you fill in the blanks? Your interpretations of what you see are through your filters and biases. The meaning you bring to a situation depends on your interpretation. Whichever interpretation prevails at any given moment is what has power over you - and it's not necessarily the truth.

Spiritual Contemplation: When has your interpretation of an experience led you astray? Is there an area of your life where you might be heading in the wrong direction because the filter you are looking through is biased? How can you see it differently?

Affirmation: I step beyond my present interpretations to see and understand the situation in a new light!

AUGUST 27

Play for Your Health

Rest and Play are as vital to our health as nutrition and exercise. – Brene Brown

Play is an integral part of who we are as humans. Children have an innate capacity for play. Their natural urge expresses itself creatively and individually. Something happens as we grow and are taught that to be an adult means to be serious. We lose the connection to our natural creative sense within. It can be seen in people's relationship to exercise. As adults, we know that exercise is important and yet we drag ourselves to the gym or the exercise class (or not) like it's a chore.

Play is important for our health. Engaging in sports, dancing, or outdoor activities promotes physical fitness, mental well-being, and overall health. Playful exercise is enjoyable and makes it more likely for us to engage in it regularly. This leads to improved heart health, reduced risk of chronic disease, and increased energy and vitality.

Spiritual Contemplation: Think about ways that you can engage in physical play in a new and enjoyable way. Try something new. Maybe it's pickleball, swimming, or dancing – it doesn't matter what as long as it's fun for you and gets you moving in a new way!

Affirmation: I embrace play to enhance my health!

AUGUST 28

Precarious Moments

~❧~

Never look at that which you do not wish to experience. – Ernest Homes,
Science of Mind, page 186

High on a peak, hidden away from peering eyes, there is a monastery whose dizzying heights look down upon birds soaring, as it often rises above the clouds. To reach this hermitage, which rests on a precipice, one must first trek an exhausting journey through rugged terrain. Then, on approach, a basket is lowered to haul guests up. The ride in the hand-pulled basket, along the sheer face of the cliff, is frightening. One day, a seeker on his way up was concerned as the monks charged with hauling the basket paused to catch their breath, leaving the riders dangling high above the ground. This visitor, looking up and seeing that the ropes holding the basket appeared tattered and worn, asked the monk riding with him how often the ropes were changed. The brother looked up and with a twinkle in his eye responded, "Whenever they break."

Sometimes we don't get the answer we want, but it doesn't mean we should stress. Though we may not be suspended hundreds of feet above the ground, we are presented many opportunities to choose peace over upset and panic. A Course in Miracles reminds us, "I can choose peace instead of this." Choosing peace is liberating and transforming. Stress is debilitating and depleting. Consciously choose rather than emotionally respond to precarious moments. Don't set yourself up for a fall. Remember that form follows consciousness.

Spiritual Contemplation: Is there a precarious situation in your life causing a bit of extra energy to flow through your body? What new thought can you choose rather than the drop of doom?

Affirmation: I choose to trust this moment in life!

AUGUST 29

Playfulness at work

This is the real secret of life - to be completely engaged with what you are doing in the here and now. And instead of calling it work, realize it is play. – Alan Watts

The traditional attitude about work can be summed up by this quote from actor William Hurt. He said: "Play is play, fun is fun, and work is work. They're different. I work hard; even if it's supposed to be fun for someone else, it's work for me." Actually, research has found evidence that incorporating play into work has been shown to increase productivity and job satisfaction. When individuals are encouraged to approach tasks with a playful mindset, they become more engaged, creative, and motivated. It can also foster a positive work environment and improve collaboration and teamwork.

Playfulness at work can look like team-building exercises (think escape room or indoor skydiving), creating a "fun zone" with creative activities for breaks, incorporating playfulness and humor into internal communications and meetings, and more. It is important to strike a balance between playfulness and maintaining a professional workspace, but when implemented thoughtfully, a playful environment can have a positive impact on employee well-being, creativity, and satisfaction which can be highly beneficial for all.

Spiritual Contemplation: How can you bring an attitude of playfulness to your work life or another group that you are part of?

Affirmation: I embrace play as a way of being in all aspects of my life!

AUGUST 30

Bull

∼⚭⚮⚭∼

I never exaggerate. I just remember big. — *Chi Chi Rodriguez*

Stop telling such outlandish tales. Stop turning minnows into whales. — *Dr. Seuss*

Nothing makes a fish bigger than almost catching it. Some people feel that unless one enhances a story, no one is going to care or listen. Yet others feel that unless you embellish, you can't tell the truth. Communication can be tough. It's been said, "If you add bull to bull you get more bull." The Talmud points out, "If you add to the truth, you subtract from it."

There is a story of a bird who was in the field chatting with a bull, sharing how it would like to be in the tree but didn't have the strength to fly up there. "Why don't you peck on some of my dung, there are plenty of nutrients there?" The bird went ahead and did just that and found the strength to make it to the lower branches of the tree. The next day, after partaking in some more, his energy rose to the level where he finally got himself proudly perched on the top of the tree. There, he sang out with exaggerated exuberance. This is when the farmer saw him, grabbed his shotgun, and shot the bird right out of the tree.

Moral of the story: Bull might get you to the top, but it won't keep you there.

Spiritual Contemplation: Are there some areas of your life where you might be overdoing your storytelling? Is there any need to clarify your communication for a greater level of integrity?

Affirmation: I am a clear channel of truth telling!

AUGUST 31

Abandoning Who You Are

Just because you are happy it does not mean that the day is perfect but that you have looked beyond its imperfections. — Bob Marley

Happy people don't go around saying they are happy; they are just happy. Spiritual people don't go around saying they are spiritual, any more than an honest person goes around saying they are honest. It is who they are. It is time to be who you are without the need to verbalize it to the world. As Ralph Waldo Emerson would tell you, what you do speaks so loudly that he cannot hear what you're saying.

Be like a young child who is excited to get out and play every day for the wholehearted joy of self-expression. Can you remember what the full abandonment of self-conscious concern feels like in order to be present in a moment? Just because a situation or game is unfolding less than perfectly doesn't mean you must abandon who you are and become someone you are not. Who you are doesn't need to be dictated by circumstances. If you are a spiritual, happy, and loving person, then that is who you can be in the highs and lows of your enchanted journey.

Spiritual Contemplation: What qualities of your being do you want to speak so loudly that it doesn't matter what you say; people will still know who you are?

Affirmation: I consistently express who I am through the various facets in the game of Life!

SEPTEMBER

Authenticity

September 1-7
Living Authentically

September 8-14
Beholding

September 15-21
Seeing Clearly

September 22-30
You'll Know When You Know

SEPTEMBER 1

Is Your Soul Trapped At Work

I have learned that it is no one else's job to take care of me but me. — Beyoncé

Labor Day is a peculiar holiday that is celebrated without any formal rituals, except maybe shopping and barbecues. There seems to be very little family drama around it like Thanksgiving or religious holidays. Labor Day is a relatively noncontroversial holiday that is the demarcation for the end of summer. Yet, controversy in the early days of unionization helped birth Labor Day. It was a day set aside for factory workers to take a day off to strike, to come together, have a cookout in Central Park, or participate in a parade, rather than protest. These early factory laborers brought about the awareness of a more humane way to be in the workplace other than 70-hour work weeks of six or seven days. Remember, even God rested on the seventh day.

One might think those intense unending workdays and hours are gone? Maybe in manufacturing, they are. However, there is a plague sucking the life out of skilled white-collar workers who carry responsibility 24/7, unable to leave it behind when they go home, if they go home. Work has crept, or rather roared, into family time thanks to technology. When your head is constantly engaged in thoughts, keeping you connected to the workplace rather than those you are with, you are not "off" or taking a break. Your body may not be at the workplace, but your soul is trapped there. If that is you, today, unplug your electronics and your head, find a party, and make this a true day off and wonderfully different from all the other days of the year. Find your sanctuary.

Spiritual Contemplation: Where are you overdoing it in your life with no end in sight? How can you reduce the demand on yourself and schedule some time away from that demand?

Affirmation: I honor this day by resting from my workload!

SEPTEMBER 2

Live Your Authentic Life

Authenticity is a collection of choices that we have to make every day. It's about the choice to show up and be real. The choice to be honest. The choice to let our true selves be seen. — Brene Brown

This quote from Brene Brown comes from her personal journey to living an authentic life. Early on, Brene followed a conventional path in pursuit of a successful career as a professor and researcher, but soon she realized something was missing in her life. She had avoided vulnerability and was living in fear of judgment and failure. With this realization in tow, Brené embarked on a journey to understand and embrace vulnerability. Through her research, she delved into the complexities of human emotions, discovering that by embracing vulnerability and living authentically, people could cultivate deeper connections, resilience, and a sense of worthiness. Through her viral TED Talk and her willingness to be vulnerable and share her own struggles, she became a catalyst for change in her own life and the lives of countless others.

Living an authentic life is a personal journey requiring self-reflection, self-awareness, and a willingness to embrace who you truly are. Being true to yourself and living in alignment with your core values, beliefs, and dreams instead of conforming to external expectations or societal norms helps you build a life based in truth and will connect you to your own sense of purpose, passion, and meaning.

Spiritual Contemplation: What stands in the way of living your authentic life?

Affirmation: I recognize my true self and live my authentic life!

SEPTEMBER 3

Becoming Your True Self

I alone cannot change the world, but I can cast a stone across the waters to create many ripples. – Mother Teresa

Often, people will come to me with a deep desire to do something beneficial for the world. They want to help and make a change that makes a difference. A common theme is a feeling of overwhelm and frustration over their inability to do anything that would make a difference. I've even heard the idea that some want to make a lot of money just so they can do something good with it. It's a worthy impulse in a misguided way.

The best way we can serve the world is to allow ourselves to become fully expressed in our own uniqueness. Doing our own healing to let go of past wounds and feelings of unworthiness will allow each of us to show up in our wholeness and power. When we live from that place, we can direct our creative energy in positive ways both big and small. As we become more of our true self, using our unique voice to speak words of peace, compassion, and love, we inspire others to do the same. As each person is given permission (from themselves) to be who they truly are without holding back, it is as if they are a light illuminating the space around them. This is the ripple that Mother Theresa speaks about in the quote above. The light spreads as each awakens to their gifts and it unfolds across the world. Let us each be the spark that brightens the world right where we stand.

Spiritual Contemplation: In what ways are you holding yourself back from expressing your true self? What fears or hurts need to be released to do this? Trust the Divine that created you knew what it was doing and see if you can open a bit more to share your light with the world.

Affirmation: I am a light of love shining in the darkness!

SEPTEMBER 4

It's In Everything

Children are happy because they don't have a file in their minds called "All the Things That Could Go Wrong." — Marianne Williamson

Young ones naturally love God. They are intimate with this life force that is not an intellectual conception. They feel it, know it, and express life with a passion. Their essence commands the attention of the room without even trying. All eyes are on the children, not because they are supposed to be but because of something they are that touches your heart. It is only as the young ones grow and are taught what God is, that their connection to Spirit moves from what their heart knows to be true to their head. They fully learn what religion is, forgetting what the real spiritual connection to the Infinite feels like.Learning to be more self-conscious of what's outside of them, they forget to trust what's inside, losing contact in their attempts to sync with this world. They are systematically guided "for their protection" away from their Divine link by dishonoring its relevance.

Allow the young master in your world to intimately awaken the innocent love you once had for the wonderful life you've been given and for how you saw God in everything without ever having to call it that.

Spiritual Contemplation: Have you gotten so busy doing life that you have forgotten that you are Life expressing? Look out with childlike wonder once again and see everything sparkle with God.

Affirmation: I am dazzled and in love with God as my life!

256

SEPTEMBER 5

You Be You!

Authenticity is the daily practice of letting go of who we think we're supposed to be, and embracing who we actually are. – Brene Brown

Embracing authenticity is a core practice of living a wholehearted life. You cannot be an integrated whole without embracing and expressing the totality of who you are. The word authenticity has been overused in recent years and sometimes it seems to have lost its true meaning. Yet, the core message is critical in moving forward on your path. You are here to express your uniqueness in everything you do.

An easy way to tell if you are not being authentic is to notice if you shift who you are to fit someone else's idea of what's right. Maybe it's just holding back an opinion in conversation with a friend or conceding to eating at a place you don't like. It is often seen in small choices you make against yourself and at some point, you wake up to the fact that you are no longer being yourself. This is the time to pause, take a deep breath and recommit to being the truest expression of yourself. It takes some courage and practice, but it is worth it! Your authentic self is a gift to the world and you have come into this life to give it!

Spiritual Contemplation: Notice when you are trying to please someone else or catch yourself worrying about what someone else thinks. Shift back to your authentic self and note how you could have handled those situations differently.

Affirmation: I am the authentic expression of me!

SEPTEMBER 6

Your Unique Delivery

While we have the gift of life, it seems to me the only tragedy is to allow part of us to die - whether it is our spirit, our creativity or our glorious uniqueness. – Gilda Radner

An honorable warrior went to a temple to find inner peace. Coming upon the spiritual leader in tranquil contemplation filled the warrior with emotion. He knew he'd fought courageously and honorably throughout his time, yet he was distraught to sense he would never have the presence of peace as did the teacher who stood before him.

As the day passed and the night rose, the great warrior felt melancholy. When the two stood in the middle of the moonlit courtyard, the humble teacher pointed to the exquisite moon and said, "As the moon crosses the heavens the sun will rise, much brighter, lighting up the sky and landscape in entirely different ways. I never heard the moon grumbling, how come I'm not as bright as the sun, I must be less than." The sun and the moon are different, each with its own unique gifts. You must not compare yourself to others. Trusting your uniqueness challenges you to leave yourself vulnerable. We are all different people, expressing in our own unique ways to make the world a better place. Is that not what matters?

Spiritual Contemplation: Where do you find you're comparing yourself to others? What is your purpose in the world? How is your delivery style uniquely you? Can you love that about yourself?

Affirmation: I am happy to be on purpose delivering my gift in my unique way!

SEPTEMBER 7

Who Do You Want to Be?

To be yourself in a world that is constantly trying to make you something else is the greatest accomplishment. — Ralph Waldo Emerson

Toward the end of his life, literary giant George Bernard Shaw was asked what person in history he would most like to have been. His response was that he would most like to have been the George Bernard Shaw he might have become but never did. What a powerful concept to consider for ourselves – how can we become the greatest version of ourselves in this life? To live a wholehearted life, we must connect with our true selves and live from that place of knowing who we are and why we are here.

It takes courage to be a unique expression in a world that desires conformity. It takes empowerment to speak truth to power. It takes faith to keep our hearts soft and open when it feels like we are being judged. But each of these things are necessary to first realize who we are and then to share our unique perspective with the world. This is why we are here.

Spiritual Contemplation: What kind of person do you want to be in this life? If you could make life better for those around you, what would you change? When your life is over, how do you want to be remembered?

Affirmation: I am the greatest expression of myself that I can be!

SEPTEMBER 8

Know Thyself

This above all-to thine own self be true, and it must follow, as night follows day, thou canst not then be false to any man. — William Shakespeare

Basketball legend LeBron James is considered one of the most intensely focused competitors ever to play basketball. He was once asked what could possibly cause an MVP like him to lose his rhythm on the court. His response: "I get off my game when I start playing for others rather than playing for myself." This is a universal truth. We fall off course the minute our intention shifts from following our heart to responding to what we think others want from us.

We are called to know ourselves and we are all in a process of discovering who we are again and again. We can stand firm and strong in our lives when we know who we are, and we can move in the direction of our dreams from that place of knowing. When we find ourselves changing who we are or censoring ourselves just to make it comfortable for others, it is a clear indication that these are not our people, and we need to find a place where we can be ourselves. We should not waste our time striving to please other people by changing what we believe in or by acting a way that is outside of what we really want to do. When we know ourselves and act in alignment with that, we live a life of fulfillment and joy.

Spiritual Contemplation: Take some time to consider today what you know about yourself. What do you believe in? What is important to you?

Affirmation: I listen to my heart and hear the truth of my unique expression!

SEPTEMBER 9

Quiet Mind

~e/&ve~

All men's miseries derive from not being able to sit in a quiet room alone. —
Blaise Pascal

An elder was walking with one of her young students on a jungle path.
The apprentice spoke thoughtfully about the spiritual perspective of "as
within, so without". This is the idea that what you think about manifests in
your world, and what's in your mind reflects in your surroundings. The wise
one kept silent throughout their stroll. After some time the two came across
an enormous boulder on their path. The master teacher simply asked, "There
is a large rock before us. Do you consider this inside or outside your
thoughts?"

The neophyte quickly responded, "In my spiritual practice everything is
an out picture of what's in my thoughts. Therefore, that boulder is definitely
in my mind." The master gently smiled and said, "Your head must be very
heavy if you are carrying a boulder like that in your mind." The two
completed the rest of their stroll in the serenity of silence.

Spiritual Contemplation: Where is your mind too full with chatter and
interpretation that you are not available to experience the creative expression
of what actually is before you?

Affirmation: I am open and available to the inspiration of my serene self!

SEPTEMBER 10

Find Your Rhythm

Find your own rhythm, and confidently go with that rhythm. When you become one with the rhythm and flow of your own life, you will encounter the rhythm of the universe that bestows harmony and order upon all things: the pulse of the cosmos, Yullyeo. — Ilchi Lee

There are moments in our lives when we feel in sync with life, when harmony flows and everything unfolds with ease and joy. There are also moments in life when we feel out of sync, when everything feels off and out of alignment. This is the time to become aware of your individual rhythm. We each have our own unique needs regarding the rhythms of our lives. How much rest we need, what kinds of interactions feed and nurture us, and how we operate in our days all contribute to how synchronized we feel with life.

If you are in a moment when you feel out of sync with life, it means it's time to wake up to your own individual rhythm and explore how to proceed in a new way. Honoring your needs is an act of radical self-care. It will give you the chance to be the best expression of yourself since honoring your rhythms will support coming from your wholeness and not someone else's ideas of what's right for you. When you find and honor your own rhythm, you open to a greater connection to the Life of the Universe where you can welcome infinite blessings into your experience.

Spiritual Contemplation: When do you feel most connected to the rhythm of your life? What kinds of interactions feed and nurture you? What kinds of interactions drain you?

Affirmation: I allow my natural rhythm of life to flow with ease!

SEPTEMBER 11

Behold

~~ell&ve~

Look inside yourself. You are more than what you have become. – Mufasa (The Lion King)

Step out of your humanhood and recognize your spiritual identity. Develop a state of consciousness that witnesses your mental chatter, emotional choices and operating belief systems. Behold, you are not those things you are watching! You are the beholder who is observing the choices being made. This kind of awareness instantly frees you to overcome the tug of your world.

Learn to rely on this inner perceiving plane, placing your reliance on the infinite nature of your being and its direct revelation of the Divine. Spiritual freedom and the peace which passes logic doesn't depend on anything in the manifested universe. God is always present in the consciousness of those who are conscious of God's presence. Drop the demanding thoughts of what has been and what you've become. Dive deeper within your awareness until you receive the God-response. Behold, this is your greater yet to be.

Spiritual Contemplation: Find a quiet place, close your eyes and ask yourself, "Show me more of who I am." Listen to the answers with your whole being. Then ask, "Show me more." Then listen with your whole being. Then ask, "Show me more." Repeat this over and over.

Affirmation: I am more than I've become!

SEPTEMBER 12

Your Flaws are Your Gifts

God enters through the wound. — Carl Jung

Dr. Temple Grandin is one of the top scientists in the humane livestock handling industry. She has a PhD in Animal Science from the University of Illinois and is a professor at Colorado State University. She has authored six books, including two bestsellers. She is autistic and says "Autism is part of who I am." Her "disability" is the gift that allows Grandin to understand animals. She has changed livestock handling and influenced an entire industry.

So often we judge ourselves harshly for those things that we consider weaknesses or flaws. We try to hide what makes us different. Yet, more often than not, these are the unique gifts that we're meant to share with the world. They allow us to see life differently and open our capacity for creativity and compassion. These differences are what make us unique and are to be honored and celebrated because these are the special attributes of God made manifest as us.

Spiritual Contemplation: What do you consider to be a personal weakness or flaw? How can you look at this as a gift to you and others? What capacities have you developed because of this? Note this in your journal.

Affirmation: I am a beautiful expression of the Divine! Whole, perfect and complete - just as I am!

SEPTEMBER 13

Stained Glass

People are like stained - glass windows. They sparkle and shine when the sun is out, but when the darkness sets in, their true beauty is revealed only if there is a light from within. — Elisabeth Kubler-Ross

Standing before a stained-glass window during the day, its colors casting light upon you, is awe-inspiring. At night, the experience is even more magical as the windows come alive when you stand outside in the darkness, gazing at the towering portals of sparkling color illuminated from within. This soul-stirring sight transports your awareness beyond where you stand.

You are much like the stained-glass window. When you allow your light to shine from within, you bring it to the dark times. Those twinkling eyes of yours are like a stained-glass window, a transparent partition between your soul and the world.

When you choose to turn up your heart light, what you bring to the dark times around you is a transferring illumination, inviting others to step into a brighter time.

Spiritual Contemplation: How did it feel to bring some light and a greater possibility to another when they were in pain or fear? What did it feel like to turn on that inner light?

Affirmation: I am a bright light in the world!

SEPTEMBER 14

Take a Good Look in the Mirror

We have two strategies for coping; the way of avoidance or the way of attention. – Marilyn Ferguson

One of the reasons we keep ourselves so busy in our day-to-day lives is that we are actually avoiding the pain and discomfort we feel sometimes. We avoid resting and slowing down because it is too painful to take a good look at the state of our lives. Instead, we fill our time with distraction, excuses, or self-imposed numbing. Our vices, which can be positive or negative, keep us separated from the truth and from solutions that could bring peace and positive change.

Taking time to slow down and observe where we are requires us to be vulnerable and honest in allowing our feelings to express. When we do this, we hear what we need to hear so we can give attention to where it's needed. We can look at where we are in our lives, see how we got here with eyes of compassion and acceptance, and surrender the pain and discomfort gently knowing we are right where we need to be.

Spiritual Contemplation: Contemplate what area of your life you may be avoiding looking at and take some time with eyes of compassion and acceptance to explore your feelings in your journal.

Affirmation: I look at my life with eyes of love, compassion and acceptance!

SEPTEMBER 15

Nebulous Messages

The single biggest problem in communication is the illusion that it has taken place. — George Bernard Shaw

Have you ever caught a glimpse of something you knew was going to show up in your life, but it didn't arrive how you thought it would? Metaphorically, consider that the UPS driver was expected to drop a package off at your workplace on a particular day. Tracking said it would arrive, but it didn't. You rationalize that it will probably come another day and then forget all about it, only to get home and unexpectedly meet a FedEx driver in your driveway. You realize, to your total surprise, you never verified on the tracking, who would be delivering it and where it was to arrive. Your mind logically filled in the blanks differently than what was written.

When you catch a glimpse of a message from the universe, it is often obscure. At this point, your mind wants to take control and get a handle on the unknown. It does not like nebulous messaging without clear content. However, the universe speaks in images, inklings, feelings, vibrations and revelations. Learn to trust that the glimpses of life's coming attractions are enough to prepare you to be in the right place at the right time to be the recipient of the unexpected good that awaits your arrival.

Spiritual Contemplation: By paying attention to vague messages from the universe and how they ultimately unfold into form, you'll discover how to more accurately interpret them with your whole heart rather than your logical mind. Give it a try today and you might discover the Universe is continuously seeking to communicate with you, with all the information already available.

Affirmation: I clearly feel and understand my connection with the Universe!

SEPTEMBER 16

Time to Unlearn What You Know

The illiterate of the 21st century will not be those who cannot read and write, but those who cannot learn, unlearn and relearn. — *Herbert Gerjuoy*

When you are feeling stuck and aren't sure which way to go, it may be time to pause and let go of what you think you know about yourself, life, and God. Our thoughts and beliefs, both conscious and unconscious, determine our experience and when we get to a place of confusion or stagnation, a new idea is the only thing that will shift our experience and get us moving forward again.

When you are too full of your own beliefs about how life is supposed to be, you can't take in new information and you can't deal with those moments that do not align with your ideas. This is the time to practice unlearning. You unlearn by undoing your worldly conditioning and everything you've been taught to think. It's an active process of choosing an alternative paradigm by stepping out of your comfort zone to view things differently. When you let go of the ideas that no longer serve you, you are open to relearning a new way of being in the world and welcome new possibilities for your life.

Spiritual Contemplation: Think about what idea you may be holding about yourself that is currently limiting your experience. Can you let that idea go and embrace a new concept about yourself that will expand your idea of what's possible? Write your new idea in your journal.

Affirmation: I let go of the beliefs that no longer serve me. I welcome a new idea of what's possible and I step into my greatness of being!

SEPTEMBER 17

Shattering the Reasoning Mind

When I was a child, I spoke and thought and reasoned as a child. But when I grew up, I put away childish things. – 1 Corinthians 13:11, NLT

So much of what you believe has to be cleared away before there is space for the Divine to be known. You must empty your mind in order to know peace. The glass must be cleaned in order to allow the light to shine. The cleaning, purifying, and purging all take place through your commitment to spiritual practices.

When you catch a glimpse of the celestial realm, the heart's desire is for more. What evolves is an expansion and ultimately unification, shattering the reasoning mind. The Divine Light will burn away anything unlike Itself. The child is gone, and the living presence of the Almighty dances with delight as you. The face of God will only be unveiled to those who are lost in love. There is no way to know this Divine Love other than direct transference of love between you and the Beloved until you are one.

Spiritual Contemplation: How can I integrate more of my spiritual practice of prayer, meditation, contemplation, and journaling, into my daily activities?

Affirmation: I see the face of God!

SEPTEMBER 18

Tell a New Story

You cannot swim for new horizons until you have the courage to lose sight of the shore. — William Faulkner

Do you remember the last time you went to your childhood home? It's funny to me that, even as an adult, after living out on my own for many years, I would visit my parents in my childhood home and suddenly, I would be acting as if I were 12! Crazier even still, not only did I start acting that way, but they all treated me that way! It occurs to me that if we do not question our old stories or get present and wake up to the stories we are carrying around about ourselves, they will remain unchecked. This will chain you to someone you may have been 25 years ago but are no longer.

When you shift the story, the limitation that goes with it shifts, too. You are constantly evolving, and you are not the same person you were back then! You want to embody and integrate the parts of the old you that served and helped you become who you are now and let go of those parts that limit you. Let your stories catch up to who you are now and watch with curiosity how you can experience your brand-new story filled with adventure and joy!

Spiritual Contemplation: Think about your past. What part of your story no longer applies to you? What are you ready to release and what new ideas about yourself are you ready to embrace?

Affirmation: I honor and celebrate who I was, who I am and who I am becoming!

SEPTEMBER 19

Seeing More Than Has Been Seen

Man's mind, once stretched by a new idea, never regains its original dimensions.
— Oliver Wendell Holmes

One of the beautiful things about learning is no one can take it away from you, even if others try to challenge it with their facts and opinions. You are not here to sanctify the known, but to investigate it and discover what's not known. Small minds will criticize what they don't understand, shaming and guilting what is not in their frame to witness or comprehend. Schools that use the fearful motivation of failing grades, your class advancing without you, or negative narratives like "you'll never amount to anything unless you learn what I tell you" are squashing the inquisitive spirit. Instruction is good, but it is encouragement that inspires the curious spirit to see more than has been seen.

True teachers are the bridge from here to the beyond that their students traverse. Happily, they willingly collapse behind their explorers of truth so they cannot return the same way. It is when you are outside your element, over the bridge in new territory, that you come to discover yourself the most. You may stumble now, but it often prevents the fall later in life. Don't allow tough lessons to harden your heart. Love life and learning. Lessons are to make you better, not bitter. There is an oriental proverb that states, "Learning is a treasure that will follow its owner everywhere."

Spiritual Contemplation: What was it like to have a teacher who focused more on having you repeat what they wanted you to learn? Compare that to the influencer who inspired your hunger to know more. Which one do you want to emulate in the world?

Affirmation: I am an inspirer and discoverer of the richness of life!

SEPTEMBER 20

You are a Gift from God

What you are is God's gift to you, what you become is your gift to God. – Hans Urs von Balthasar

There is a Buddhist story about a blind turtle that lives on the ocean floor and surfaces just once every hundred years. A golden yoke (hoop) floats on the vast ocean, blown every which way by the wind. The chances of the turtle surfacing at just the right moment and in just the right place to be able to put its head through the yoke is as rare and precious as your human incarnation.

We forget sometimes how miraculous it is to be alive and what a gift our lives can be to the world. When we remember that we are precious and purposeful, we begin to rise out of the negative feelings that come from the belief that we are unworthy and not enough. This realization is all that is needed to change course and begin creating a life that makes a difference not only for ourselves, but for those around us. When one person lives from the realization of their divinity and worthiness, they give permission to others in their life to do the same. As we each awaken to this truth, we become the spark lighting up the space around us, calling out to those who are also ready to become that spark. The influence spreads and we all step into the light together.

Spiritual Contemplation: Think about those things that make you unique and special. What talents, traits or experiences make you uniquely you? How are these things blessings not only to you, but to the world?

Affirmation: I am a gift from God and I shine my light brightly!

SEPTEMBER 21

It's A Puzzle

~~ഛ~~

There are no extra pieces in the universe. Everyone is here because he or she has a place to fill, and every piece must fit itself into the big jigsaw puzzle. — Deepak Chopra

Do you ever have pieces of your life that just don't seem right? They are crazy, or ugly, or just don't seem to make sense in the overall scheme of things? They don't seem to fit the picture you had for your life. Have you ever opened a jigsaw puzzle whose picture was exquisite on the box? It was so appealing that it enticed you to purchase the puzzle. Your creative nature loves a good challenge! As you pour the pieces out on the table and start turning them image-side up, you begin to wonder. Looking closely at some of the puzzle pieces, you ask yourself, "Where in the world might this piece go? This one is certainly a strange shape, and this other one seems quite ugly compared to the beautiful picture I saw. What was I thinking when I bought this puzzle?"

Those questionable pieces cannot be forced where they don't belong. Nor can they be hidden or thrown away. There are no extra pieces and every piece has its place. You must continue asking yourself, "What is the whole picture I'm working on here?" Eventually, with your creative tenacity, those unique pieces of your life will find their perfect place completing the image you had in mind. Each distinctive piece of your life is absolutely necessary. Your life is much like that puzzle. Every experience you have has its distinctive place in the overall arrangement of the unfolding picture. Who you are is an integral part of the grand jigsaw puzzle of the universe that would be incomplete without you.

Spiritual Contemplation: What pieces of your life would you like to throw out? How can you now see their perfect placement in your life?

Affirmation: I love the creative process of the unfolding puzzle of my life!

SEPTEMBER 22

Bring Forth Your Gifts

If you bring forth what is within you, what you bring forth will save you. If you do not bring forth what is within you, what you do not bring forth will destroy you. — Jesus, The Gospel of Thomas

The quote from The Gospel of Thomas by Jesus is a powerful statement that resembles a Zen koan. A koan is a statement or story that helps students of Zen Buddhism reach a higher insight that transcends the usual thought processes. At first glance, this quote seems like a puzzle that doesn't make sense, but with a deeper look, we can see that there is wisdom here. In this life, we each learn to put on masks and facades to shield our true selves from the world. We learn how to protect ourselves from challenging situations and relationships by not showing the world who we truly are. Unfortunately, in this process, we can lose sight of ourselves.

This statement by Jesus is an invitation to do the inner work to discover who we are and then find a way to reveal it to the world. If we can do this, we will be saved. If we cannot find a way to do this, we will never experience the fullness of our lives and the joy of being truly expressed and seen. This experience of being stunted and stagnant will destroy us. It's up to us to do the hard work of inner discovery. The payoff is meeting yourself at the core and realizing you are so much more than you ever imagined.

Spiritual Contemplation: What aspect of yourself are you holding back from the world? How can you begin to open up and share that? Make a list of five new ways you can share your gifts.

Affirmation: I open my heart and share my gifts with the world!

SEPTEMBER 23

I Know When I Know That I Got It

And those who were seen dancing, were thought to be crazy, by those who could not hear the music. — Friedrich Nietzsche

As a young student began his schooling, the teacher taught the class how to draw a straight line like the number one. As the other students moved on to the next assignment of curved lines, this student wholeheartedly continued practicing the first design. After a couple days of not moving on from the straight line, his practicing of the letter "one" continued for weeks. The teacher eventually sent him home because he was making a mockery of the lessons by not learning. At home, he continued on the same design with the straight line, until his parents were fed up with him.

This child would say, "I have not yet mastered this lesson," and continued to practice. The other children moved on to the next grade, as the teacher and parents gave up on the little one. Thereafter, the child would go off to the woods and get lost for days at a time practicing this straight-line lesson. Eventually, after a long time, the boy returned to the school, and upon seeing the teacher, he proclaimed that he had finally learned the lesson. He said he would show the teacher by drawing a straight line on the wall. When he did, the wall split in two.

What you wholeheartedly see as possible, others may not. Do not allow another's limited vision to entice you to conform to their ways, just because it might be easier or quicker. When your whole heart sees, all things are possible.

Spiritual Contemplation: Where have you acquiesced to another's vision of being less than you knew was possible for you?

Affirmation: I know when I know that I got it!

SEPTEMBER 24

Be Bold!

Whatever you can do, or dream you can, begin it. Boldness has genius, power and magic in it. — Johann Wolfgang von Goethe

No one ever created the life they imagined for themselves by being meek and scared. There is an innate urge within each of us to be bold and to express our uniqueness with the world. Often, we hold that urge back, afraid of being judged or ridiculed for our beliefs and who we are. This leads to an experience of sadness and depression because we know that holding back and hiding from life is not why we are here.

It's time to rewrite the story of your life. No longer will you hold your voice back or be afraid of shining your light brightly in the world. Live boldly and you will open to a whole new level of possibility. More joy! More abundance! More freedom! It's a whole new life! It takes courage and boldness to step into your magnificence and today is the day to begin!

Spiritual Contemplation: Think about one thing you want to experience in your life but have been holding yourself back from. Decide how and when you will do it. Share your desire with a trusted friend for support. Know that you can do it! Be bold!

Affirmation: I am bold! I am courageous! I am free!

SEPTEMBER 25

Path of the Past

~ado~

You can live your life angry, bitter, mad at somebody or even guilty, not letting go of your own mistakes, but you won't receive the good things God has in store. –
Joel Osteen

You think you have a past that disqualifies you from being an expression of Spirit? It didn't stop these bible characters from making a difference:

Moses stuttered.	Naomi was a widow.
David's armor didn't fit.	Paul was a murderer.
Timothy had ulcers.	So was Moses.
John, Mark were rejected by Paul.	Miriam was a gossip.
Jacob was a liar.	Samson had long hair.
David had an affair.	Peter was afraid of death.
Solomon was too rich.	Lazarus was dead.
Abraham was too old.	Gideon and Thomas both doubted.

Every saint has a past and a path they walked. What matters is whether you are available to be used by God to make a difference today?

Spiritual Contemplation: What mistakes, from your past, do you keep telling yourself are the reason why you are not good enough? Are you ready to let those go and move on?

Affirmation: I am fully present and available for my God assignment today!

SEPTEMBER 26

Who are you?

An unexamined life is not worth living. — *Socrates*

As you commit to living and walking a spiritual path, it is important to begin by getting clear about who you are and why you are here. When you understand this, most everything in your life will begin to make sense. You will understand what motivates you and brings you joy. You will begin to create an inner vision for what's possible for your life and move in the direction of more of that! Without a vision and clarity you tend to wander. You'll feel unmoored and miss the opportunities that will feed your soul and bring you greater happiness.

Spend some quality time alone daily. Explore your thoughts, ideas and desires and you will begin to introduce yourself to who you truly are. You will realize what you value, are passionate about, and what you'd like to see out in the world. This will lead to a bigger vision for yourself and your life.

Spiritual Contemplation: Make a list of 100 things that you would like to be, do and/or have in your lifetime. Allow your mind to stretch and expand your concept of self as you begin to form a vision for your life.

Affirmation: I am a unique expression of God sharing my passion and love with the world!

SEPTEMBER 27

Do You See What I See?

I see you. – Neytiri and Jake, Avatar

A new student, who had been expelled from a couple of previous schools, arrived at his latest school. The first teacher who came into the classroom took one look at him and thought, "Where do these kinds of kids come from?" When the second teacher walked in and saw him, he said, "There is no lack of delinquents like you around here." When the third teacher came to class, she celebrated with, "Do we have a new student here?" She approached him, shook his hand and looked into his eyes saying, "Good morning. I've been waiting for you! Welcome to my class!" The student's life changed after being seen for his positive potential, rather than the label of "delinquent" placed upon him.

Sometimes, it takes only one person to see the good in another to help bring it out. You live up to the perceptions the world places upon you. What positive perceptions are you laying on the world?

Spiritual Contemplation: Are there some people in your life about whom you hold less-than-divine ideals? Do those individuals fulfill your perception of them? How can you change your view about them?

Affirmation: I choose to see the best in people!

SEPTEMBER 28

Not Everyone Will Like You

Hold onto who loves and honors you. Not everyone will know how to. Some souls don't even know how to love and honor themselves, let alone you. – Lalah Delia

One of the ways we step into our fullest authentic expression is by accepting the fact that not everyone is going to like you, no matter how hard you try. There will always be people who will like you and some who will dislike you. The best way to handle this is to stop trying to get them to like you. When you start appreciating yourself first, you begin to realize that being liked is not as important as being authentically you.

Everything in life is energy and when you are focused on making the other person like you, you are wasting your energy. When you strive to make someone like or love you, you become someone you aren't just to try to gain their love. Instead, use this energy by redirecting it to support yourself. Focus your energy on understanding yourself, your goals, dreams and values, so you can work toward living from your whole heart as an authentic expression instead of living a life that is false.

Spiritual Contemplation: Is there anyone in your life that you are trying to get to like you? How can you reframe this relationship to see if it is serving you or not? Today, commit to putting your own feelings and well-being first and begin to let go of anyone who can't appreciate the amazing person that you are.

Affirmation: I am loved and lovable!

SEPTEMBER 29

Lane Departure

There are times when logic seems to choke The mysteries that we invoke.
— Ernest Holmes, Voice Celestial, page 179

These days some cars seem to have a mind of their own. Have you ever gotten behind the wheel and possibly drifted a tad out of your lane and a voice booms, apparently from out of nowhere, saying, "Lane Departure?" Really, how does it know that? It's one thing to have a satellite giving you GPS directions but to interrupt your space with "lane departure?" is a whole new level of knowingness.

When you start drifting in life, an internal warning system goes off because it's been pre programmed to warn that you are off track. The challenge you face comes when you override the system with the volume of other mental activities. There are a lot of available stations on that mental radio, but you don't need to have them blasting. As in your life, there can be a lot of unnecessary tunes going through your mental world. Remember to turn up the volume to your inner guidance system and tune out the other distractions.

Spiritual Contemplation: Your internal tracking system is even more acute than rhetoric in the world. Have you turned its volume down and turned up the chaos in your awareness? Where do you need to turn the volume down so you can once again hear your pre-programmed internal guidance?

Affirmation: I hear and am led by my divine guidance!

SEPTEMBER 30

Check Within

Wall Street is the only place that people ride to in a Rolls Royce to get advice
from those who take the subway. — Warren Buffett

A young man bought a parrot to keep him company. After a couple days, the man went back to the pet shop and told the owner his bird hadn't spoken a word. The shopkeeper asked if the bird had a mirror. The response was no, so he bought a mirror and took it home. The next day, the new pet owner returned to the shop to say his bird still hadn't talked and was looking lethargic. The shop owner asked if the bird had a ladder for some exercise. The response was no, so he bought a ladder and took it home and put it in the cage. The next day the man went back to the pet store to inform the owner that there was still no talking. The shopkeeper asked if his bird had a swing in order for it to relax. The response was no, so he bought a swing and gave it to his bird. The next day, the man returned to the store to inform the owner that his bird had died. The shopkeeper was shocked and wondered if the bird said anything before it died. Yes, with its last breath, it asked, "Why don't they sell any food in that pet store of yours?"

Are you looking at the obvious? Are you taking advice from those who don't know you or the situation? Are you receiving prescriptions for betterment from experts who aren't actually listening to you? Be cautious before following any guidance, no matter how good it may be, until you have checked in with your heart and soul and found, in the depths of your being, that the given direction is yours to take.

Spiritual Contemplation: When given advice, check within to see if it is yours to do.

Affirmation: I honor and respect the insights of my internal reviews!

OCTOBER

Abundance

October 1-7

Dreaming Big

October 8-14

A Giving Heart

October 15-21

Plugging In

October 22-28

Being Intentional

October 29-31

The Fullness of Life

OCTOBER 1

Multiplying Your Good

For whoever has will be given more, and they will have an abundance. Whoever does not have, even what they have will be taken from them. – Matthew 25:29, NIV

This scripture makes more sense when we understand that God is speaking about having gratitude in our hearts. For the person who has gratitude, calls to themselves more abundance of all things. The one who has no gratitude, can't sustain, and loses the little good they have.

Recall that we are energetic beings and what we give out to the world, we get back from it. If we are grateful for the abundance and the blessings we experience, they multiply and expand. We share gratitude with the Universe, and it responds with abundance. If we are not in gratitude, we stop the energetic flow and end up empty and lost. If we dole out judgment and complaint, the Universe will give us something more to complain about! It is truly up to us how we experience life, and one simple way to shift towards an awareness is through the practice of gratitude.

Spiritual Contemplation: In what areas of your life is it difficult to see the blessings of abundance? Take some time to explore how you can cultivate gratitude in your experience and watch for the shift as the good in your world multiplies.

Affirmation: I am grateful for the fullness and abundance of my life!

OCTOBER 2

Divinely Endowed

Understand and accept the cycles of money. The setbacks you may have today or next year will not keep you from financial freedom. If you hold on to your goals and dreams, you will get there. — Suze Orman

If you have ever played a board game like Monopoly, then you already know. you win some choices and you lose some decisions. What matters is if you are further ahead of your opponent at the end of the game. It's crucial that you don't stop buying when one of your choices doesn't pan out, though. Sometimes you lose it all when someone clears the board game like a giant recession. But then you can start over and play another game. You have been divinely endowed with the ability to succeed, but you have to stay in the game.

One of the vital lessons from childhood board games that translates into your investing today is, you win some and you lose some. The question to ponder is whether you are further along today than when you left the house as a teenager. Too often people get fixated on their losses and don't jump back into the game of life. There will be losses along the way, but that is just part of the risk of playing the money game. If you are still caught up and talking about the financial hit you took a few years back, it's time to pass go. Leave that experience in the past, and start loving, talking about, and moving toward your new prospering intentions and plans for the Infinite Abundance of the Universe to lavishly source your life with good.

Spiritual Contemplation: Got any old stories of financial loss you keep reminding yourself about? Remember, you may win some and you may lose some, but it's all part of the total money experience. Are you better off today than when you started? Are your creative financial intentions of today focused upon past losses or abundant creation?

Affirmation: The Omnipresent Infinite Source of all good is lavishing blessings upon my life now!

OCTOBER 3

What Abundance is All About

Abundance is not something we acquire. It is something we tune into. — Wayne Dyer

In the mid-1970s, a wave of evangelism rose across America consumed with the idea that God rewarded believers with health and wealth. Fueled by several television evangelists, the Prosperity gospel found a grasp on the minds of many. This was damaging to the psyches of those who lost faith because they were struggling and couldn't reach the heights that preachers told them they could if they truly believed.

It's important to realize that the spiritual concept of abundance is not about manifesting excessive wealth or possessions. It's about recognizing and appreciating the abundance that already exists in our lives. It is a way to find contentment and joy in the experience of life, right where we are. This realization leads to a more fulfilling and purposeful life journey, as you understand that there is enough for everyone. It is freely given because you are a part of the Divine creation and are here with a purpose. You have innate worth and the Universe pours itself freely upon you simply because you are here.

Spiritual Contemplation: Can you accept that you are a Divine gift to life and deserve to have an abundant and full life? What gets in the way of your abundance? Think about this and journal about your thoughts and beliefs.

Affirmation: I am a Divine emanation and am supported by the Universe in all ways!

OCTOBER 4

An Abundance Awareness

When you are able to shift your inner awareness to how you can serve others, and when you make this the central focus of your life, you will then be in a position to know true miracles in your progress toward prosperity. – Wayne W. Dyer

There is something within you that knows how to receive your good. Don't be embarrassed or ashamed of your prosperity. The law of supply shows up where it is welcomed. Share with joy and appreciation that which you have received, for you are a divine distributor. That which you give, continues to grow. Think without limitations, and you become an unlimited receiver, enabling you to be a limitless giver. You must accept your good to be in this ever increasing circular flow.

You talk about what you think about. Allow your thoughts of abundance to be spoken to the world and backed up by a practice of circulating good. Know that only good goes forth from you. As a result, only good comes back into your life. All that is needed to continue this reciprocating wealth is now in your abundance awareness. You have the right attitude to call forth good in all things.

Spiritual Contemplation: Where is your stinking thinking limiting you? How can you be a greater distributor of the Divine in order to break free from the constricting feelings that are encroaching?

Affirmation: I give generously of love and wealth! As a natural result, I am a blessed receiver of Life's perfect circulation of limitless good!

OCTOBER 5

Develop an Abundance Mindset

*We don't create abundance. Abundance is always present. We create
limitations.* — *Arnold Patent*

There exists a general belief in the world that there is not enough of anything for everyone. Just look at what happened with the hoarding of toilet paper across the country at the beginning of the COVID-19 quarantine. People went crazy to make sure they had enough. Fights broke out at stores, and people were shamed across social media. There is a deep belief that each person needs to fight for a small piece of the finite pie of life. This way of being is damaging and keeps everyone stuck in limitation and separation. However, life doesn't have to be this way.

When you develop an abundance mindset, you realize that there is more than enough for everyone and that success, happiness, and prosperity are not limited resources. Studies have shown that there are enough resources on the planet to support all of the humans and creatures that live here. It is a matter of cooperation and collaboration rather than separation and conflict. What happens on a large scale is also true for the individual. When you develop an abundance mindset, you realize the importance of collaboration, generosity, and the willingness to share knowledge and resources. When one person prospers, with an abundance mindset and way of living, everyone around them prospers too.

Spiritual Contemplation: Contemplate your current mindset on abundance and limitation. Do you know that there is enough of everything available for you? How can you expand your thinking to include an abundance mindset?

Affirmation: I open my mind and see the abundance all around me!

OCTOBER 6

I am Enough

When we are focused constantly on the next thing—the next dress, the next car, the next job, the next vacation, the next home improvement—we hardly experience the gifts of that which we have now. — Lynne Twist

The stream of abundance does not cross the threshold of the belief in scarcity and inadequacy uninvited. No matter what financial level you are playing at, being caught up on what you don't have, rather than being grateful for what you do have, keeps you in a lack mentality. To reside in the consciousness that you live in a world where there is enough is a transforming state from scarcity to sufficiency.

Sufficiency isn't about cutting back, rather, it is a demonstration of your healthy relationship with the affluent flow of life. It is a deep knowingness that you are enough residing within you. You will interact in life with the knowledge that Infinite resources are available for you to direct in wholehearted ways, rather than giving your power away by rushing after something outside to fulfill yourself. There is a newfound freedom, confidence, and calm that comes when you know you are enough in doing what is important to your heart and soul.

Spiritual Contemplation: Where do you feel you are not enough in your life? How can you refocus your attention on what you already have? Reclaim your power by directing that life force to what has value in your life.

Affirmation: I am enough, I am wonderful!

OCTOBER 7

Let Yourself Dream Big

All dreams start from the core. Unless you are in total alignment with whatever you envision, the dream will get derailed. Your intention has to be pure. —
Oprah

In the manifestation process, it's important to clarify what you want in your life. This alone can be a challenge because many of us don't listen to our own wants and needs. Maybe we weren't encouraged by our families to honor our own needs and we never learned how to do it. It's not about being selfish and trying to get everything you want at the cost of those around you. You need to learn to balance your own desires with the needs and desires of others.

As you work on creating the life of your dreams, you need to start by being clear about what those dreams really are. This is where spending some time daydreaming and using your imagination can be helpful. When you pause and get out of your normal routine, you create space that allows your thinking mind to calm down and open to innate creativity to guide you. Take the time to let your mind wander to all sorts of possibilities and see what speaks to you. You will form a vision for yourself, and the manifestation process will open to you revealing all the situations that can bring your dreams to life.

Spiritual Contemplation: Take time to let your mind wander today and imagine all the things that would bring you joy and happiness. Make a list of what you'd like to experience and how you will feel when you manifest this.

Affirmation: I am allowing my deepest dreams and desires to manifest easily in my life now!

OCTOBER 8

Congratulations, You've Won

It is only in your thriving that you have anything to offer anyone. — *Abraham Hicks*

If you had just won the lottery, you would head on over to the lottery office, present your winning ticket and claim your winnings. Congratulations! You wouldn't show up beseeching and imploring to be paid, as if you weren't worthy. Nor would you ask what you have to do to earn this payout, or who you need to please in order to receive the income? You'd simply march right in and claim what is rightfully yours.

When working with the creative process, you claim what is already yours. As an expression of the Infinite, it's all available to you now. You are already a winner as an expression of God. Go claim what has already been given. The principle of success prospers you now! You'll find success surrounds you with all that is necessary for you to step into your good. And, the principle of success will be manifested for those you love, too. Everyone we are with will also be prospering. Everything your thoughts touch, prospers because you have claimed your good.

Spiritual Contemplation: Where have you been apprehensive or apologetic in claiming your good?

Affirmation: I joyously and gratefully now claim my good that is waiting for me!

OCTOBER 9

Take Inspired Action

Inspired action comes from the guidance of Spirit, not ego. When in doubt, don't. Inspired action is responsive, not reactive. — Annette Vaillancourt

Are you taking inspired action or just going through the motions? Inspired action comes from a place of allowing the joyful manifestation of your desires. When you are "going through the motions" you are living by default, doing what you think you "should be" doing or what others expect you to do. "Going through the motions" will leave you frustrated, while inspired action will lead you to create the life you truly desire.

When you act from a place of inspiration and alignment within your true self, you create a positive momentum that attracts opportunities and resources to you. Taking inspired action initiates a flow of energy and momentum that propels you toward your goals. This momentum can lead to a chain reaction of positive outcomes and abundance. When you align with your true purpose and passions, you naturally attract circumstances that support your dreams and aspirations. By taking inspired action, you tap into the abundance that exists within and around you, creating a positive ripple effect that attracts more opportunities and prosperity into your life.

Spiritual Contemplation: In what ways are you "going through the motions" instead of taking inspired action? How can you shift to act from a place of inspiration?

Affirmation: My intuition guides me to take inspired action to fulfill my dreams and desires!

OCTOBER 10

Find Your Place

When you undervalue what you do, the world will undervalue who you are. –
Oprah Winfrey

A father wanting to pass along to his son a 200-year-old watch given to him by his grandfather, asked him to go to the local watch shop and see how much they would give him for it. When he returned he told his dad they offered him ten-dollars for the watch because it was old. His dad then asked him to see what he could get for the watch at the local coffee shop. When his son returned he said the best he could get for it was five-dollars because it was old. Finally, his father told him to take the watch to the museum and show it to the curator. When he returned to his father he was stunned because the museum had offered him one-million-dollars for this rare piece.

The father wanted his son to know the right places value you in the right way. Don't find yourself in the wrong place and getting upset if you are not valued. The right places for your unique gifts honor what you have to offer. Don't stay in places where your worth is not valued. Find a place that recognizes your creative gifts and share yourself there.

Spiritual Contemplation: Is there a place in your life where you are not valued and seen for the gifts you bring? Are you using your energy to strive and prove your value to others, rather than channeling it into your creativity?

Affirmation: I find myself with those who appreciate who I am!

OCTOBER 11

Clarity + Purpose = Abundance

If one advances confidently in the direction of his dreams, and endeavors to live the life which he has imagined, he will meet with a success unexpected in common hours. – Henry David Thoreau

The key to building an abundant and prosperous life is having a clear vision of what you want and aligning your actions with your purpose. This involves understanding your values, passions, and long-term goals which then guides your actions and choices. It is important to become laser-focused on what you truly want to experience and where you want to go. This helps you stay on track and avoid distractions and other less-important endeavors that will try to steal your energy and time.

Ultimately, clarity and purpose empower you to live a life of intention and meaning. They guide your pursuit of abundance and encourage you to make choices that lead to a more fulfilling and prosperous existence. When you know who you are, what you want, and why you want it you can create a life that aligns with your deepest desires and values.

Spiritual Contemplation: What is your vision of a fulfilling and abundant life? What is it that you want to create in your life and why? Allow a fully formed vision for your life to emerge, and then focus on keeping it at the forefront of your mind, guiding your actions and choices.

Affirmation: I know who I am, what I want, and why! The Universe supports me in manifesting all I desire.

OCTOBER 12

House Of A Thousand Mirrors

Life is a mirror and will reflect back to the thinker what he thinks into it. –
Ernest Holmes

A guy was griping to a wise woman about how much of a struggle his life was. He carried on about never having enough money, people betraying him, no one listening to him and never being able to get ahead. He wanted to know what he could do to change it all. The woman chuckled and told him the story of the house of a thousand mirrors. In the tale, a young child sneaks in every day to play with a thousand of her friends. She claps her hands and a thousand children clap theirs. She smiles and sees a thousand happy children around her.

An angry man once visited this same house of a thousand mirrors. Inside, he saw a thousand vicious faces staring back at him. When he raised his fist to strike, a thousand fists raised against him. He found it terrifying and couldn't leave the house fast enough. A wise woman explained, "Your life is like a house of a thousand mirrors. What you give out comes back multiplied. You live in an expanding universe that amplifies what you project. Heaven or hell—it's up to you."

Spiritual Contemplation: Take an objective look at your life and see what is increasing right now. Do you like what is going on? Consider that your life is just a mirror of your consciousness. Do you feel like changing the original thought? Do that now, and hold a new image up for your enchanted journey.

Affirmation: The mirror of my mind reflects my ever increasing abundant good!

OCTOBER 13

Cultivate a Giving Heart

~~◦◖◊◗◦~~

Do not judge, and you will not be judged; do not condemn, and you will not be condemned. Forgive, and you will be forgiven; give, and it will be given to you. A good measure, pressed down, shaken together, running over, will be put into your lap; For the measure you give will be the measure you get back. — Luke 6: 37-38, NRSVA

There is a law of Cause and Effect that affects each of us, and our life experiences stem from our core attitudes, including our mindsets, ways of being, and the choices we make in life. The scripture from Luke gives us clear direction on how to shift from a limited experience to one of freedom and abundance. We do this by cultivating a giving heart.

A giving heart is one that doesn't judge or condemn. It forgives and does not hold on to resentments and grudges. It is generous, giving of its time and kindness. The generous heart is the new cause that creates an experience of abundance and overflow. The gifts we receive are more love, more joy, and a deeper connection to Spirit and Life. As we open and share our hearts freely, we are gifted with all the blessings and abundance of Life itself.

Spiritual Contemplation: Today, practice opening your heart in a new way. What judgments are you holding onto? What past resentments are you ready to release? Who are you being called to forgive? Write a letter to the universe sharing what you are ready to do to cultivate a more giving heart.

Affirmation: My heart is open and I share my love with the world!

OCTOBER 14

Pennies from Heaven

If it's a penny for your thoughts and you put in your two cents worth, then someone, somewhere is making a penny. — Steven Wright

When pennies are given as change, they are often left on the counter. If they aren't thrown out, they may end up in a penny jar, never seeing the light of circulation again. Though much attention is not given to a penny anymore, like the days of penny postcards and penny candy, it's amazing how when one is spotted on the ground, it can stop the most affluent in their tracks to bend over and pick it up.

The recipient of that penny will often smile as if they have found gold. Placed before the beneficiary, is a message dropped from heaven, In God We Trust. That receiver's thoughts have been transported to check in with God. Their momentary contemplation to remember, to trust God, adds blessings to them and the collective consciousness. This momentary reflective affirmation instantly changes mental dynamics from concerns, to blessings. What great value that little copper coin carries!

Spiritual Contemplation: When was the last time you stooped down to pick up a penny? Did you think about the statement, In God We Trust? Did it shift your mood for a moment, as if you had been blessed?

Affirmation: I trust in God in all things!

OCTOBER 15

Struggling Financially? Check Your Self-worth

True abundance isn't based on our net worth, it's based on our self-worth. –
Gabrielle Bernstein

How you esteem yourself can get in the way of experiencing abundance and prosperity in life. Your sense of self-worth can influence your financial abundance. If you feel undeserving or unworthy of success, financial or otherwise, you may struggle with managing the components of your life effectively, especially your money.

The good news is that when you learn to value yourself and your self-esteem increases, your relationship to success shifts, creating a healthier relationship with money. People with a healthy sense of self-worth are more likely to recognize and pursue opportunities. Self-worth enhances confidence and belief in your own capabilities. When you believe in yourself, you are more likely to take inspired action leading to positive outcomes. When you believe you deserve success and abundance, you are more open to seizing opportunities as they pop up in your life. The truth is that each of us is a uniquely special spiritual being worthy of all life's blessings.

Spiritual Contemplation: Take some time to journal about your experience of self-worth and abundance. Look at your relationship to finances and abundance as well as how you esteem yourself.

Affirmation: I am a unique spiritual being worthy of all life's blessings!

OCTOBER 16

Plugging into the Current

Thoughts are mental energy; they're the currency that you have to attract what you desire. Learn to stop spending that currency on thoughts you don't want. – Wayne Dyer

Current is movement, and where there is movement, there is life. Imagine that you could plug yourself into a socket that would permit you to connect into the electrical current of the universe. Because this source of energy is omnipresent and infinite, it would give you direct access to immeasurable resources. You are plugged in, and you are the one who turns it on or off, controlling the level of flow.

God Energy never diminishes. It is the constantly available life-sustaining field where you live, move, and have your being. Your intentionality is the plug that opens you to the abundance of the new current. Your enthusiasm is the wholehearted access that strengthens your body, mind, and soul by calling forth the circulation of prosperity. You become the action of God Intelligence made manifest. The energy of the God Mind is your mind and is vitally expressed as your health, abundance, and love.

Spiritual Contemplation: Is there anything blocking the abundance of your incoming Good? How can you be a stronger conduit of God's Good in your world? Where can you give more of who you are?

Affirmation: I am an abundant expression of the affluent flow of life!

OCTOBER 17

You Can Change the World

Pay it Forward people who are crazy enough to think they can change the world are the ones who do. — Steve Jobs

Many years ago the movie Pay It Forward showed what happened when 11-year-old Trevor was given a school assignment to, "Think of an idea to change our world and put it into action." He decided to do a good deed for three people and then asked each of them to 'pay it forward' by doing similarly difficult favors for three others. Before long, his project became a movement, demonstrating how a little love and kindness can really make a difference in the world.

Trevor didn't go out with the intention of changing everything he thought was wrong in the world. He did a small act for someone in his circle and that kindness and generosity was contagious and began to spread. It is part of our nature to give and receive. When we allow ourselves to be part of the Divine Flow of life, our inner life deepens and we experience greater satisfaction. When we are willing to share our lives, our time, our talents and our money with others - everyone wins. We can change the world simply by consciously choosing to be a light to others in great and small ways. Start with a smile and a kind word and you will see how quickly it spreads.

Spiritual Contemplation: Today, think about what small acts you can do to 'pay it forward' and then go out and give! Whether through a smile, kind word or small gesture, allow your presence to be the gift in someone else's day.

Affirmation: God's love flows through me and brightens the world!

OCTOBER 18

Pay It Forward

"You don't pay love back; you pay it forward." - Lily Hardy Hammond, In the Garden of Delight

One day, Nancy Joy, a longtime beloved member of the Seaside Center for Spiritual Living, shared she was gifting $25,000 to start a 'Pay It Forward' Program. Nancy was fulfilling her vision by providing financial support to help others bring their gifts to the world, enabling them to make the difference their hearts desired. She knew the recipient's gift would inspire others to also make a positive difference, creating a ripple effect into the future.

Her gifts brought much opportunity. One artist used her gift to paint an 18'x20' mural in the Center's sanctuary, spreading beauty and peace to all who sit nearby. Visitors carry its healing energy with them, touching lives wherever they go. Another gift helped a naturopathic doctor keep the doors open, allowing healing to continue and joy to spread throughout the community. Support went to many, including a group that created a midweek healing service, attracting attendees who then spread positive vibes. One gift aided a heart attack victim, a sound engineer who returned to oversee soul-inspiring, life-changing events.

This book was published with the aid of Nancy's gift. 100% of its proceeds are directed to Katherine's daughter's college fund. Katherine, who passed away before this book came to fruition, will touch lives into eternity. Her daughter intends on attending medical school. So, your book purchase will help launch a new M.D. in the world.

Spiritual Contemplation: How can you pay a gift forward in a way that inspires someone else to be a blessing, creating a ripple effect that continues to spread into the future?

Affirmation: My gift is a gift that inspires others to give!

OCTOBER 19

Sharing Your Good

Be willing to share your blessings. The only riches that last are the ones that are given away. – David Khalil

Sharing your good or developing what Stephen Covey calls "having an abundance mindset" is a powerful practice in personal and spiritual development. The abundance mindset supports you in realizing that there is always good to share with others. There is no lack of resources for you or anyone because your good is a part of a never-ending wellspring that cannot run dry. It is one whose source is and always will be the infinite wellspring of the Divine.

When you live with an abundance mindset, you experience the pure joy of seeing others succeed, give generously to where you are spiritually fed, and practice random acts of kindness as you give your time, talent, and treasure. When you commit to living a sacred life whole-heartedly, you also commit to walking the altruistic path, realizing that we are all in this life together. As we are generous with one another, we all reach higher ground and prosper.

Spiritual Contemplation: In what areas of your life do you find it easier or more difficult to share your Good? How can you increase your abundance mindset, realizing on a deeper level that you are supported by the abundance of the Universe?

Affirmation: I am Abundant and Prosperous and share my good with the world!

OCTOBER 20

Know You Know before You Go

All misfortune is but a stepping stone to fortune. — Henry David Thoreau

Three monks sat on the shore of their still lake, beginning their morning meditation together, when one stood up and said, "I forgot my mat." He got up, walked serenely across the water to the other side, grabbed a mat from his hut, and returned. The second meditator stood up and said, "I forgot to put my wet laundry out to dry. I'll be right back." He ran across the lake, did his task and came back the same way. The third, and newest monk of the trio, not wanting to be outdone and figuring this was a test, stood up and boldly professed, "Think your skills are greater than mine; watch this!" He sauntered down to the edge of the water, took a large step forward, and proceeded to sink up to his knees. Unflustered, he tried again, and then again. After being amused by this routine for a while, the first monk leaned over to his buddy and asked if they should show the new kid where the stepping stones were located?

Don't allow others' abilities to discourage you or make you feel less than who you are. Remember, it takes learning and developing the secrets of the craft before showing them off. Be patient, gentle, and kind to yourself in your learning process. It will go a long way in evolving your skills.

Spiritual Contemplation: Do you remember a time you knew you weren't ready, but felt you needed to act as if you were, and it didn't turn out so well? What did you learn from that premature display?

Affirmation: I am confident in what I know and what I don't know!

OCTOBER 21

How Comfortable are you with Money?

Your wealth is hiding under the very thing you are afraid to do. It's time to face your fears and take action. Expect Miracles. — Joe Vitale

How comfortable are you with the subject of money? Most people are not comfortable talking about or dealing with issues around money because they have been programmed with limiting beliefs about money. These ideas may sound familiar to you, including "Money doesn't grow on trees," "You have to work hard for every penny," "Money is the root of all evil," and so on. These limiting beliefs cause fear in various ways, including stress, anxiety, confusion, frustration, anger, etc. Though it is easy to become consumed with these fears, we also have an opportunity to elevate our perspective and transcend our fears about money.

Overcoming the fear of money and embracing abundance requires addressing your limiting beliefs and negative thought patterns. This process includes looking closely at where you are now financially and how you got there. Diving into your mind state about your self-worth and fears about money will reveal where your blocks lie. Developing a healthy financial mindset through prayer, gratitude, and education will support you in moving forward in a new way. Money is just money. It is a tool you can use to fulfill your goals and isn't anything to be afraid of. By acknowledging and working through the fear of money, you can open yourself up to the abundance life offers and create a more fulfilling and prosperous journey.

Spiritual Contemplation: How comfortable are you dealing with financial issues and money? What messages did you receive from your parents about money? How do you want to be in relationship with money?

Affirmation: I love money, and all it can do to help me fulfill my dreams!

OCTOBER 22

Be Intentional About Your Prosperity

Plant seeds of happiness, hope, success, and love; it will all come back to you in abundance. This is the law of nature. – Steve Maraboli

Living a spiritual existence includes all aspects of your life, including your finances. When you dedicate yourself to a spiritual path, you no longer operate under the world's laws and limitations, instead you fall under the laws of the Spirit. This means that your financial circumstance is the same as your health, relationships, creativity, and work life. You are called to be proactive in creating the inner mindset of abundance and possibility to manifest the experience of prosperity in your experience.

Being intentional and proactive in your financial life empowers you to build a strong foundation for your future and increases your ability to weather any financial challenges that may arise. Taking charge of your finances cultivating an abundance mindset and understanding the principles of prosperity. This knowledge empowers you to make informed decisions that can lead to a sense of security, freedom, and abundance in your life.

Spiritual Contemplation: How intentional are you in your finances? How can you work proactively to build your abundance mindset and trust of yourself and the Universe?

Affirmation: I trust the infinite nature of the Universe and embrace my abundance and prosperity in all ways.

OCTOBER 23

Bedazzled

Pursue what catches your heart, not what catches your eyes. — Roy T. Bennett

Have you ever found yourself chasing the shiny things? Do you jump from one pursuit to another because you have quickly lost interest with what you are working on? Why do you sometimes become bedazzled by what's just beyond your reach, getting sidetracked into pursuing it when you're trying to focus on something else? Dissatisfaction can be a creative state, but it can also be a distraction from going deeper. Remember, you have to go below the surface if you want to find the true gems.

Either you are the master of your world or it masters you, pulling you from one undertaking to the next. You can either be the chess piece moved around in the game of life or the chess master who does not fall prey to alluring traps. You have to see things as they are and, sometimes, sincere people are sincerely wrong. Take time to reflect and listen to your heart before chasing after something else.

Spiritual Contemplation: When did you chase a 'sparkling opportunity' that pulled you away from what you were really supposed to be doing? What did you lose? Was what you gained worth it?

Affirmation: I choose wisely from the choices presented to me!

OCTOBER 24

Givingness is Godliness!

It takes time to practice generosity, but being generous is the best use of our time.
— Thich Nhat Hanh

There is a kind of vegetable grown in Vietnam called he (pronounced "hey"). It belongs to the onion family and looks like a scallion. The more you cut the plants at the base, the more they grow. If you don't cut them, they won't grow very much. But if you cut them often, right at the base of the stalk, they grow bigger and bigger. This is also true of the practice of sacred giving. If you give and continue to give, you become continually richer in terms of happiness and well-being. This may seem strange but it is always true.

Our experience is measured not by who we are but by what we give to the world around us. Giving of yourself in sacred service to others and the world, sharing your time, talents and treasure all open a channel of giving and receiving in your experience. We move into a space of Divine Flow and everything that we need and desire finds its way to us. Feeling stuck? Find a way to give and watch as that stuck-ness begins to dissolve.

Spiritual Contemplation: As you contemplate this idea today, look for areas in your life where giving is challenging. What is difficult for you to give? Your time? Expertise? Money? Be gentle with yourself and observe which areas feel more stuck than others. Take a few moments to breathe into the idea of giving and see if it shifts and changes. Note this in your journal.

Affirmation: I give of myself freely to the world around me!

OCTOBER 25

Working Smart

Learning how to be still, to really be still and let life happen - that stillness
becomes a radiance. – Morgan Freeman

Two lumberjacks argued over who could chop more wood in a day. They started at the same pace, but within an hour, the first lumberjack noticed his friend stop chopping. Seeing a chance to pull ahead, he worked even harder. Ten minutes later, his friend resumed chopping, and their paces matched again. This cycle repeated, with the second lumberjack stopping every hour while the first kept working. By the end of the day, the first lumberjack was confident he had won, but to his surprise, his friend had cut more trees. He asked his partner, "How could you have possibly cut more trees than me, when you were stopping every hour?" The second lumberjack answered with a grin, "I was sharpening my ax."

Working smart enhances hard work. There are 'tricks-to-the-trade'. When applying spiritual principles to your life, you can try to coerce the Universe to respond to you. Or, you can choose grace by allowing the Universe to work through you. Forcing your way through life quickly creates resistance, whereby allowing Spirit to guide your life sharpens your spiritual tools. Remember to pause throughout the day to reconnect with source.

Spiritual Contemplation: Where are you attempting to muscle your way through life? Where can you step back for a bit and allow love to guide your work?

Affirmation: I work at my perfect pace with God!

OCTOBER 26

What Have You Got to Give?

When we're not receiving all the blessings we desire, it is because we're not sharing with others the blessings that we have in a wise and openhearted way. – Ernest Holmes

Practicing giving-ness and cultivating generosity are creative acts that cultivate energy and movement in your life. These are some of the best healing practices you can do. For example, if you are feeling stuck and stagnant, facing a financial challenge, or experiencing feelings of loneliness or being lost, that is precisely the moment to lean in and give something to get the energy moving again.

Most of us hit a rough patch and pull back, separate, and hold back. But this alone will stop the Divine flow. It is the act of turning off the faucet when what we actually want to do is open it wide that is flawed. What can you give? It may not be a financial gift, but you have so much to share with the world. Maybe your gift is one of sharing your time with a worthy non-profit or in the service of a friend in need, or you have some items you are no longer using that can be better served with someone else. Or perhaps you share your gift simply through a a kind word to a stranger in the grocery line. When we share ourselves in a "wise and openhearted way", we open the spigot and welcome the Divine flow into our lives.

Spiritual Contemplation: Contemplate the ways you are currently sharing your blessings and wisdom with the world. See if you can think of three new ways you can share yourself.

Affirmation: I give my love to the world and I receive the blessings of God!

OCTOBER 27

Every Step of the Way is The Way

Your life's work is to find your life's work-and then to exercise the discipline, tenacity, and hard work it takes to pursue it. – Oprah Winfrey

In the business world, keeping the faith longer than most is called tenacity. Before a person is successful they may appear to others as crazy, impractical and irrational. If you are to succeed you must hold your vision while others can't see what you can see, even if they are calling you names. When you align your energies and actions with the Spirit that gave you the vision, all that is needed to make it a reality is already known within that Divine Mind. You are its outlet.

Keep the vision before you, making it more real than all the signs that say it's over. When you continue to put one foot in front of the other in the direction of your vision you'll experience your success as the sum of the many small steps totaling up to your triumph. So continue to put yourself wholeheartedly into every step so every step becomes part of your manifested destiny.

Spiritual Contemplation: Write out the vision you are wholeheartedly giving yourself to now. What is calling you to pursue it with time, energy and treasures? If this page is still blank, where is your time and energy being spent?

Affirmation: Every step I take with its twist and turns leads me to my destiny!

OCTOBER 28

Make a Contribution and Give Back

Remember that the happiest people are not those getting more, but those giving more. — H. Jackson Brown Jr.

Making a contribution and giving back are powerful in building abundance and enriching your life in meaningful and fulfilling ways. Acts of kindness and charitable giving not only benefit others, but also foster a sense of happiness and contentment within yourself. A series of studies found that neurons in the portion of the brain associated with a sense of satisfaction start firing when a person chooses to donate their time or money to an organization or person in need. When you give back to others and contribute to the well-being of your community or the world, you not only make a positive impact but also experience a sense of purpose and abundance within yourself. Finding ways to give back and contribute to causes you care about is important in living wholeheartedly and can support not only the person/group you are serving but enrich your life also.

Spiritual Contemplation: Think about a group or individual whom you are inspired to support. In what ways can you give back with your time, talent, or treasures?

Affirmation: I give freely and support those in need around me with my time, talent and treasure!

OCTOBER 29

No Need for Leftovers

Nature abhors a vacuum. — Aristotle

Abhors is a strange word; it means to despise or strongly dislike. Yet, Aristotle made his lasting point that nature contains no vacuums because the denser immediately fills the void. When you get out of a hot tub, the space in the water from your body does not remain. It doesn't matter how many waves you may have been making, it doesn't hold its shape when you are gone. Maybe you have noticed when you donate some clothes in your closet, it doesn't seem to take long for it to be filled again.

This is why it is important for you to be proactive and conscious of what you want to fill the new available space with after you have done the work to clear out the old. Life will tend to fill it rather quickly with the denser leftovers. You'll want to be clear what new clothes you now want to fill that space. You wouldn't want last year's styles in today's world. If you have cleared space for a new relationship, you wouldn't want somebody's else's rejection sporting the issues you've worked hard to leave behind. If you have cleaned up your finances, you don't want to fill the void with the next poor decision. Get clear about what you want in your available space, and go get it.

Spiritual Contemplation: What clutter needs to be cleared from your life and mind? What does the new occupant of this space look like?

Affirmation: The space I clear, I fill with good!

OCTOBER 30

How Full is Your Fullness of Life?

Gratitude unlocks the fullness of life. It turns what we have into enough, and more. It turns denial into acceptance, chaos to order, confusion to clarity. It can turn a meal into a feast, a house into a home, a stranger into a friend. – Melody Beattie

Shrink wrap was a brilliant invention. The scientific genius of it is that it always shrinks down to the exact size of whatever it has been wrapped around. Whether it's a piece of beef jerky or a mattress being delivered, the plastic molecules contour to the shape of the item to preserve and protect it. Lack and limitation work in a similar manner in our lives, but in a negative way. They confine us to a limited perspective that prevents us from experiencing the abundance and fullness of life all around us. We can't reach it because we are held back by our own ideas of worthiness."

We can break free from this confinement through a regular practice of contemplating possibility and potential. When we remember that this is an abundant universe and we are part of it, we begin to remember not only our worthiness but also, our ability to experience the fullness and joy of life itself.

Spiritual Contemplation: What ideas are keeping you shrink-wrapped to lack and limitation? How can you break free and accept your Divine birthright?

Affirmation: I am one with the Divine and experience the fullness of life here and now.

OCTOBER 31

All-Hallows Eve

They who dream by day are cognizant of many things which escape those who dream only by night. – Edgar Allan Poe, The Tell-Tale Heart

Halloween celebrations can be found all the way back to the ancient Gaelic festival of Samhain. At that time, November 1st was the beginning of the New Year. This day marked the end of summer, the harvest, and the beginning of the dark, cold winter, a time of year that was often associated with human death. The Celtic belief was that on the eve before the new year, the boundary between the worlds of the living and the dead become blurred. The spirit world becomes visible. The Celts believed it was important to have the harvest in from the fields before Samhain, otherwise the spirits would play tricks with the harvest on the eve of the dark half of the year. They felt it was smart to leave treats or harvest offerings to placate the spirits.

Since then, Christians folded some of the ancient celebrations into All Saints' Day or All Hallows' Day to honor those who have departed this world. It can be empowering to connect with your ancestors. You don't need to hang out at their grave and have a picnic while watching a Netflix show on your computer with your departed loved one, as some cultures might practice today. Yet, with so many believing in this day that the connection is clearer, just maybe, the veil is a little thinner? Though, there is always "magic" in the multidimensional connector of love that transcends time and space. Why not invite a beautiful memory of a loved one who has moved on from this world into your awareness this evening?

Spiritual Contemplation: Create a sacred space where you can sit uninterrupted for a while. Activate your heart to call in memories of loving times with special people who are no longer in this world. Your treats await at the portal of time.

Affirmation: I am available to the omnipresent love connection that transcends time and space!

NOVEMBER

Gratitude

November 1-7

Frequency Shifter

November 8-14

Eyes of the Beholder

November 15-21

The Divine Flow

November 22-30

I am Blessed

NOVEMBER 1

Heaven on Earth

⚘

An attitude of gratitude is most salutary and bespeaks the realization that we
are now in heaven. – Ernest Holmes

Many holy ones, including Jesus, taught that we can create heaven or hell right here on earth. Our experience of life can be one of freedom and joy or it can be painful and fraught with challenge. It is up to us as to which we choose to create. We have the power in any one moment to shift and change our experience. We do this through our minds, thoughts, and subsequently, our actions.

When we begin to realize that we are part of a larger life, part of God, itself, and that we are the manifestation of the Divine, we see ourselves and live differently. We trust Life to bring opportunities to us for our growth and expansion. We share our gifts more freely, no longer hiding who we are from the world, and that makes all the difference. When we fully express ourselves in the world, we welcome the Divine into our day-to-day experience and when we practice gratitude on top of that – watch out! We begin to call all the things that bring peace and joy to us and we begin to live in heaven, right here on earth.

Spiritual Contemplation: Are you currently creating Heaven or Hell in your world? How can you shift to welcome more of the Divine into your day-to-day experience? Begin creating more Heaven and less Hell.

Affirmation: I am One with God and Grateful for my Life! I create Heaven right here and now!

NOVEMBER 2

Praise It To Raise It

God made man merely to hear some praise of what he'd done on those Five Days. — Christopher Morley

If you want to put a twinkle in someone's eyes, praise them. It is something that instantly lifts their spirit like a balloon lifting off. Mark Twain said, "I could live for two months on a good compliment." We often underestimate the power of a kind word, warm smile, or attentive heart. More people than you know are struggling. With a touch of encouragement and praise from you, it can improve their day and even turn things around for them.

A compliment is like a kiss, it can really get things going. Charles Fillmore stated, "We increase whatever we praise. The whole creation responds to praise, and is glad." Everyone is happy to receive a sincere compliment. It doesn't cost you anything to give a little love that way and it instantly transforms the moment. In the presence of a compliment, fear drops away and the vibrational frequency becomes lighter and brighter. If someone is about to step into a meeting, onto a stage, or faces an intense moment, remember, your words of praise and encouragement do make a difference.

Spiritual Contemplation: Give at least three compliments today, four tomorrow and five the next day. Experience the vibrational shift your encouragement makes in the recipient … and yours too!

Affirmation: It's my joy to praise, encourage and give compliments!

NOVEMBER 3

Seeing the Fullness

As you wander on through life, sister/ brother, whatever be your goal, keep your eye upon the donut, and not upon the hole. – Sign in the Mayflower coffee shop in Chicago

Where we put our attention makes a big difference in our lives. The difference between an optimist and a pessimist is that the pessimist exercises muscles of negativity, while the optimist is grateful they have muscles to exercise at all. The quote above reminds us how easy it is to overlook the abundance in our lives and focus on the areas that may be lacking. It is easy to fall into the habit of only acknowledging where we are missing out or struggling, often overlooking the areas of our lives that are working and abundant.

Truthfully, it's all there at any one moment. The practice of Gratitude helps us see the blessings already happening around us more clearly. A regular Gratitude practice also increases the abundance of our lives as it is magnetic and attracts even more blessings to us. If you are feeling low or lost, begin to look around your world to find what you are grateful for. It may be as simple as having a roof over your head or your next full breath. This will help you begin to shift your sight and then your experience will reflect that shift from one of lack to one of the fullness of life.

Spiritual Contemplation: Today, make a list of 50 things that you are grateful for in your life. Take the time to dig deep to find the areas that are working and begin to expand your spiritual sight and experience.

Affirmation: I am grateful for my life, and I live from the fullness!

NOVEMBER 4

Gratitude, A Frequency Shifter

Appreciation is a wonderful thing: It makes what is excellent in others belong to us as well. — Voltaire

People work better and put forth a greater effort with approval than with criticism. It's been said that encouragement is oxygen for the soul. People want to be recognized and appreciated for their contributions. Achievement is motivating, but it feels even better when noticed. What does it cost you to say, "Way to go, nice job!"? The key is to be sincere. No one wants to be manipulated with false praise. It dissolves trust and the relationship.

Keep your eyes open and try to catch people doing something right and then praise them for it. Unexpressed gratitude is like having a gift for someone and not giving it to them. What value is there to that? Keeping your appreciation silent is not much of a blessing to another. Showing gratitude is a simple, transformative and uplifting gift you can give another person. It's also impossible for you to feel depressed and grateful at the same time. Gratitude is a frequency that shifts everything.

Spiritual Contemplation: Catch people doing good and gratefully praise them.

Affirmation: I feel good about the good people are doing!

NOVEMBER 5

Ever-Available Cosmic Current

The contemplative mind, attempting its return to divinity, is constantly dragged
back toward the senses by the life currents. — *Paramahansa Yogananda*

If you break a lamp at home, you still have electricity. If your body breaks down, for whatever reason, you still have the life force that is available to you. You bring health and harmony back into your experience by plugging back into the source. When a lamp breaks, you sweep up the pieces, get a new lamp, and plug it into the same wall socket. The energy was still available, unchanged by the lamp's breaking. Your body is a bit different in that you don't get rid of it when it breaks. Instead, you adjust what is broken in your finite thinking by reconnecting with the still ever available Infinite Source.

Your wellspring is inexhaustible and serves your health and well-being. Stop trying to patch up conditions with your prayers. Spiritual harmony isn't something you add to human situations; it's always available. Transcend your desire to fix the physical world by staying centered in the Omnipresence of God. In this state of mind, you will know peace, safety, and wholeness, and your world will naturally shift for the better. It's not that Spirit suddenly comes along to fix the human realm; it's that you are no longer at the mercy of fragmented circumstances. By connecting with the ever-available cosmic current, you feel the Divine Presence, which naturally shines in your life as wholeness, harmony, and abundance.

Spiritual Contemplation: How often do I attempt to understand the Infinite with my limited human perspective rather than feel it with my unbounded soul? Where can I better realize the Divine Presence in the midst of my confusion?

Affirmation: I go to God for God!

NOVEMBER 6

Take a Walk

The true miracle is not walking on water or walking in air, but simply walking on this earth. — *Thich Nhat Hanh*

Another way to practice gratitude is by taking what's called a 'mindful walk'. This is a form of mindfulness that involves being fully present during your walk. It can be done in any setting, whether it be a busy street or quiet trail. This practice involves waking up to where you are and taking in the environment around you. When you combine this mindfulness with a feeling of gratitude, you begin to appreciate the world around you in a new way.

To begin your walk, start by noticing your environment and engaging all your senses. Listen for the birds, feel the air on your skin, see your surroundings, smell the odors of nature or the city. Become present and take in these sensations. Then, as you are walking, identify the things you are grateful for. This can be anything including what you are experiencing, the strength of your body allowing you to walk, or even just for having the gift of a moment of peace in your day. As you acknowledge each thing you are grateful for, say a silent "thank you". After your walk, take a few moments for reflection to deepen the experience. The goal of a mindful gratitude walk is not to force feelings of gratitude but to create a space where you can notice and appreciate all the things you're grateful for in your life.

Spiritual Contemplation: Take a mindfulness walk as your spiritual practice today. Notice how it feels to become present and engage with your surroundings in this new way. Journal your reflections after completing your walk.

Affirmation: With each step, I am awake and aware of all I have to be grateful for in my life!

NOVEMBER 7

Drop a Sticky Note!

Gratitude can transform common days into thanksgiving, turn routine jobs into joy, and change ordinary opportunities into blessings. — Proverb

I was moved by a story I saw recently about a young woman and her stepfather. Upon her high school graduation, she gave him a beautiful gift. Each day of her high school career, he wrote a positive message on a sticky note and added it to her lunch. She saved all the notes and framed them and gave them back to him on her graduation day as a gift of appreciation. His small daily act of support made a huge difference in her life. She shared that there were times when she felt discouraged and alone until she opened her lunch and there, she found his beloved words of wisdom and comfort. It supported her through the rough times and she wanted to give that loving support right back to him.

We talk about the powerful exercise of writing gratitude letters and how it supports both the sender and receiver. But shorter notes and cards, even electronic ones, can be equally effective and moving. The message can be brief, it simply needs to be honest and heartfelt. Just a few sentences to remind someone of their impact on you and how it made you feel is really all that is required. Send that email or write that sticky note and you will share your love and light out into the world.

Spiritual Contemplation: Who can you send a quick note or email of gratitude to today? Take a moment to write a brief message and send it. Share your love with the world. Notice how it feels to do this, and jot down your thoughts in your journal.

Affirmation: I am a channel of divine gratitude and thanksgiving! I share my love freely with all!

NOVEMBER 8

Grateful for it All

In all things, give thanks. – 1 Thessalonians 5:18, DRA

The bible reminds us of the importance of a regular gratitude practice. It is reminding us that we are to practice gratitude for the totality of our lives, not just the moments of peace and plenty. It teaches that we are to be grateful for it all – the good, the bad and everything in between. We mustn't wait until everything is okay with us or the rest of the world in order to be grateful because we might not ever get there.

This scripture calls us to expand our ability to practice gratitude, even for the difficult things that challenge us. When we do this, we start to experience the magic of gratitude. While gratitude may not eliminate suffering, it makes it easier to bear and amplifies the good in our lives. We don't deny suffering or hardship, but we also don't let it blind us to the beauty and joy around us, regardless of what else is happening. Regularly practicing gratitude for all experiences opens us up to welcoming greater blessings into our lives.

Spiritual Contemplation: Take some time today to contemplate how the biggest challenge you are currently facing is actually a blessing in your life. Write about it in your journal.

Affirmation: In all things I give thanks!

NOVEMBER 9

The Past as a Gift

Bitterness is like cancer. It eats upon the host. — *Maya Angelou*

Do not waste your time on needless regret and bitterness. Being bitter impacts every aspect of your life. The poison moves not only through your mind but through your body as well. If you wonder why your vitality is low, it's time to recognize that living in bitterness sucks out your life force. You might have a valid reason for your upset, but is it worth ruining your life over? Stewing in your upset only circulates the poison, denying your availability to life-healing opportunities.

Are you still angry about what happened to you as a child or in a past relationship? Do you keep rehashing a devastating financial loss in your mind? Maybe you were treated unfairly, and you just want someone to understand how badly it hurt. You weren't created to suffer, but disappointments can happen. Through forgiveness, you can transform pain into revelation by seeing every experience in your past as a gift. Any action that seems to block your good, Infinite Intelligence can turn into a blessing. The Creative Mind always knows how to make things right, but are you open to allowing it?

Spiritual Contemplation: Where have you allowed the root of bitterness to grow into bitter fruit? What can you do to uproot those bitter thoughts of the past that you are allowing to poison your life today?

Affirmation: I now find calm clarity guiding my thinking!

NOVEMBER 10

You've Got A Text

The more you praise and celebrate your life, the more there is in life to celebrate.
— *Oprah Winfrey*

When you text a message of appreciation to someone, it feels good. Often, the blessing of gratitude is as much for the giver as it is for the receiver. When you receive a thank-you text, it brings joy and a sense of connection, knowing you touched someone's life.

So, when was the last time you texted yourself a note of gratitude for a life well lived so far? How about a pat on the back for navigating this amazing journey without a map? Have you taken a moment to thank yourself for the lessons learned—and even those not yet learned? Have you recently sent yourself a love note of appreciation, acknowledging the incredible job you're doing in this human experience, despite all its twists, turns, and surprises?

Spiritual Contemplation: Go ahead and text yourself a wholehearted gratitude note now.

Affirmation: I am grateful to myself for how I have made it to this point in my life!

NOVEMBER 11

Veterans Day

~~⁓℘⁓℘⁓

The willingness with which our young people are likely to serve in any war, no matter how justified, shall be directly proportional to how they perceive the Veterans of earlier wars were treated and appreciated by their nation. – George Washington

Take a moment of silence this Veterans Day at 11 o'clock to honor those who served in the United States Military. This time and date honor when the Allies and Germany implemented an armistice at the eleventh hour of the eleventh day of the eleventh month in 1918, marking the end of the 'War to End All Wars.' You will be joining other allies in Canada, Australia, and Great Britain who observe November 11th Remembrance Day.

Norman Schwarzkopf stated, "It doesn't take a hero to order men or women into battle. It takes a hero to be one of those who goes into battle." As a nation, we have learned that in war, there are no unwounded soldiers. Yet the brave knowingly go out to meet the danger and glory that awaits them. There was something inside these young men and women that was more than muscle; it was a will to do whatever it takes. Douglas MacArthur said, "Americans never quit." American Veterans embody the ideals upon which America was founded in 1776 and those ideals of freedom still live to this day because of the United States Military Veterans of War.

Spiritual Contemplation: At 11 A.M., take a moment to fully appreciate those who served in the military to secure your freedom. Then, reflect on how you are using that freedom in your life.

Affirmation: I am grateful to those who fought for freedom!

NOVEMBER 12

Being Grateful Even if You Don't Feel It

Be thankful for what you have; you'll end up having more. If you concentrate on what you don't have, you will never, ever have enough. — Oprah Winfrey

Sometimes it is hard to be grateful for the situations in your life. Maybe you got laid off, received a scary diagnosis, or are in the midst of a challenging financial situation. No matter the case, it can be hard to feel appreciation in difficult times. It is important to remember that cultivating gratitude isn't always easy. It is a practice that takes patience, consistency, and commitment. But practicing gratitude does always make a difference. Over time, a consistent gratitude practice changes your outlook on your life. You become more optimistic, hopeful and can see that even though you are in a rough spot, there is always something to be grateful for.

You can still express gratitude even when things don't go as planned. Perhaps you received a gift that wasn't what you hoped for, or a gathering didn't turn out as expected. By finding something to appreciate, even in these moments, you create a gratitude feedback loop that brings you closer to what you want. This practice helps you recognize and value the people in your life, which, in turn, multiplies positivity. Committing to daily gratitude can lift your spirits and help you bounce back from any challenge you face.

Spiritual Contemplation: How can you practice gratitude when you don't naturally feel it? Make a list of five ways you can share appreciation in the midst of a challenge.

Affirmation: No matter the situation, I am always grateful for my life!

NOVEMBER 13

Eyes of the Beholder

~⚬⚬⚬~

People often say that 'beauty is in the eye of the beholder,' and I say that the most liberating thing about beauty is realizing that you are the beholder. This empowers us to find beauty in places where others have not dared to look, including inside ourselves. — *Salma Hayek*

There was a caring and involved father who wanted to teach his son that not all families were as affluent as theirs. He arranged for them to spend the day at a family farm outside the city. On the ride home, the father asked his son if he had learned anything. "Oh yes, Dad," the boy replied. "I learned that we have a dog and a cat, but they have a whole barn of animals. We have a pool in our backyard, but they have a lake in their front yard. We have a porch where we watch cars go by, but they have a horizon where they can see the sun rise on one side of their house and set behind the mountains on the other. We have imported lamps to see at night, and they have fireflies and stars. Thank you, Dad, for showing me how poor we are."

Perspective lies in the eye of the beholder. How you choose to see life is how life responds to you. You are living in an abundant universe that expands right where you place your gratitude.

Spiritual Contemplation: What are some of your perspectives that could use an uplift?

Affirmation: I see the abundance of God in all things!

NOVEMBER 14

Mark the Moment

When you arise in the morning give thanks for the food and for the joy of living. If you see no reason for giving thanks, the fault lies only in yourself. — *Tecumseh*

Many studies have shown that expressing gratitude regularly can increase your happiness and reduce symptoms of depression. When you realize what you are grateful for, you focus on the positive aspects of your life, which helps shift your mindset and boost your mood. This is called cultivating a Gratitude Mindset. Over time, you will find it easier to notice and appreciate the positive aspects of your life, which can improve your overall mental and emotional well-being.

One way to cultivate a Gratitude Mindset is to mark the moment. When you find yourself enjoying something—a delicious meal, a beautiful view, a favorite song, or time with a trusted friend—take a moment to express your gratitude. Pausing to breathe and recognize that all is well in that moment will help you see the blessings in your life more clearly, guiding you to live with a Gratitude Mindset.

Spiritual Contemplation: Practice cultivating a Gratitude Mindset today by marking the moments when you feel grateful. It could be for any reason, large or small. Take the time to breathe and feel your appreciation.

Affirmation: I am grateful for each and every moment of my life!

NOVEMBER 15

I Remember Forgetting

Without forgetting it is quite impossible to live at all. – Friedrich Nietzsche

Picture a young lad going to school, already deeply spiritually aware but socially awkward. He walked through the schoolyard to the beat of a different drummer. In elementary school, one of the bigger kids always made fun of him. In junior high, the same kid continued to harass him. By high school, he began to appreciate his intuitive sensitivity more, though it made the bullying situation even more unpleasant. A couple of decades later, the tormentor started seeking his own path to spirituality. He decided it was time to immerse himself in a spiritual program and find a community to deepen his journey.

He enrolled in a spiritual school and joined several self-help programs. To his surprise, the spiritual leader he admired turned out to be the very kid he had harassed in school all those years ago. To his amazement, he was welcomed with open arms and a big hug by the master teacher. One day, he decided to address the cruelty he had shown the spiritual leader in their childhood. But the teacher seemed not to remember the behavior. When the former tormentor asked, "Don't you remember?" the sage replied with a smile, "I clearly remember forgetting it!" They both then burst into laughter.

Spiritual Contemplation: How could your relationship with someone you love improve if you let go of a past incident?

Affirmation: My life is richer because I choose love over pain!

NOVEMBER 16

Verbalize Your Gratitude

Feeling gratitude and not expressing it is like wrapping a present and not giving it. – William Arthur Ward

When we take the time to share gratitude for those in our lives, we strengthen relationships and deepen our connections. It can be challenging for some at first, but speaking our appreciation directly to the person we are grateful for, can be a powerful experience that shifts how we relate to our friends, family, and the world. Verbalizing our gratitude helps others feel appreciated and valued. We strengthen our social connections by thanking those around us for their help or telling a friend what we appreciate about them. This opens lines of communication and shows we care, which can encourage others to be more open with us.

To enhance your relationships, start by sharing your appreciation. Thank someone each day for something they've done, no matter how small. Acknowledge a colleague, friend, family member, or even a stranger. Make a habit of appreciating others, and you'll find your relationships becoming more supportive and strong. It might feel awkward or forced at first, but as you discover your own way of expressing gratitude, it will naturally become a part of your interactions.

Spiritual Contemplation: Take time today to share your appreciation for a friend, colleague, or family member. Tell them what a difference their kindness has made in your experience. Notice how it feels to speak this to them and write about it in your journal.

Affirmation: I speak my love and gratitude freely with those around me!

NOVEMBER 17

Beyond Computer Grasp

~~◦◦◦◦◦~~

Computers are like Old Testament gods; lots of rules and no mercy. — Joseph Campbell

Siri and her friends got us used to conversing with Artificial Intelligence as a common practice. Open AI has gathered its data from the internet, books, websites, articles, social media and has been trained on hundreds of billions of words. Chatbots now generate responses that seem friendly and intelligent. In a style request, they now are producing essays, articles, poetry, and passing the bar. This brings both blessings and deep concern. Is it possible there could be a new common world religion created by an "Unknown Intelligence" where people could actually talk to the "Creator" of the Holy texts for clarification?

The aspect of religion that cannot be replaced by AI, is the felt sense of connectedness with the Living Spirit of God. It is a feeling of gratitude and awe. A perceived reality is in the brain, while the heart and soul is where spirituality thrives. The mystical is a deep connection with the incalculable, a merging with a full spectrum of emotions and feelings, both sensual and soulful. The challenge isn't that computers will think like humans but that humans will begin to think like computers. Life is more than just an intellectual amalgamation. It is a blending of the multidimensional aspects of your being. The wonder of a community of loving family and friends will never be felt and experienced by a computer program. The simple key that takes you beyond a computer's grasp is a feeling of gratitude. Computers do not feel, they compute.

Spiritual Practice: Are there any areas of your life you would like to take back from your time? Reclaim your freedom and power now!

Affirmation: I now feel my inner guidance integrating all aspects of my life!

NOVEMBER 18

Gratitude and Divine Flow

Acknowledging the good that you already have in your life is the foundation for all abundance. – Eckhart Tolle

Practicing gratitude is an important state of consciousness that keeps us aware of our oneness with divine flow. You do not need something to be grateful for. Gratitude is as spontaneous as happiness can be. It is a state of being that flows out from your center and changes not only your own mindset and experience but the experience of all around you. In 1 Thessalonians 5:18, St. Paul urges us to give thanks in all things. This is advanced spiritual work to find a way to be grateful for all things. Being laid off, having a relationship that sours, and losing your health are all things that happen in the normal course of life, and it would be difficult for some to find a way to be grateful for them.

But again, the spiritual path is purposeful and brings experiences to support your growth and evolution. These things may be happening in your life because you have cut yourself off from that divine flow. This is a call to recenter yourself in the awareness of the infinite, abundant nature of the divine and remember that you are connected to it at your core. When you reconnect to your source, which is God, you open that channel of flow and the frustrating experiences will right themselves.

Spiritual Contemplation: What situations in your life arose to remind you of your divine connection? How do you recenter yourself when you feel cut off from the divine flow? Share this in your journal.

Affirmation: I am one with Divine Flow and my life is abundant! I am grateful!

NOVEMBER 19

Lens of Perception

Gratitude is the healthiest of all human emotions. The more you express gratitude for what you have, the more likely you will have even more to express gratitude for. – *Zig Ziglar*

It is through gratitude for the present moment that the spiritual dimension of life opens up. – *Eckhart Tolle*

Make sure you practice gratitude every day. It's a powerful force that energizes everything it touches and instantly refreshes a dreary perspective. It's easy to focus on shortages or problems, but shifting your attitude with gratitude can bring blessings to what you want to enhance. Your finances, business, and relationships all flourish under a shower of gratitude. Gratitude connects you with the source of all blessings.

When you feel overwhelmed, pause and reclaim your thoughts and emotions. Consciously choose to focus on what you're grateful for, and it will feel as if everything has changed in an instant. By changing how you view your challenges, you transform them. Gratitude is a powerful catalyst for positive change, shifting your perception and brightening everything in its path.

Spiritual Contemplation: For the next 21 days, start your mornings writing down a dozen things you are grateful for in your life.

Affirmation: I clearly see and feel how blessed I am!

NOVEMBER 20

Thank a Teacher

As we express our gratitude, we must never forget that the highest appreciation is not to utter words, but to live by them. – John F. Kennedy

Most mothers make a big deal about sending thank-you notes in a timely manner. They will often stand over their child after a birthday party, bar/bat mitzvah or any special occasion pressuring the child to get them done. This is a beneficial habit to have, but the truth is there is no expiration date or statute of limitations on gratitude. It is always beneficial to express your gratitude for someone or something, even if our mothers would cringe at how long it took us to share it! One group I find most appreciative of gratitude is teachers. Teachers are a foundational part of our life's structure. They play an important role in our lives and though sometimes we don't realize it, they have helped shape our paths.

It is never too late to thank a teacher whose presence made a big difference in your life. Reaching out to share your gratitude with that special teacher, whether they were from elementary, middle, high school, or college, can bring you great satisfaction and joy. Imagine the joy a teacher would feel receiving a thank-you note from a student from 20 years ago! If they are no longer teaching or if they have passed from this life, you can still honor them in some special or meaningful way. Let us take the time to honor those who give their gifts for our benefit and thank a teacher today.

Spiritual Contemplation: Make a list of the teachers that made a difference in your life. Choose one person to honor with a note, email, social media post, or any personal way that suits you. Notice how you feel acknowledging their gifts and how you were changed by being in their class.

Affirmation: I am grateful for the many teachers I have had in my life!

NOVEMBER 21

The Broken Tea Cup

When I let go of what I am, I become what I might be. When I let go of what I have, I receive what I need. — *Tao Te Ching*

A Zen master, known for his wisdom, once taught his clever young apprentice a lesson with a precious, ancient teacup. One day, the student accidentally broke the teacup and was deeply unsettled. Hearing his master approach, he placed the pieces on a table behind him and stood before them. When the master arrived, the student asked, "Why do people have to die?"

"It's part of the natural cycles of life," the master explained. "Everything has a time to live and a time to die." The apprentice then revealed the shattered cup, saying, "It was time for your cup to die."

All physical things have a lifespan. There is birth, life and transition. It's true in nature and it's true in the human form. Do not give your power away to form when you are the essence of the power. Appreciate what is in your life and when it is complete do not lose yourself in the loss but be glad and rejoice for the time shared.

Spiritual Contemplation: Where are you holding on to that which has moved on? How can you practice an appreciative release?

Affirmation: I am grateful for the good that has blessed my life and energetically release the good that is no longer part of my world

NOVEMBER 22

Heal with Gratitude

Gratitude is the great multiplier, so say thank you for your health every single day. — Rhonda Byrne

After being diagnosed with stage four metastatic breast cancer, I had a choice to make. I could either succumb to the fear of the unknown, or I could step forward and keep living no matter what I was faced with. I chose the latter and eight years later, here I am typing these words for you. I found that the best way to keep going was by practicing gratitude every day. I found a way to find something within each day that I was grateful for – my husband, who delivered tea to my bedside each morning, the beautiful view at our home, or a kind word shared by a friend or stranger. As I made a point to practice gratitude and appreciation, it snowballed and I found lots of things to be thankful for, even in the really hard times.

We may think that a gratitude practice only supports our emotional and mental well-being, but studies have shown that individuals who practice gratitude regularly tend to take better care of their health, exercise more often, and experience fewer physical symptoms including aches and pains. Practicing gratitude can also help to improve the quality of your sleep, which is very important when you are working on healing physically because it helps to shift your focus away from negative thoughts and worries that can interfere with your rest. You sleep better, your cells recover more easily, and you feel better in your body. This is healing.

Spiritual Contemplation: Are you experiencing any physical challenges in your body? In what ways can you express gratitude to increase your health and vitality? Share your thoughts in your journal.

Affirmation: I am grateful for my life! I am grateful for my body and my health!

NOVEMBER 23

Little Details, Big Impact

Feeling gratitude and not expressing it is like wrapping a present and not giving it. — William Arthur Ward

A woman had worked as a janitor for a company for over two decades— a demanding, thankless job with little recognition. When the company was sold, the new owner took the time to handwrite a thank you note for every employee and had his assistant personally deliver them.

When the janitor received her card, she opened it and began to cry, requesting a moment alone. The assistant, initially concerned for her health, later learned that the janitor had never received a thank you from previous management. She had been contemplating resigning now that the company had changed ownership. The heartfelt note from the new owner moved her deeply, making her feel recognized and valued. The small gesture of appreciation had such a profound impact that she decided to stay with the company.

Spiritual Contemplation: Are there people in your world who you haven't acknowledged lately? Make a list of their names and let them know how much you appreciate them being part of your life. Express the difference they make; you might be surprised what a big impact a little detail might have.

Affirmation: It's my joy to recognize and acknowledge all those who are part of my journey through life!

NOVEMBER 24

Seeing the Good

You cannot have a positive life and a negative mind. — *Joyce Meyers*

Negativity bias refers to the brain's inclination to focus on negative experiences over positive ones. This survival mechanism evolved over millions of years and was a key factor in keeping humans safe from potential dangers and threats. In modern times, however, this bias can cultivate stress and anxiety as it keeps us focused on the negative aspects of life. It skews our perception of the world and our experience in it, training us to overlook positive aspects.

Practicing gratitude helps counteract our natural bias by shifting our focus to the positives in our lives and fostering appreciation for ourselves and our abilities. It trains us to recognize and value the good, cultivating emotions like joy and contentment that can diminish fear and worry. Regular gratitude practice helps rewire the brain to be more attuned to positivity, allowing you to notice and appreciate the good rather than just the negative. While rewiring the brain takes commitment and time, a consistent gratitude practice sets you on the right path.

Spiritual Contemplation: In what area of your life do you have a difficult time seeing the positive? Can you find something within that area to be grateful for? (It could be as simple as being grateful for seeing the problem there!)

Affirmation: I am grateful for it all! I find something to appreciate every day!

NOVEMBER 25

Thought Thieves

The world will persist in exhibiting before you what you persist in affirming the world is. — *Emma Curtis Hopkins*

When there is discord in your life, it reflects discord in your thoughts. If your body is not at ease, it indicates unrest in your thinking. Limitations in your life mirror constrictions in your mindset. As within, so without—form follows consciousness, and the creative process operates on the principle of "It's done unto you as you believe." Just as you wouldn't invite a thief to roam freely in your home, why allow thoughts that can rob you of your greater good and stifle your dreams?

Cherish the sacred space of your inner realm by rejecting unwanted thoughts. When you've had enough of certain mental guests, it's up to you to escort them out of your consciousness. Many thoughts will come knocking, seeking your attention, but you are the one who decides which thoughts are allowed to enter your mental space.

Spiritual Contemplation: When have you allowed your thinking to run off on unhealthy tangents? What were the ensuing results before you evicted the unwanted thought guests? Where might this be happening now?

Affirmation: I am clear in my discernment of the mental guests that come knocking on the door of my consciousness!

NOVEMBER 26

How Blessed I Am

I don't have to chase extraordinary moments to find happiness - it's right in front of me if I'm paying attention and practicing gratitude. — *Brene Brown*

A man was walking along the road, carrying a bag of worldly possessions over his shoulder, visibly upset and mumbling disparaging words He came upon an old man who asked him what was wrong. The disturbed one threw down his bag, kicked it and grumbled, "I can carry everything I own in this miserable old sack." The old one said, "That's too bad," and laughed as he snatched the sack and ran off with it.

Having just lost everything he had, the unhappy one began to cry and contemplated his devolving life now with the loss of all he owned. Eventually, he wiped his tears and headed back down the road, now more depressed than ever. In the meantime, the man who had swiped the bag ran around the corner and left it in the middle of the road. When the downtrodden one turned the corner and found his sack sitting there, he jumped with joy with wholehearted appreciation for what he had.

Sometimes one doesn't realize their own good until it's gone. Losing what is taken for granted can remind you of how blessed you are now. Happily-ever-after is a day-to-day experience. Choose to get your mindset right without the need for loss.

Spiritual Contemplation: What are you taking for granted in your life? How would it feel to be without these? Pause and take a moment to be grateful for the small things in your life.

Affirmation: I see and feel how blessed I am by the small and large things in my life!

NOVEMBER 27

A Letter of Thanks

I awoke this morning with devout thanksgiving for my friends, the old and the new. — Ralph Waldo Emerson

Often, we practice gratitude by making lists of things we appreciate, either in a journal or in our minds. This solitary activity can warm our hearts and uplift our spirits. However, sharing our gratitude with the people we appreciate can be even more healing. Writing a letter of thanks has profound positive effects, even if you never send it. Studies show that writing such letters significantly reduces stress hormones and triggers the release of hormones that support the immune system. Scientists suggest that expressing gratitude activates the brain's reward center, shifting our perspective on the world and ourselves.

Reflecting on those who have supported and loved you fosters feelings of love and appreciation. Taking the time to write a gratitude letter plants these positive emotions deep within you, enhancing your relationships and leading to greater satisfaction and happiness.

Spiritual Contemplation: Write a letter to someone you're grateful for but haven't had the chance to properly thank. You don't have to send it, just writing it can foster feelings of gratitude. If you do decide to send it, journal your experience and see if adding a letter of thanksgiving each week could be a beneficial part of your spiritual practice.

Affirmation: I am grateful for those who support and love me in my life! I share my love and gratitude freely!

NOVEMBER 28

Thanksgiving Initiates Love's Flow

It is through gratitude for the present moment that the spiritual dimension of life opens up. — *Eckhart Tolle*

Thanksgiving embodies a deep love for life, revealing endless things to be grateful for when you truly pay attention. Gratitude shifts your perspective from limitation to abundance, drawing you closer to the spiritual realm. It transforms a routine day into one of thanksgiving, elevates a simple meal to a feast, and turns challenges into opportunities.

The more you express gratitude, the more you find to be grateful for. All that is needed for your fulfillment is already part of Infinite Consciousness, which is your true identity. Thanksgiving resonates with the frequency of Love's expression, moving gratitude from mere thought to heartfelt experience.

Spiritual Contemplation: Make a list of everything you're grateful for in your life, including the challenges you've faced. Consider how these difficulties might be viewed as blessings or opportunities for growth.

Affirmation: My life is blessed and I am grateful!

NOVEMBER 29

Practicing Gratitude with the Family

When we focus on our gratitude, the tide of disappointment goes out and the tide of love rushes in. — Kristin Armstrong

Gratitude is an important and powerful practice for us all. It helps our mental well-being by promoting positive thoughts and emotions, which lead to greater satisfaction, happiness, and decreased stress and anxiety. It is a tool that anyone can use no matter their age or ability. This is why creating a family gratitude practice is an activity that can bring a family closer and more aligned with one other. This deepens your relationships, fostering better communication and compassion within the family unit.

The practice can be done in many ways. Each night at dinner, you can go around the table and have each person share what they are grateful for. You could create a special gratitude jar where each family member writes down things they are grateful for on small pieces of paper and adds them to the jar. After a certain amount of time or when someone is feeling down, you can pull out pieces of paper to remind you all of something positive. You could take time regularly to speak your gratitude for one another face-to-face, by letter or small love note. Sharing appreciation deepens relationship bonds and enriches your experience together.

Spiritual Contemplation: What are three ways that you can think of to practice gratitude within your family?

Affirmation: I fully and freely share my appreciation for my family! They are a blessing in my life!

NOVEMBER 30

Gratitude & Resilience

When I started counting my blessings, my whole life turned around. — Willie Nelson

American icon Willie Nelson is an award-winning country singer/songwriter who has sold countless albums over the past 70 years. After moving to Nashville in the 1950s, he found himself disillusioned with the corporate Nashville music scene that wanted him to be something that he was not. He had a little success in Nashville but when he moved to Texas in the mid 1960's to focus on his family and his music, he found himself again. He summarizes this experience in the quote above. He remembered who he was and started practicing gratitude for his life finding great joy and success with his music.

Shifting your focus from an external goal to connecting with what is authentically true for you, can be a transformative experience. Practicing gratitude can help you deal with adversity and bounce back from challenging experiences. As you shift your focus to the positive aspects of your life, you build resilience and learn to cope amid difficulty. Your self-confidence will build as you awaken to your personal strengths and realize that you are stronger and more capable than the voice in your head leads you to believe. This fosters greater optimism and joy in your life.

Spiritual Contemplation: What challenges are you currently facing? How can you use gratitude to build self-confidence, optimism, and resilience?

Affirmation: I am grateful for all aspects of my life! I face each day with thanksgiving and know that I am enough!

DECEMBER
Happiness/Joy

December 1-7

The River of Joy

December 8-14

Happiness is a Choice

December 15-21

Living in the Joy

December 22-28

Choosing Joy

December 29-31

The Joy of Completion

DECEMBER 1

Family Comes in Many Shapes and Sizes

Family is not about blood. It's about who is willing to hold your hand when you need it the most. – Anonymous

Sarah was crushed to find out that her mother and family would not be attending her wedding to her girlfriend of two years. She had been openly gay since she was 15 and was surprised and disappointed by her family's choice. She shared her raw thoughts and feelings in a TikTok video that went viral. Daniel Blevins, founder of the support group Stand in Pride, saw the video and immediately decided to offer himself up as a stand-in parent for the wedding. He flew across the country and stood next to her as her stand-in dad. Sarah said: "I'm so happy to meet him — I'm going to treat him just like he's my dad. It's nice to know that someone like Dan has my back. Having his support makes all the difference."

Sometimes your family of origin is not able to support you in the ways that you need. But this does not mean that you are alone. The Infinite brings people into your life who can see, accept and honor you for who you are. You just need to be willing to see them and welcome them into your experience. Acquaintances can become friends, and friends can become family when we open to creating a space for acceptance and belonging for one another.

Spiritual Contemplation: Who in your life is like family though not related by blood? How do those relationships serve and support your well-being?

Affirmation: I welcome love and acceptance from those friends who are like family in my life

DECEMBER 2

Trusting The Process

How long a minute is depends on which side of the bathroom door you're on. —
Zall's Second Law

It's easy to get tired of waiting for business to grow, relationships to flourish, or a chronic health situation to turn around. The possibility of instantaneous healing, floodgates bursting open with affluent flow pouring forth, and a one-and-done prayer with immediate results are all real possibilities. Yet, sometimes it can take the unfoldment of life a bit longer to catch up with your vision of the Good that's possible.

In the meantime, avoid letting discouragement take hold. Focusing on problems rather than possibilities can cloud your perspective. Instead of dwelling on anxiety, which can drain your enjoyment of life, take charge of your thoughts. Focus on where you want to be, trust the process, and allow it to elevate your perspective. You'll find that the end is closer than you think.

Spiritual Contemplation: Where are you getting anxious about not having the results you want? How can you shift your thinking to trust the process more?

Affirmation: Breathe in and say, "Peace now," then exhale, "I trust the process!

DECEMBER 3

Let Go and Allow

Learn to let go. That is the key to happiness. — *Buddha*

Many people struggle with change, clinging to the past and using their energy to keep things the same. This fear of the future can prevent them from enjoying the present and exploring new possibilities. Letting go and allowing are key practices for finding happiness and joy, regardless of circumstances. These practices involve releasing attachment to outcomes, accepting the present moment, and adopting a more relaxed and open approach to life.

Recognize that life is constantly changing and nothing stays the same forever. By embracing this impermanence, you can let go of specific expectations and remain open to new opportunities. Trust in the perfect unfolding of life, knowing that everything happens for a reason, even if the outcome isn't immediately clear. Letting go and allowing life to flow can be exhilarating when you realize that the Universe wants you to have everything you desire—and even more than you can imagine.

Spiritual Contemplation: Journal about the areas where you have a challenge trusting the flow of life. How can you embrace change and find excitement for what is to come?

Affirmation: I surrender and allow life to flow with joy and excitement!

DECEMBER 4

Opener of Doors

~~·ᘛᘚ·~~

When one door closes another door opens; but we so often look so long and so regretfully upon the closed door, that we do not see the ones which open for us.
— *Alexander Graham Bell*

A big part of faith is trusting that Higher Wisdom is operating through you when you don't know what's next in your life. You might not understand why a particular door has closed for you, why the relationship ended, why the fulfillment at work has waned, or why you have lost interest in what you were once passionate about. Stepping across a threshold to what's next in your life is a natural transition. Sometimes letting go or having life take that interest from you before you are ready to relinquish it is what's needed for you to find a new level of wholehearted happiness awaiting you.

There are keys to unlocking the door to your greater potential. Joseph Campbell famously said, "Follow your bliss and don't be afraid, and doors will open where you didn't know they were going to be." To find greater happiness, embrace adventure and become an opener of doors. Sometimes you may need to open many doors to find the right one. If a door you open isn't the right one, adopt the attitude, "At least I know what's behind this one," and keep moving forward. As Krishnamurti said, "Nobody on earth can give you either the key or the door to open except yourself."

Spiritual Contemplation: Are you facing any closed doors in your life? What are you afraid of losing by stepping beyond the threshold? If you choose to trust life for the greater good, could you shift your focus from the old door to the new possibilities that await?

Affirmation: I trust Higher Wisdom within me knows my perfect next door to open!

DECEMBER 5

Letting Go of How it Was Supposed to Be

Happiness is letting go of what you think your life should look like and
celebrating it for everything that it is. – Mandy Hale

Many people struggle with reconciling their expectations of life with its actual outcome. The dreams of youth that never materialized, the potential left untapped, and the adventures never undertaken often bring a sense of sadness and disappointment. This can weigh heavily on the mind and heart.

Realizing that every choice along the way has led to this moment of awareness reveals a surprising gift: the power of choice and creativity. When we bless our disappointments and perceived mistakes, we start to see that there was always a purpose to our path. Everything that did and didn't happen had its reason. By awakening to the present moment and accepting our journey, we can move forward with power and purpose. It's never too late to create joy in our lives. Letting go of 'shoulds 'and self-judgment opens the door to greater peace and happiness.

Spiritual Contemplation: What judgments are you holding about your past and the mistakes you think you've made? Take some time to journal about how those experiences were exactly what you needed and what you've learned from them.

Affirmation: My Life unfolds with ease, grace and joy! I am happy!

DECEMBER 6

Get Off the Nail

The pain pushes until the vision pulls. — *Michael Bernard Beckwith*

It's not uncommon to hear someone complaining about their life, their job, or their relationship, feeling stuck in their situation. There's an amusing story that illustrates this point: An older man is rocking in his chair on the front porch of his farmhouse, alongside his moaning old dog. A woman walking by stops to chat with him and asks, "Why is your dog moaning all the time?" The man replies, "It's because the dog is sitting on a nail." She then wonders, "Why doesn't he move?" "I'd guess," the farmer says, "it's because it doesn't hurt him enough to move."

This story reflects an issue many people face in life. They would rather endure discomfort than make the effort to change their circumstances. Instead of wholeheartedly embracing what will bring joy and happiness, they choose the familiarity of misery. During this holiday season, you have the opportunity to decide whether to spend your time where it brings you delight and happiness or return to a toxic situation that will diminish your holiday joy. Remember, the choice to sit on the nail or not is yours.

Spiritual Contemplation: What situation in your life might it be advantageous to remove yourself from? What reasons are you giving yourself for staying on the "nail"? Do you recognize that, with your freedom of choice, you are actively choosing to remain in this toxic situation?

Affirmation: With my freedom of choice, I choose wholehearted happiness!

DECEMBER 7

Open Your Heart

Life can't give to you if your hands are closed. Open your mind, open your heart, and open your arms. — *Louise Hay*

Parker Palmer shares a story about a pupil who asks his rabbi, "Why does the Torah say to 'place these holy words upon your hearts' rather than 'in your hearts'?" The rabbi responds, "Our hearts are often closed, making it difficult to place the holy words inside. So, we place them on top of our hearts. They remain there until, one day, when the heart breaks open and the words fall in."

This story reminds us that no matter what happens in life, the challenges and difficulties are here to soften and open our hearts. We cannot understand how loved and supported we are by God until we allow God's presence to be active in our daily experience. For many of us, it is difficult to be vulnerable and share our emotions freely. Life's challenges force us to do this and often, when this happens, we realize just how loved and supported we are. Do not let the difficulties of life close your heart even more. Instead, let it open and welcome the love that is already here for you.

Spiritual Contemplation: Look at the challenges you have faced thus far in your life. Can you see how those challenges were there to show you how supported you are? Note this in your journal.

Affirmation: I allow Life to show me how loved and supported I am!

DECEMBER 8

Happiness, Your Choice

If more of us valued food and cheer and song above hoarded gold, it would be a merrier world. — *J.R.R. Tolkien*

Whoever is happy makes those around them happy.

Drew Barrymore said, "Happiness is the best makeup. I think happiness is what makes you pretty. Period. Happy people are beautiful." Give up the pressure of trying to be who others think you should be and find happiness in being who you are. It comes down to realizing that your personal happiness depends on you.

During the celebrating season, find the joy of food, music and laughter with the people you love being with and who love you for who you truly are. Rather than fulfilling self-imposed, tension-filled obligations with people who are disappointed that you are not who they think you should be. Happiness comes when you are wholeheartedly living your truth rather than someone else's expectations for you.

Spiritual Contemplation: Why go somewhere that will make you miserable when you can go somewhere that makes you happy? Silly question, but worthy of contemplation during the holiday season of invitations.

Affirmation: I sing and dance and feast with those who love me for who I am!

DECEMBER 9

Let Go of Negativity

We need to learn to let go as easily as we grasp, and we will find our hands full and our minds empty. — Leo F. Buscaglia

As metaphysicians, we know that what we put our attention on expands. This is a fundamental truth, and it is no more apparent than in the experience of negativity in our lives. Negativity is a damaging and toxic energy that can affect our decisions and actions if we allow it. Every day we encounter numerous toxic people who deliver subtle negative messages and try to instill negative ideas constantly. Even if we try to stay positive, we are repeatedly bombarded with negativity from external sources that can affect our physical and mental health.

It would benefit us greatly to release negativity, grudges, and past regrets, as holding onto these emotions can block our ability to fully experience joy. We should be mindful of the media we consume, limiting exposure to negative news and content that may weigh us down. Instead, choose to surround yourself with positive messages and people who bring joy and lightness into your life. This shift in your environment will help transform your internal landscape, allowing you to recognize the silver linings and experience greater happiness and joy.

Spiritual Contemplation: Journal about your relationship to negativity and negative media. Are you naturally optimistic or pessimistic in your worldview? How can you embrace more positivity?

Affirmation: I let go of all negativity in my life and surround myself with positivity and joy!

DECEMBER 10

Duck Stuck

When we clear the physical clutter from our lives, we literally make way for
inspiration and 'good, orderly direction' to enter. —Julia Cameron

It all started innocently enough when we purchased a wooden duck decoy on a mountain trip with some buddies. Word got around that one of our friends liked ducks. On his birthdays he started receiving various duck expressions, like pictures of ducks in flight and shirts with duck images. When his parents saw this newfound passion, they added to the holiday cheer with a deluge of ducks in various forms - porcelain ducks, duck wall hangings and, of course, duck towels. Then came the lame duck sayings on bumper stickers, stuffed ducks, duck slippers and pajamas, books and plates with duck images. The wall space and shelves were beyond full. The poor guy was running out of room in his house and was really done with ducks.

How many years does something need to be out of control before you work up the nerve to speak up about it? Your new position isn't going to match what others perceive you to be. They will be surprised, if not shocked, and maybe even hurt, when you speak your new truth. You suspect it's not going to be received well, but how long are you going to let others tell you what you should like? You can stay duck stuck for years - or you can speak your present truth. Rather than rustling other's feathers by disappointing them that you are no longer 'that person 'they believed you to be, be authentically you and refuse to live the tale that no longer is.

Spiritual Contemplation: Where in your life are you holding onto illusions or deceptions that clutter your world and no longer serve you? Consider where you need to confront these falsehoods and express your current truth to others.

Affirmation: I boldly speak my Truth!

DECEMBER 11

Don't Worry – Be Happy!

Now and then it's good to pause in our pursuit of happiness and just be happy. – Guillaume Apollinaire

Happiness is not just a destination; it's a state of mind that can be experienced in the present moment. It isn't solely about what we have or achieve but how we choose to perceive and appreciate the world around us. Even in challenging situations, there is always something to be grateful for. This is evident in places like the chemo ward, where patients facing life-threatening illnesses often continue to smile, laugh, and find joy. They understand that life is precious and choose to embrace it fully, rather than dwell in negativity.

We are called to shift our focus from seeking happiness in external pursuits to finding contentment and joy in the present. Happiness is not a constant state; it's okay to experience moments of joy alongside other emotions. By pausing to appreciate the happiness that exists now, you can create a more balanced and fulfilling life.

Spiritual Contemplation: How can you find happiness and joy in your everyday experience, no matter what is happening?

Affirmation: I embrace happiness and joy no matter what is happening in my life!

DECEMBER 12

Holiday Blues

~ơໄ∕ᴑ

I always like walking in the rain, so no one can see me crying. — *Charlie Chaplin*

The solution to loneliness is to love. Love yourself so you can be at peace in those solo moments and love others to find engagement in life. Wholehearted living is the key to an enchanted journey. When one is thinking about others with kindness and love, the law of attraction opens the opportunities to get involved in life. You'll no longer be attempting to escape from loneliness, rather you find a sense of belonging to that which matches who you are in this busy season of sentiments and demands.

Even people who love the holidays can experience the blues. While reminiscing about past holidays can be magical, it's important to remember that things change and focus on who is with you now. Children grow older, people move on, and new friends enter your world. Create new traditions to embrace what is available to you this season. Be realistic and kind to yourself when deciding on your engagements. There's no need to overcommit, as you're not obligated to attend everything. Make your choices from a place of joy. Spend time with those you truly want to be with and go where your heart leads you.

Spiritual Contemplation: If you're feeling lonely, where can you engage in holiday cheer? If your obligations are taking you where you don't want to be, how can you step away? If you are overcommitted, where can you back off?

Affirmation: I find the perfect balance with this season of Joy, to live the Joy!

DECEMBER 13

Find Joy in Your Day-to-Day

Being excited about what we do every day and sharing our gifts with the world is how we cultivate joy and energy. – Deepak Chopra

It's easy to get caught in the drudgery of daily routines, weighed down by life's stresses, and forget the journey that brought us here. Many lose sight of the excitement and passion they once had for their work, leading to a sense of heaviness and difficulty. Depression, anxiety, and loneliness are prevalent in our culture, but it doesn't have to be this way. Reigniting enthusiasm and excitement in our daily activities can rejuvenate our energy and bring joy back into our lives.

Embracing a purpose-driven, enthusiastic approach to life encourages you to tap into your passions, utilize your unique talents, and contribute positively to the world around you. Cultivate an enthusiastic mindset for everything you do. Begin each day with a sense of excitement and curiosity, and let your enthusiasm shine through in all of your actions and interactions. You will find that your days will be filled with more joy and vitality than you ever imagined.

Spiritual Contemplation: Have you lost joy in any one area of your life? How can you embrace an enthusiastic approach to this? Use your curiosity and sense of wonder to foster more joy and energy in your experience.

Affirmation: I wake up excited for each new day! I step forward open, ready and curious for the adventure that lies ahead!

DECEMBER 14

Hanukkah, A story of Faith

Look at how a single candle can both defy and define the darkness. – Anne Frank

Hanukkah is an epic story of freedom of religion against all odds. It has as much significance for those today as it did over two thousand years ago when the Maccabees chose to keep their love of their faith rather than succumbing to the paganism that the Greeks and Syrians attempted to impose upon them. The light of religious freedom must overcome intolerance. Unless we all have the right to worship freely, then no one is truly free. Remaining indifferent when a human right is denied supports the oppressor. While some allowed their religion to be toned down to keep the peace, others rose up and refused to have their tradition assimilated into another culture. They took a stand for what they believed.

This miraculous saga of faith, with revolt against overwhelming forces of a mighty oppressor, shows how faith overcomes fear. Hanukkah reminds us how trust in the Divine triumphs over despair. In the darkest places, at the darkest hour, if you stand up to the shadow with your light of faith and action, God works through you in miraculous ways and transforms the darkness into day.

Spiritual Contemplation: Where in your life do you feel you are abdicating your right to what you believe just to keep the peace? How can you take a more honest stand in the face of oppressing authority?

Affirmation: In the face of adversity, I fearlessly stand up and speak out for what I believe!

DECEMBER 15

The Pause

The capacities by which we can gain insights into higher worlds lie dormant within each one of us. – Rudolf Steiner

Seeing your lawn in the middle of winter can be disconcerting. What was once a lush green carpet now looks closer to dead than alive, which was never your intention. When you check in with your gardener, you inadvertently give them a good laugh. They reassure you that there's no cause for concern   your lawn is simply going through its natural winter dormancy. It's taking a well-deserved rest and will be ready to reach for the sun when spring's warmth returns.

When it appears life is not flowing, spiritual connection feels closed off, or romance is less passionate as you'd like, there is no need to worry. Remember, life has its cycles and a restful pause is a natural part of the phases of living. Your pause is meant to be regenerative, renewing and revitalizing. When you come out of this restful time, you feel the stimulation pulsating through your body, soul and spirit. Trust the process, all of nature does it and so do you.

Spiritual Contemplation: How can I more greatly appreciate the regenerative moments of my life?

Affirmation: I appreciate and enjoy my regenerative pauses

DECEMBER 16

Choosing Happiness

Happiness is a choice. There's going to be stress in life, but it's your choice
whether you let it affect you or not. – Valerie Bertinelli

If you ask anyone what they truly want in life, they are more than likely going to answer that they want to be happy. But most people are not happy. Viktor Frankl, who shared his experiences as a Holocaust and concentration camp survivor in his book Man's Search for Meaning, asserts something remarkable. In it he says that everything can be taken from a person except one thing. That one thing that can never be taken away is the power to choose one's attitude in any given set of circumstances. His words remind us that happiness, as well as any other feeling, is a choice. No matter what happens around us, even under the most horrific of circumstances, we are the only ones who can control our attitude.

Some people believe that achieving a certain level of material comfort will bring them happiness. While material possessions can provide comfort, they do not guarantee happiness. True happiness comes from embracing your fuller self-expression and making a conscious choice to live fully and be happy. Start by acknowledging that you have the right to be happy. As the Declaration of Independence asserts, every person has the right to life, liberty, and the pursuit of happiness. This is both a spiritual truth and a fundamental reality. Every day, remind yourself that you deserve to be happy and walk through your day with contentment and joy.

Spiritual Contemplation: Ask yourself what is holding you back from experiencing happiness. Reflect on these barriers and shift your perspective to recognize that you deserve to be happy. Consider how you can invite more joy into your life and embrace the possibility of greater contentment.

Affirmation: I am Happy! I am Joyful! I am Free! Today is a GREAT day!

DECEMBER 17

Your Soul's Adventure

Life is either a daring adventure or nothing at all. – Helen Keller

Your soul incarnated in this life to have an adventure. You might have convinced yourself that your goal is to reach Easy Street—retirement and rest—ultimately wanting to stay safe and cozy in your small, comfortable life. This is just not true! Your soul came into this life to grow, expand and experience great joys and unique delights! It is up to you to step out of your comfort zone. Embrace the excitement of the adventures waiting for you!

It is easy to get on a track of life where all you do is work at creating all the structures you think are meant for you. You wake up to the fact that you have wasted years trying to create something that you don't even like! You end up living a safe little life that doesn't reflect your passion in the least! It's time to wake up and step out in a new way! Move out of your comfort zone and try something new! Travel. Meet new people. Do something you've always wanted to do but never allowed yourself to try. Welcome some new adventures and see how your soul lights up. Your life will become more fulfilling than you ever could have imagined!

Spiritual Contemplation: Think about something you've always wanted to try and journal about how you can step out of your comfort zone to pursue it. Outline a plan for how you will take this new step, setting achievable goals and identifying any support you might need. Taking this initiative will open new opportunities and experiences in your life.

Affirmation: I open to the joy and adventure my soul desires here and now!

DECEMBER 18

Cultivate Joy

As we cultivate peace and happiness in ourselves, we also nourish peace and happiness in those we love. — *Thich Nhat Hanh*

Cultivating joy in your life is a spiritual practice that involves adopting daily exercises and mindset shifts focusing on appreciating and finding happiness in everyday experiences. Practicing mindfulness, gratitude, and making meaningful connections work together to support you in opening to the gift of happiness that comes from living from a deep place of awareness.

Making time for the activities you love, like hobbies, creative endeavors, or exercise, brings joy and fulfillment and contributes to your overall well-being. Even appreciating the simple things in life, like a gorgeous sunset, laughter with friends, or that first cup of coffee in the morning will bring joy to your day-to-day life. Set an intention to cultivate joy daily, and you will see how happy your life will become.

Spiritual Contemplation: What are the activities and experiences that you love? Have you made time in your life for these activities? How can you include at least one practice per day to cultivate joy in your experience?

Affirmation: I cultivate joy in my life each and every day!

DECEMBER 19

Love Yourself Happy

Self–worth is so vital to your happiness. If you don't feel good about yourself, it's hard to feel good about anything else. – Sandy Hale

Cultivating a strong sense of self-worth is important because it can profoundly impact your overall experience of happiness and well-being. When you value and respect yourself, it positively influences your experience of the world and your interactions with others. This can be challenging for those of us who grew up with less than supportive messages about who we are. But by practicing self-compassion, recognizing your unique strengths, and setting healthy boundaries, you'll reset your experience and begin building a new relationship with yourself.

Building self-worth is an ongoing process requiring consistent effort and self-awareness. Be patient with yourself and remember that your worth is not defined by either external factors or the opinions of others. As you embrace your inherent value and cultivate a positive relationship with yourself, you make space for happiness and contentment in all aspects of your life.

Spiritual Contemplation: Make a list of 10 of your most unique strengths and talents. Take a few silent moments to honor yourself for these and how you show up for others. Practice gratitude and appreciation for yourself today.

Affirmation: I know my unique talents and embrace who I am!

DECEMBER 20

Feel the Joy

When we lose our tolerance for vulnerability, joy becomes foreboding. — Brené Brown

Foreboding joy is a concept that researcher Brene Brown teaches about in her books and lectures. It's that feeling when a moment of joy is quickly overshadowed by thoughts of worry and dread, with a sense of impending doom, as if something bad is about to happen and the other shoe will drop. The joy you are experiencing is real but so is the worry and fear. This holds you back from a full experience of joy in your life.

You don't have to let foreboding joy disrupt the happy moments you experience. Becoming conscious of your mind-state is the first step to releasing your negative thought cycles. Observing how you relate to happiness and joy will show you where you are holding onto beliefs of scarcity and lack. You can counteract these thoughts by practicing gratitude, self-awareness, and cultivating resilience. These are all ways you can allow yourself to embrace joy without any 'what ifs 'attached.

Spiritual Contemplation: Take some time today to contemplate your relationship with happiness and joy. Do you believe that you deserve to be completely happy? Are you carrying around ideas of foreboding joy and waiting for things to unravel? Practice gratitude for your life to start embracing joy.

Affirmation: I am Happy! I am Joyful! I am Free!

DECEMBER 21

Winter Solstice

In the depths of winter, I finally learned that within me there lay an invincible summer. — Albert Camus

Celebrate the Winter Solstice as a sacred time for reflection, release, restoration, and renewal. In the northern hemisphere, the Winter Solstice marks the turning point of the Sun's journey, where light begins to be reborn, symbolizing death and rebirth. This moment invites us to bid farewell to the old and welcome the new. Across cultures, deities such as Horus, Mithras, Amaterasu, Lucia, and Baldur are honored, each representing light and renewal.

The story of Persephone, who splits her time between the underworld with Hades and the surface with her mother Demeter, highlights the dual nature of spiritual journeys. It underscores that growth involves both ascending into light and descending into shadow, gaining wisdom in both realms. Persephone's journey illustrates the balance required to embrace both roles with equal passion. The Winter and Summer Solstices symbolize the necessary cycles of expansion and contraction in life. Embracing these changes reveals the options available in our adaptability and self-expression.

Spiritual Contemplation: How can I better surrender to the restorative energies of my soul by becoming more introspective?

Affirmation: My soul finds balance as I embrace the restoration of the night and self-expression by the light of the day!

DECEMBER 22

A River of Joy

When you do things from your soul, you feel a river moving in you, a joy. — Jalaluddin Rumi

This Rumi quote speaks to the power of authentic self-expression that leads to an experience of deep joy and fulfillment. Tapping into your true self, embracing your values, passions, and purpose, and allowing them to guide your choices and actions leads to a full and fulfilling life that brings great joy and happiness.

When you act in alignment with your soul's purpose and desires, there is a sense of harmony and flow. You engage in activities that resonate with your deepest intentions, and this alignment creates a powerful and enriching experience. Living this way brings a deep sense of joy and fulfillment that is not temporary or fleeting but arises from a deeper source, providing lasting contentment and satisfaction.

Spiritual Contemplation: What are the activities that align with your soul's purpose and desires? What are the values and passions guiding your choices and actions?

Affirmation: I align with my true self and float on that deep river of joy!

DECEMBER 23

Time for Baḳalava and other family Traditions

It's true, Christmas can feel like a lot of work, particularly for mothers. But when you look back on all the Christmases in your life, you'll find you've created family traditions and lasting memories. Those memories, good and bad, are really what help to keep a family together over the long haul. – Caroline Kennedy

Every December, my daughter and I spend a day in the kitchen making Baklava, the sweet Greek layered pastry. I have been doing this since I was a small child in the kitchen with my own mother, who learned how to make it from my Greek grandmother Yiayia. This is one of our family holiday traditions that brings a sense of connection with the past and fosters a sense of joy and appreciation for our family. It's one of our favorite days of the year, and we love sharing our creation with friends during the holidays.

Traditions play a significant role in shaping a family's identity, fostering a sense of belonging, and creating lasting memories. These traditions provide a framework for shared experiences and values, helping to strengthen relationships and pass down cultural heritage from one generation to the next. Whether they are traditions passed down for years or something new you are starting this year, participating in traditions will enrich your holiday experience with greater love and joy.

Spiritual Contemplation: What are your annual holiday traditions? Are there any that you have let go of that you could reintroduce? What new traditions would you like to create? (favorite holiday movies to watch, dishes to cook, activities to participate in, etc.)

Affirmation: I honor my family traditions and create new ones to serve my family.

DECEMBER 24

This Moment

Maybe Christmas, the Grinch thought, doesn't come from a store. — Dr. Seuss

Clement Clarke Moore wrote, "T'was the night before Christmas, when all through the house, not a creature was stirring, not even a mouse." Can you remember as a little child, Christmas Eve, your mom or dad getting you settled into bed, their hand tucking you in before the big morning? There is an enchantment that settles in the night before Christmas. The streets twinkle with lights, many people have paused to join the ancestors from the beginning of time in lighting a candle, there is joy and music in the air, and people are festive and kind with their expressive loving hearts. It's almost as if the previous year's mood shifts, at least for this night when the world waits in a stillness for the magic to unfold, often forgetting that the kindness, caring and nostalgia of this moment is the magic itself! Something fresh is about to commence. Expectancy is the birth place of miracles.

With the smell of pine, fire crackling, stories, laughter and songs filling the night air, the invitation for the Christ expression to fill this moment is answered with love. Bob Hope would say, "If you haven't got any charity in your heart, you have the worst kind of heart trouble." Those who haven't found Christmas in their hearts aren't going to find it under the tree. It is what's birthed within you that touches the hearts of family and friends. Become like a child and believe once again.

Spiritual Contemplation: Can you live Charles Dickens' decree through the awakened Scrooge of A Christmas Carol, "I will honor Christmas in my heart, and try to keep it all the year."

Affirmation: I remember to honor the Spirit of Christmas throughout the year!

DECEMBER 25

I Am The Light of My Path

Seeing is believing, but sometimes the most real things in the world are the things we can't see. — The Conductor, The Polar Express

It is during our darkest moments that we must focus to see the light. - Aristotle

Imagine a teenage girl sitting alone when an angel appears, telling her she's favored by God and will give birth to a baby boy destined to be the savior of the world. This child will heal the sick, raise the dead, walk on water, and be known as the Christ. The angel assures her that she will be loved, adored, and remembered as the Beloved Mother Mary, even considered a saint. She eagerly agrees, as it sounds incredible. However, what wasn't mentioned was the hardship in between: traveling long distances while heavily pregnant, giving birth in a stable, fleeing from King Herod's wrath, and ultimately watching her son be betrayed, mocked, whipped, and crucified. Had she known all the details, she might have thought twice about the deal.

Spirit places a vision in you but doesn't reveal the details of the journey. Who would willingly choose the struggles you've faced to reach your destiny? Yet, it's in the dark times that you discover a new strength and a greater consciousness. The light returns when you dig deep into the darkness. You must believe in the star-like vision of your heart more than the darkness. When you do, you become the light in your journey. The world changes because you had a faith stronger than death, and a new life was born.

Spiritual Contemplation: Where are you caught in the struggles of the middle on your journey to creation? Remember the star-like vision that first called you on this path. Let that light guide you once again.

Affirmation: I believe I am the light that illumines my path!

DECEMBER 26

Kwanzaa

~echo~

During the holiday, families and communities organize activities around the Nguzo Saba (The Seven Principles): Umoja (Unity), Kujichagulia (Self-Determination), Ujima (Collective Work and Responsibility), Ujamaa (Cooperative Economics), Nia (Purpose), Kuumba (Creativity) and Imani (Faith). Participants also celebrate with feasts (karamu), music, dance, poetry, narratives and end the holiday with a day dedicated to reflection and recommitment to The Seven Principles and other central cultural values. – Dr. Maulana Karenga, creator of Kwanzaa

Kwanzaa, meaning "first" in Swahili, is not a religious ceremony, rather it is a culturally inclusive one. Swahili is the language of Kwanzaa, chosen because it is widespread across the "mother continent" and has a lack of tribal association. Kwanzaa delivers an ancient and living cultural message which reflects the best of African thought and practices. This annual celebration of African-American culture that is held from December 26 to January 1, culminates in a communal feast called Karamu.

A kinara, "candle holder" with seven candles — one black, the first to be lit, to represent the people; three red to represent the struggle; and three green to represent the prosperity — placed upon a mat and an African cloth, flanked with at least two ears of corn to represent the communal harvest tradition, and a unity cup from which to pour libation, are the only symbolic requirements. It is recommended that the final day is a sober meditation, asking: "Who am I? Am I really who I say I am? Am I all I ought to be?

Spiritual Contemplation: Take these three questions into your deep reflection. Do they connect you with any of your ancestral memories?

Affirmation: With self-determination, I creatively contribute my purpose to the collective unity of life!

DECEMBER 27

The Stone Cutter

I believe much trouble would be saved if we opened our hearts more. — Chief Joseph

There was once an unhappy stonecutter who felt insignificant. One day, he saw the luxurious life of a rich woman and wished to be wealthy. His wish was granted, but soon he was uncomfortable with people's envy. He then desired to be a powerful ruler, but even that left him discontent. He envied the sun, became it, but found he caused suffering. He wished to be the clouds, then the wind, but each time he brought misery. Finally, he craved to be an immovable rock, finding contentment in his solidity. However, this contentment didn't last long as he heard and felt the pounding of a hammer and chisel. Who could have such power to change him? Looking down the face of his towering stone cliffs, he saw a small figure at his base—a stonecutter.

Spiritual Contemplation: Are there places in your life where you want to dominate and be the strongest power in the room? Put that desire on hold for a bit and open your heart to the power you already are and love that!

Affirmation: I am now as much a part of nature as the sun in the sky or the winds of heaven!

DECEMBER 28

A Few Extra Days

Life is what happens while you are busy making other plans. — *John Lennon*

What would you do if you had a few extra days of life given to you? How would you make the most of those days? Would you go somewhere, spend some quality time with someone special, go on a meditation retreat, clean out a long overdue cluttered up space, finish an unfinished project or maybe start a new one? There is a magical interval where time expands between Christmas and the New Year that seems to just evaporate if not intentionally embraced. It could be described as a lull or pause before life launches into your fast moving action packed New Year's plans.

There's no need to feel anxious over the next few days about not sticking to your usual work routine. It will be waiting for you in the new year. These few extra days are a longed-for gift to allow life to happen to you beyond your typical plans. Be available, spontaneous, unstructured, and even impulsive to the call of your soul during this magical period. There is an opening in your calendar to say yes to this urge, but will you allow yourself to come out to play?

Spiritual Contemplation: What would you do if you found you had a few extra days for fun? Would you talk yourself out of the pleasurable by getting anxious around your pending workload or lack of work? Go embrace this moment.

Affirmation: I allow the call of my soul to find joy in this day!

DECEMBER 29

Think On These Things

What we demonstrate today, tomorrow and the next day, is not as important as the tendency which our thought is taking … the dominant attitude of our mind. — Ernest Holmes

If each day your life is getting brighter and happier, and your dominant attitude is positive, then you're moving in the right direction. What can happen, however, is something or someone can disrupt the tendency of your thinking. Be careful not to allow someone to capture your mind with what he or she said or did. When someone else's action jolts you off your trajectory, you have to take your mind back.

If you find yourself rehashing a disturbing scene in your field of awareness, it's a call to kick that thought to the curb. Don't give what you don't want a free ride into your tomorrow. If you find yourself obsessing over something, it becomes clear where the hijacker of your consciousness is hanging out. The captor must be tossed out and you can do that by no longer feeding it your energy. Place your inner conversations and images of the God qualities of your desired wholehearted direction and be done with the captor's dialogue. Then the dominant attitude of your mind will, once again, place you back on track for a brighter and happier today, tomorrow and the New Year.

Spiritual Contemplation: What freeloaders are lingering in your awareness that you'd like to leave behind in the outgoing year? What are the God qualities of your enchanted journey for the New Year? Fill your thoughts, inner conversations and mental images with these!

Affirmation: I am the fiery essence of the Divine made manifest!

DECEMBER 30

A Moment of Appreciation

You yourself, as much as anybody in the entire universe, deserve your love and affection. — Sharon Salzberg

As the year and our journey wind down, pause and reflect on where you are now compared to where you were when we started. Spending time each day contemplating a spiritual aspect of your life and learning how to live wholeheartedly has brought you to this moment where you are ready to step out in a new way.

So rarely do we give ourselves credit for our accomplishments, fearing that we will come across as arrogant or boastful. This is not the truth. You have many things to be proud of. You have come a long way from where you started, and today is the day to acknowledge and claim it. Even if you didn't work through every page of this book, the fact that you have it, spent time with it, and have integrated the learnings into your life, will make a difference in how you move forward and create your next chapter. Today is a day of integration and appreciation for yourself and how far you've come. Then, start the new year ready for the greatest adventure yet.

Spiritual Contemplation: Spend at least 10 minutes in meditation today with your hands folded over your heart, breathing gently. Breathe in appreciation and gratitude, and breathe out love for yourself, for all you have accomplished up to now, and for all that is to come. Know that you are blessed.

Affirmation: I honor my path and celebrate all that I am and all that I ever will be.

DECEMBER 31

Time for Reflection

The way we experience the world around us is a direct reflection of the world within us. — *Gabrielle Bernstein*

No need to wait until tomorrow to start your year in review. The wisdom from your experiences has already been circulating and ruminating in your subjective mind, just waiting to be harvested. Love the fruits of this year's labors. They are ripe and ready for you. Here are some questions to begin your wisdom gathering.

- What are some standout moments and achievements from this year?

- What were some moments from this year that fill you with gratitude?

- What experiences and memories do you intend to leave in this year?

- Do you have anyone or anything to forgive and forget before moving into the New Year?

- What is your vision for the New Year?

- What are some specific intentions you intend to accomplish in this coming year?

- Is there anywhere you want to travel or people you want to see this New Year?

- What would bring you great joy to do this coming year?

Affirmation: I have learned from this year's journey. I see my greater good and hear its calling. I integrate my past with now to create an amazing New Year!

Acknowledgements

Progress on this book came to a halt during its editing phase due to Katherine's transitional period. After her passing, author and longtime Seaside member Lori Gertz came to the rescue of Wholehearted Living. She lovingly dedicated countless hours to editing and publishing the manuscript, transforming it into this book. Without Lori, this book would still be sitting on a hard drive instead of in your hands. I had the chance to share with Reverend Katherine, just a couple days before her passing, that Lori would be taking our project across the finish line. Katherine and I wholeheartedly express our gratitude for her heart and the love she put into bringing our work to life in this book.

Many thanks to Beckie Celikel, who has joyfully been 'cleaning up' my daily guides and sending them out to the world for the past decade. I feel blessed by my wonderful spiritual family, Seaside Center for Spiritual Living, who have continued to support our enchanted journey together.

A huge amount of love and appreciation to Doctor Katherine who came wandering into my world 25 years ago on her soul's enchanted journey. It was obvious then, Spirit had high intentions for her wholehearted work in the world; how grateful I am that included me with, Wholehearted Living, An Enchanted Journey For The Soul.

Christian

Deep gratitude to my prayer partners, Rev. Angela Geary, Rev. Patti Paris, Rev. Tracy Earlywine and Don Taylor, RScP for your continued support during this process. I could not have completed this book without your weekly words of encouragement and love. I am grateful to the Center for Spiritual Living Temecula Valley congregation, who I had the honor of serving for over eight years. I witnessed such magical growth and expansion during our enchanted journey and I am forever blessed by our time together. To Reverend Doctor Christian, who in a simple phone message put me on yet another new path, I am deeply grateful. Who knew 25 years ago when I stumbled into Seaside Center for Spiritual Living that it was the beginning of my life's path and work. My heart is filled with love and gratitude for all you saw in me, then and now. You inspire great things in those you serve and love with your whole heart. Thank you for choosing me to partner with on this book. What a gift!

Katherine

About the Authors

Christian Sørensen

A gifted and eloquent speaker and author with a unique and engaging style, Christian has been lighting up audiences all over the world for more than four decades with his expansive vision, passion, and wholehearted enthusiasm. He has authored eleven books, numerous articles, blogs and podcasts ,and hosted two television programs on spirituality, New Thought, and growing one's consciousness. Christian was the last appointed president of the Church of Religious Science and their first elected Community Spiritual Leader. His intention is that his life be his message.

Reverend Christian Sorensen, D.D. is the spiritual leader of the Seaside Center for Spiritual Living in Encinitas California and his weekly talks can be viewed at www.seasidecenter.com.

Katherine Economou

An engaging and articulate speaker, teacher, and facilitator, Katherine was renowned for inspiring personal growth and spiritual transformation for over 25 years. She had a gift for translating spiritual and mystical concepts into understandable and usable tools to cultivate and create the life one desires. Through her classes, retreats, writing, and circles, she fostered connection with the self and others to deepen one's walk in life. Her intention was to empower others to discover their inherent worth and create a life of joy. Katherine lived in Fallbrook, California, with her husband, Steve, daughter, Emilie, Maltipoo, Daisy May, and her ten beloved chickens.

Rev. Dr. Katherine facilitated retreats, classes, and circles. Her talks and more information can be found at www.cultivatewithkatherine.com.

For More Information

For more information on Spiritual Living, Science of Mind, and a practical, positive spirituality that teaches tools for personal transformation and making the world a better place or to find a community in your area, go to www.csl.org.

Index

FEBRUARY 29

A Day for You - Leap Day!

What will you do with your one wild and precious life? - *Mary Oliver*

Every four years, we get an extra day on the calendar. If you are reading this on one of those years, we have an additional 24-hours to decide what to do with! So often, I hear people lament about wanting more time. "Oh! If I only had an extra day!" Well, today, you have it, and the question is, how will you spend it? Will it be just another normal day? Or will you spend your bonus time doing something you love, something you've always wanted to try, or something to feed your soul?

As this month is all about love, let us complete it with a day that is focused on appreciating and loving yourself. Choose activities and experiences that feed and nurture yourself. If you must work, allow this theme of self-care and self-appreciation to flow through your day during your breaks, in and through what you eat, and how you spend your time outside of work. If you can take the day for yourself, plan your time caring for yourself in a new way. You will get back at it tomorrow, more relaxed, centered, and ready for what comes next!

Spiritual Contemplation: Care for yourself today in ways that nurture and support your well-being.

Affirmation: I love and appreciate myself and spend my time caring for my soul!

Made in the USA
Las Vegas, NV
05 December 2024

13348077R00216